**"Just take the pill,"** Sean insisted. "It's harmless, and you'll be able to sleep."

Margie took the pill with reluctance. Instead of making her feel better, a few minutes later she felt sick to her stomach. She ran and locked herself in the bathroom and threw up violently. Sean came to the door and demanded to be let in. Weakly, Margie opened the door. Sean picked Margie up in his arms and carried her to bed.

The hours that followed were filled with images fading in and out of her mind in bits and pieces. Was she dreaming? She wasn't sure. Over her, she saw those piercing eyes narrowed with hatred. Manicured fingers with fists clenched. She felt herself trying to scream into the darkness of the night. The screams died in her throat. Then she lapsed into merciful unconsciousness again, only to feel more of the scene unfolding like a nightmare from which there was no escape. At some point she felt her own tears falling into her open mouth, her head slammed back. She thought she saw blood on the hands of the shadowy figure looming above her, parting her legs. And then there was pain, pain which blotted out everything else . . .

# TAINTED ROSES

A True Story of Murder,
Mystery, and a Dangerous Love

## MARGIE DANIELSEN

St. Martin's Paperbacks

Published by arrangement with New Horizon Press

TAINTED ROSES

Copyright © 2000 by Margie Danielsen.

Library of Congress Catalog Card Number: 99-70159

ISBN: 0-312-97685-2

Printed in the United States of America

New Horizon hardcover editon published 2000
St. Martin's Paperbacks edition / November 2000

St. Martin's Paperbacks are published by St. Martin's Press, 175 Fifth Avenue, New York, N.Y. 10010.

10  9  8  7  6  5  4  3  2  1

To my beautiful daughters:
Julie, my sunshine.
June, my inspiration.
Jessi, my guiding light.

# Contents

## Author's Note

THIS book is based on my experiences and reflects my perceptions of the past, present, and future. The personalities, events, actions, and conversations portrayed within the story have been taken from my memories, extensive interviews, research, court documents, letters, personal papers, press accounts, and the memories of participants. I have used a reasonable literary license within narrow confines of truth and credibility. Nonetheless, all scenes are recounted as closely as possible to how I witnessed them or how they were told to me.

In an effort to safeguard the privacy of certain people, I have changed their names and the names of certain places and in some cases, altered otherwise identifying characteristics and chronology. Some minor characters are composites.

# Acknowledgments

A SPECIAL thank you to Pat, for her generous help, support, and encouragement. To Andrea, for her time and unselfish advice. To my lifelong friends, Nila and Darrel, who stood by me through it all. To May, for her daily conversations of emotional comfort. To Randy, for his help in finding the truth. To Stan, for his financial assistance. To the leader of the women's group, who shines a light to women who are lost and navigates us in the right direction. To Char, a kind and fun friend who helped me get through the most difficult time of my life. And, to June, for her kindness, love, and inspiration.

## Prologue

# Dream Lover

MARGIE paused as she caught a glimpse of her reflection in the mirror that hung in the front hall. A divorced thirty-seven-year-old woman with long, golden brown hair and saucer-like dark brown eyes stared back at her.

"Not bad," Margie murmured. "A little too thin to be beautiful."

She stared a moment longer. "You're not a little girl anymore, Margie. You've got three beautiful daughters whom you have to support," she said to herself. "Get on with your life!"

But her mind spun backwards. Tears burned her eyes and blurred her vision as Margie shook her head and gritted her teeth. Margie's father had died when he was seventy-six and she was eight years old. Not too many years later, she had lost her mother from whom she had been separated for so long after her father's death. She thought of the devastation she felt when her mother abandoned Margie to marry her stepfather when she was eleven years old. Shuffled from one to the other of her seven brothers and five sisters, lonely and feeling as though she was somehow responsible for her mother's desertion, Margie had been a fragile young girl. She didn't see her mother for three years, and during that time she attended a multitude of schools, never being able to maintain friendships. When she did see her mother again and began to live with her and her stepfather, they never spoke a word about the abandonment. Margie kept all her childhood secrets buried deep inside. No one else knew of her pain and broken heart.

Though her mother tried to make up for those lost years by reassuring Margie of her love, she could not prevent the pain caused by her husband's alcoholism in scene after scene where he berated Margie and robbed her of what little self-esteem she had. Those memories of her stepfather still haunted Margie. The legacies of alcoholism and abandonment had carried into her relationship with Joel, her first husband, and destroyed their marriage. Though she had longed to get away, she had rushed headlong from an alcoholic heritage into a too young marriage. Even though she was now divorced and a single parent supporting three children who were the good part of a bad situation, Margie was terribly insecure. She never ventured far from her immediate environment in Utah, not even to the nearby states of Idaho and Wyoming.

Suddenly, her daughter Jessi bounced in the front door, her blond hair tousled, turning Margie's attention from the painful memories of the past to her pleasure at seeing her youngest child.

Jessi was seven years old and small for her age, strong-willed, very loving, and beautiful. She was eager for her mother's attention.

"Hi, sweetheart. Tell me about school."

Jessi's brown eyes gleamed. "Mom, I got a hundred on my math test. I have to go get packed to go to Dad's house. Wait till I tell him!"

Jessi's excitement about the coming weekend with her father overtook her triumph of the day. As daddy's little girl, she still felt hurt by the divorce, and she missed him. "I've put your clothes in the pink suitcase," Margie called. Jessi was already skipping to her bedroom to get ready for her big weekend away.

Soon afterward, Margie's middle child June walked in the front door. A tall twelve-year-old with long brown hair, big green eyes, and the face of a fashion model, she smiled at her mother. "How was your day, honey?" Margie asked.

"Oh, we had one of those dumb assemblies where the boys are so bored they use their gum as slingshots." She frowned. "I got hit a couple of times."

"That only means they like you, June. They're just immature."

Margie saw June as a beautiful butterfly who was emerging from its cocoon. This spring, for the first time, she had received a lot of attention from the boys at her school. The young girl, quiet and shy, seemed bewildered by all the fuss from the opposite sex but loved girl talk with her friends. Margie knew that today June's mind centered on the coming weekend of fun with the girls in her class.

Margie's oldest daughter, Julie, seventeen years old with long golden brown hair like her mother's and sparkling green eyes, arrived home from high school next. Her angelic, fair-complected face had earned her the title of "China doll" from one of her school teachers. Margie tried to give Julie space and love through her teenage mood swings and help her deal with her parents' divorce. Margie tried to give her attention now, but Julie gave her mother a few half-hearted descriptions of her day and hurried to her room to change. Margie knew she was at an age when an adult's questions seemed nosy and extraneous. Today, Julie couldn't wait to sleep over at her friend Amanda's house that night.

While her daughters were all busy with their own activities that weekend, Margie missed the times in the past when they all went out to dinner as a family on Friday nights. She felt a painful twinge of sadness for all that could have, should have, been—the family life she had dreamed of for her children, the one she had never had.

Life seemed so solitary now. Not only did the children lack a father except for isolated weekends and vacations, but she had no companion with whom to share the funny, sad, happy moments of child rearing, no less the more intimate moments. Margie dreamed of a love that did not hurt, of a man who was sensitive and cared what she was thinking and feeling, a man who made their family the center of his existence, a man who existed only in her thoughts. The dream took her from a lonely existence in the real world into a fantasy world where old wounds healed and pain disappeared.

As Margie sat transfixed, she reached for the postcard that Nila, her dear friend since high school, had sent her from her Hawaiian vacation. Margie smiled. Nila was such a good friend. Small in stature with short dark hair and blue eyes, Nila always had a kind word to say to everyone she met, though she had more than her share of life's problems. On the front of the postcard was a sensitive-looking but muscled man in a safari suit about to board a cruise ship. Margie held up the card and looked at it from different angles. She liked the man's dreamy blue eyes and his soft, wavy light brown hair with streaks of sunlit blond. The idea of cruising to some far-off island with him was a tantalizing dream.

Margie fell asleep that night with the man from the postcard on her mind. She dreamed of a romantic soulmate who brought roses to her and one red rose for each of her daughters.

In the morning Margie laughed at herself. "I'm like a love-sick teenager because of someone I created in my mind," she murmured as she began the housekeeping chores she never had time for during the week.

In the weeks to follow, when she wasn't busy working or caring for the house and her daughters, her thoughts roamed to this daydream of love and romance. She carried the postcard but kept it half-hidden in the visor of her car so that everywhere she went her secret fantasy stayed with her. *Someday, perhaps he will find me,* she told herself. *Someday, somehow, he will come.*

# CHAPTER ONE

## Cinderella's Night Out

THE humid July air hissed through the windows of Margie's home. She wiped away the steam and wished spring, her favorite season, had lasted a little longer. Spring, with its tiny buds poking out of every branch on the trees and pastel flowers peeking out of the earth to seek the gentle warmth of the sun, suited her best. Now the sun was too bright, the penetrating heat made it hard to breathe, and the trees seemed almost too green—as if they would burn themselves to death.

Summer fever hovered over Margie as she helped her three daughters pack for the special Fourth of July holiday and the vacation trip they planned with their father. Even though she would miss them dreadfully, she was glad to see their eager anticipation and good spirits as Joel drove into the driveway.

Joel's thin brown hair fell into his dark blue eyes as he opened the trunk of his car. Margie helped the girls arrange their suitcases in the back.

Margie hugged and kissed them and said, "I love you" to each daughter as she shed a few tears.

Julie, June, and Jessi waved and smiled as the car drove away.

Margie hesitated before she went back into her house. She shaded her eyes from the summer sun, looked in the direction her children had gone, and said a little prayer for them to be safe.

She slept fitfully that night, wishing her girls were home, and she spent the next day carefully straightening their rooms. Late that afternoon, Darrelette, her girlfriend since high school whom they all called Darrel, phoned and suggested a girls' night out at a country and western club for fun. For the first time, Margie agreed.

Although she had resisted the singles scene for a long time, maybe it would be good to stop worrying about the children and go out, she told herself. It had been so long since she'd gone anywhere except to work and to attend child-centered activities. She wanted to stop the pangs of loneliness. This might even be the night she'd meet her dream lover. Margie felt her face flush and went to her closet. Darrel had told her to dress Western. Slowly, she took out her blue Levis and a blue silk shirt, wondering if she really should go. Putting them on, she felt awkward and nervous. But at the sound of Darrel's car horn, she told herself she'd promised her friend she'd go, so she grabbed her purse and ran out the door.

Darrel noticed Margie's quietness as she got into the car and, as always, put her at ease. "You look great and we're going to have a great time, I promise." Darrel turned on the radio and began singing along. She tried to get Margie to sing along too, but Margie was too nervous. Darrel made small talk with Margie, trying to ease her mind. Before long, Margie was a little more relaxed as they drove under a crescent moon.

In a couple of minutes they were close to the Sagebrush Western Club. Soon the huge rustic wood building loomed before them. A statue of a cowboy stood in front. Cars and trucks filled the parking lot. Everyone they saw walking through the front door was dressed in Western attire. For a moment, Margie hesitated. Darrel linked her arm with hers. "Come on. I'll be with you. And I bet you'll see some familiar faces inside. Don't be nervous." Margie and Darrel joined the crowd.

Inside, they sat down at a table and ordered drinks. Margie watched shyly as Darrel looked around, pointing out the city cowboys and girls and waving to people she knew. As she listened to Darrel's joking descriptions, one man caught Margie's eye, because, like her, he just did not seem to fit in. Tall and slim, dressed formally in a gray blazer with a striped tie and a white dress shirt, he looked like a foreign nobleman and stuck out in the crowd of jean-clad, unshaven types with their cowboy hats and boots. *He's really attractive*, she mused. Then she sat up, startled. In fact, he reminded Margie of the picture on the postcard she carried around with her! He had longish, sunlit dark blond hair touched by gray at the temples. Just at that moment, he glanced her way. When he met her eyes, he smiled. Then he turned away to speak to someone else.

"Oh well," Margie murmured.

Margie turned and tried to see who Darrel was waving at now.

"You're doing fine," Darrel reassured her. Margie nodded self-consciously.

She didn't notice when, minutes later, the nobleman stood beside her. "Would you care to dance?" he asked formally. Taking her hand in his elegantly manicured one, he guided her to the dance floor. As he gently drew her close, he asked, "What is your name?"

"Margie!" she tried to shout over the blare of the country music. "What's yours?"

"Sean Paul Lanier," he responded in a deep resonant baritone.

He whispered his basic statistics in her ear. He was thirty-nine years old, two years older than she. He was an accomplished dancer, and gracefully led her through a few more songs, and when one of her shoes, which were a bit large, fell off, he gracefully bent down and slipped it back on her foot, looking almost princely. Then Sean walked Margie back to her table and left.

"His name is Sean," Margie shyly told Darrel. "I think his last name is Lanier." She added softly, "He's very nice."

"He's good looking and he seems gentlemanly," Darrel responded.

"We'll see," Margie said quietly.

The music started to play again. Margie looked around for Sean, but he walked right past their table without a glance in her direction.

"He's just acting cool," Darrel offered.

To hide her hurt, Margie looked away from Mr. Wonderful

and into the face of Mr. Nerd who next asked her to dance. A little flustered, she got up and walked to the dance floor.

The song seemed to drag on forever, but she tried to be nice to the stiff, balding, fiftyish man even when he stepped on her feet.

Just as she sat back down in her chair, Sean Lanier appeared again and asked her to dance. Margie's face glowed as they walked toward the dance floor.

A slow two-step began. "Do you mind this one?"

She said a quiet and shy, "No."

Sean took Margie gently in his arms as she melted under the soft glance of his dreamy blue eyes.

*Just like the postcard*, she thought.

As they continued their earlier interrupted conversation, Sean made Margie smile when he said, "I noticed how lovely you are when you first walked in."

Seemingly confessing, he said, "I'm afraid I'm younger than you are though. Thirty-five, to be exact. I told you I was thirty-nine because I thought you might not want to be with me."

Margie looked at him thoughtfully. *That seems odd. He looks older.* "You didn't have to do that." She smiled. "I hope we can be honest with each other."

"Of course we can, and should," he said, "always. My middle name is Paul," Sean stated, "and some people call me that. I think they don't always know how to pronounce Sean. I like to be called Sean Paul. Lanier is my last name."

Margie didn't know anyone who went by their first and middle names. It made Sean Paul Lanier seem different.

"Where are you from?" she asked as the music stopped. Without replying, Sean Paul led Margie back to her table. He asked first if it was all right, then he pulled up a chair and sat down.

"I'm from New Zealand, born and raised there."

Margie thought it strange that he didn't have an accent. She brushed the thought aside because she didn't know what a New Zealander sounded like anyway. The excitement of meeting someone from so far away made her heart beat faster.

Darrel, who had also been asked to dance, arrived back at the table with some friends from the dance floor, and Margie introduced everyone to Sean Paul.

Darrel, blunt and to the point, immediately asked, "Do you have a job?"

Darrel looked out for her friends and concerned herself with such matters.

Everyone at the table laughed at Darrel's forwardness. But Sean Lanier replied seriously, "Yes, I do have a job. I'm a chef at the Rosewood Restaurant. I'm getting experience so I can buy a place of my own."

Margie didn't know who felt more relieved, she or Darrel!

"You're okay then," Darrel responded, and they all laughed again.

As soon as the music started, Darrel and her friends took off for the dance floor again to find partners. Margie stayed behind at the table with Sean.

He impressed Margie when he said, "I've always wanted to have my own restaurant. I studied to be a chef in Paris, and now I'm almost ready to make it happen."

"Paris! Really?" Margie replied. "How wonderful!"

To Margie, who had never traveled anywhere and whose dreams seemed so far from fulfillment, Sean seemed full of purpose and adventure.

Two of Sean's friends stopped at the table. Steve's dark hair matched his thick, dark mustache. He looked like he worked out a lot, because his muscles were outlined by his tight-fitting shirt. Pat's bright red hair was a sharp contrast to his fair skin. Sean introduced them, they talked for a few moments about the health club Steve was buying, and then walked off.

As soon as they were gone, Sean continued their conversation.

"I've only been in town about a month," he said, "so I can't give you a lot of character references. But the friends I have made will tell you I'm a trustworthy person whom you can count on. I'd love to see you again. May I have your phone number?"

Margie hesitated slightly.

"I promise I'm okay." He smiled in his charming way, and she relented and told him the number.

Sean wrote it down on a paper napkin. "Thanks," he said, "for trusting me. I won't betray it. I'm going to call you very soon."

In the dark, smoke-filled room, they smiled and gazed into each other's eyes. Suddenly, bright lights came on.

Darrel raced up to the table. "Lights on! Time to go!" she laughed as she grabbed Margie's arm and pulled her toward the door.

Sean leapt out of his chair and hurried to catch up.

"May I take you to breakfast?" he asked.

Darrel answered protectively for Margie, "No!"

As Margie lagged behind her friend heading for the doorway, she turned back to Sean Lanier. "I'd better not. I need to know you better first, but you may telephone," she said a bit stiffly.

"I will," he called after her as Darrel hurried Margie out into the warm summer night highlighted by the crescent moon. They made their way to the car, giggling and laughing like schoolgirls as they went. Margie whispered, "I feel like Cinderella as the clock struck midnight."

"You're such a romantic," Darrel said.

When Margie arrived home, she kicked off her shoes and flopped onto the couch to ponder the night's events. Visions of dancing close to the exciting man she'd just met swam in her head.

Later, as she crawled into bed, Margie sighed. *Perhaps he's the one*, she thought hopefully. As she drifted off to sleep, the picture on the postcard and her memories of the evening with Sean Paul Lanier merged.

## CHAPTER TWO

# *First Date*

Two days passed before Sean Paul Lanier called Margie. "I really want to take you out," he pressed. Trying to be cautious about the handsome stranger, she suggested they talk on the phone for a while to get to know each other better first. He was instantly agreeable and called Margie each night all week long. They talked for hours at a time.

"I have a hard time with your two names," Margie said.

"Just call me Sean. It's okay," he answered.

"Okay, I will."

"Tell me more about yourself," Sean asked gently.

"I have three daughters," Margie informed him.

It pleased her when Sean said, "Girls are nice, not as rough and rowdy as boys."

Sean confided that he had lost his parents, a sister, and a brother in a plane crash.

"How sad," she murmured, "to be so alone."

After their conversations Margie felt more comfortable with Sean. He was certainly charming, and he impressed her with his sincerity. Finally, she agreed to go out with him. Excited that this would be her first real date since the divorce, she went to the mall to buy a new outfit. After trying on several, she settled on a gray silk dress which showed off her trim body.

The night of the date, Margie spent extra time on her hair and makeup. She was sitting in her robe in front of her makeup mirror when the phone rang.

"Hi, Margie," Sean's voice echoed. "I was so excited about our date that I bought a new outfit."

Margie smiled as she told him of the gray dress. Halfway through their conversation when she was starting to relax, she joked, "This is going to be an expensive relationship."

Unexpectedly, Sean retorted, "Well, spending like a drunken sailor won't go far with me."

This sudden criticism and the word "drunken" brought back a flood of bad memories to Margie of her alcoholic stepfather and the financial problems of her too early first marriage. "If that's how you feel, then I don't want to go out with you," she said, surprised and offended, and hung up the phone on him.

Afterward, Margie sat by the phone in disbelief at her strong reaction to Sean's words. However, in some strange way she also felt relieved. After several minutes she realized her date tonight with Mr. Wonderful no longer existed. Angry at herself and hurt, she spent the night brooding alone with the television set as her companion.

Days went by, and there were no more calls from the man whom she had just begun to hope was the answer to her dreams of Prince Charming. Then, the morning before her daughters were due home, Sean called. By this time she never expected to hear from him again.

"I called to see what happened," he said in a puzzled voice. "I don't understand. Did I do or say something wrong?"

"Sean, I'm sorry I overreacted. I've had so much pain in my life that sometimes a word or phrase brings it all back."

Sean seemed relieved. "After you hung up on me, I went to a neighbor's apartment to sulk and feel sorry for myself," he explained.

"I'm sorry I upset you, Sean," Margie apologized.

"No apology necessary as long as you agree to give me a second chance and go out with me," Sean replied. "I promise to choose my words very carefully. I really think we could be good together. What about tonight?"

"I can't," Margie said. "My daughters are coming home tomorrow, and I want to decorate the house to welcome them."

"What about next weekend?"

"Friday would be good," she said.

"Friday then. I want you to be comfortable."

After he hung up, Margie felt better. Her prince had not turned into a frog. She felt happier as she got ready for work at the cleaning business she co-owned with a friend.

At work, thoughts of Sean crossed her mind.

*Is he the one I've been waiting for?* she asked herself. *Why does he fill me with excitement and interest? Because he's from New Zealand? Or, because his family died in a plane crash? Because he looks so much like my postcard? I want to find out what attracts me to this mysterious man.*

Later that day when Margie came home from work, she took some of her eldest daughter's bath gel, drew a fragrant bubble bath, and relaxed in the tub. With Sean Paul Lanier still on her mind, she ate dinner alone, decorated the house, and thought about how much she missed her daughters.

The next morning was Saturday, and she began watching for her ex-husband's car even though they weren't due until early in the afternoon. She was standing at the window when Joel pulled into the driveway. Margie ran out the door to meet her precious girls. Jessi jumped out of the car and leaped into Margie's arms. Julie and June both ran to Margie and hugged her. All three talked at the same time telling Margie the details of their trip. Margie helped them haul their luggage and souvenirs into the house. They were pleased at the banners and balloons she had fashioned to welcome them back.

Later, at the special dinner she had fixed of their favorite, fried chicken and dumplings, the girls and she relaxed and caught up on the events they missed while they were apart. When they were eating the cake she'd made, Margie shyly said, "I have a date at the end of the week with a man named Sean."

"Is he cute?" Jessi asked.

"I think he is," Margie answered.

"Is he nice?" Julie asked, concerned.

"He's very thoughtful and polite," Margie said.

"Okay," they all answered together.

She was happy to see her daughters accepted her first date

so quickly. She knew they still felt some confusion over the divorce.

"It's just a date," she reassured them.

For the next few days the girls relaxed and called all of their friends while Margie caught up on their laundry and prodded the older girls to do their summer reading projects which they insisted didn't have to be done before the end of August. "School doesn't start till after Labor Day," they chimed in.

Thursday night she got a call from Nila, whom she'd told about her new mystery man. Nila had listened to Margie's story about the night they met, but called this time with bad news.

"I read an article in the newspaper about a murderer wanted by the FBI who may be in the area. I'm worried he could be this guy you're dating." Nila seemed concerned. "The man wanted by the FBI has a tattoo on his knuckles," she continued. "You better check him out. I'll drop the article off tomorrow."

After Margie hung up the phone, she felt a little worried too. *What do I really know about Sean? Only what he's told me.*

"I'll just check out his knuckles before I let him into the house," she murmured. "I'm probably being silly though."

Friday night, before Sean arrived, Julie left with friends and Jessi departed for her usual weekend with her father. June was to spend the night with her friend, Audrey, but the two of them decided to stay with Margie long enough to check this new man out. They giggled as Margie put on the last touch of makeup and her blue silk dress which she chose over the new gray one, because it was her favorite, and she felt more comfortable wearing it.

"You really look good, Mom." June grinned and added, "Mom, tell him that Audrey and I are sisters, okay?"

"Okay," Margie said with a smile.

The two girls kept peeking out the front window and saw Sean drive up in a blue Oldsmobile convertible. "Mom, he's here!" June called. "He's walking to the door."

Sean was wearing a navy blue blazer with an open-necked silk shirt and a medal of some kind around his neck.

"He is handsome," Margie murmured as she opened the door, but she didn't forget about looking for the tattoo.

While June and Audrey giggled in the background and before Sean could say hello, Margie blurted out, "I know you're going to think I'm crazy, but will you show me your knuckles?"

Sean looked surprised, but he did as Margie asked. She looked at the backs of his hands. There was no tattoo. She felt an enormous sense of relief.

Smiling now, she asked Sean into the house and introduced June and Audrey as sisters. Laughing, they ran down the hallway.

Margie told him about the girls' little joke and said, "Please sit down."

As Sean sat down on the couch, Margie said, "Now to explain why I asked you to show me your knuckles."

"Yes, please do," Sean said with a slight smile.

Margie pulled out the article from the newspaper that Nila had given her and handed it to Sean. "I told my friend Nila about you and she's worried that I may not know enough about you. I guess I'm a little worried too." He read it and raised his glance to meet Margie's eyes. "I heard about this guy," he responded. "Someone said he was seen in the Western club the night we met. I think I saw him. So you were afraid he might be me?"

She nodded, feeling sheepish.

"Oh, that's awful!" Sean responded. "Margie, I promised you you could trust me. Do you think they'd have hired me at the restaurant if I didn't have good references?"

Just then, before Margie could say another word, June and Audrey ran down the hallway in a hurry. They called goodbye as they headed out the door to go to Audrey's house.

"We'd better get on our way too," Sean said. "I made reservations for dinner at Henri's in Emigration Canyon."

As Sean opened the car door for Margie, he smiled and

said, "You'll have to give me directions since I'm new in town."

Margie smiled back and said, "Oh, that's right."

They were driving up the street when Margie suddenly noticed that Sean did indeed have a tattoo. It was near the medal on his right shoulder. Her heart pounded as she tried to remember the exact words of the newspaper article. Maybe the article had gotten the place wrong. But it had definitely said on the knuckles. Margie tried to make small talk and act normal. She told herself she was overreacting again. She took a deep breath to calm down and took a closer look at the tattoo. The design resembled a faded rose.

She summoned the courage to ask Sean as they entered the freeway, "What is that near your neck?"

"Oh, this stupid thing," he said, a little embarrassed. "This is supposed to be a flower. Believe me, I have regrets."

Somehow, Margie felt reassured by his answer. They sped along the freeway toward the canyon. They talked and laughed about everything and anything. Deep in conversation, Margie noticed they missed the exit off the freeway.

"I forgot you didn't know where to go," she apologized. "Turn at the next exit and we'll head back."

"I don't mind as long as I'm with you," Sean said.

Margie smiled as she blushed. "Thank you," she said.

The beauty and seclusion of the canyon surpassed the steel wonders of the city. The mountains stood high and majestic above the winding road with cars visible on the road beneath them and the starry sky above.

The magic of being one moment in the modern city and the next in a world of quiet natural beauty suffused Margie's thoughts. "I'm glad the mountains are so close to us," she said aloud.

"That's what I love about Utah, the majesty of steel and of God's mountains only moments apart," Sean said, capturing her thoughts as if they were his own.

The sound of rushing water in the stream below the road brought its music to Margie's ears. The canyon air cleansed and refreshed her as it brushed against her face. Margie felt the peace and tranquility of the Utah mountains she loved and that this stranger seemed to understand.

They soon arrived at Henri's. A young man in a black tuxedo seated them at an outdoor table to enjoy the canyon atmosphere. When he saw her shivering in the chill of the mountain air, the waiter brought Margie a sweater.

When she looked at the elaborate menu, she shook her head. "You choose," she said.

Sean ordered Caesar salad, chateaubriand for two, and a bottle of Châteauneuf-du-Pape. Then he turned toward her, his eyes drinking in hers as though they were the only two people on the restaurant terrace. "To your beauty," he said with his wine glass raised. "As wondrous as this night." As they watched, the sun drifted behind the mountains in streaks of beautiful red and pink against the navy sky. The evening seemed perfect.

As they were tasting the souffle Sean had ordered for dessert, Margie looked around and was surprised to see her friend Lara at another table with a group of people. Lara and Margie had met through their husbands several years before. They remained friends even though they were both divorced now. Lara's charming personality complemented her beautiful long brown hair and eyes. Margie excused herself from the table to go and say hello.

"Hi, Margie!" Lara said, smiling.

"Hi yourself!" Margie said. "When you get a chance, come over and meet Sean."

"Okay," Lara replied as she glanced where Margie indicated.

"Oh, cute!" Lara said, and winked.

"Yes, he's cute," Margie agreed. "I'd better get back before he disappears!"

Margie returned to Sean. He stood as she walked toward him, and like a gentleman, he pulled her chair out for her. Margie felt like a princess.

After the waiter cleared their dessert dishes, Lara walked up to their table.

"Hi, I'm Lara, Margie's friend," she said as she extended her hand toward Sean.

Sean looked up, quickly smiled, and said, "I'm Sean. Nice to meet you."

But Sean looked away as Lara tried to converse with him. His eyes never met Lara's eyes, and he seemed to be uncomfortable that she was there. Margie assumed he must be a little shy so she made conversation with Lara. Lara seemed bewildered as she said goodbye and went back to her table.

As soon as Lara left, Sean snapped out of his strange mood and returned to his thoughtful, charming self. He and Margie continued to enjoy the evening, and Margie brushed aside his unusual reaction to Lara.

*I'll call Lara tomorrow and explain that Sean is just bashful*, Margie said to herself.

As they left the restaurant, Sean picked a daisy that was growing wild on the edge of the parking area and brought it over to Margie. "A flower for a flower," he said. The romantic gesture touched her as they walked to the car holding hands.

As they drove home, the beauty of the stars hovered above them and the majestic mountains surrounded them. The eyes of prancing deer shone by the side of the road when the car lights flashed in their direction. "What a beautiful night!" Margie said.

"I think so too," Sean said.

The evening seemed to be ending too soon as Sean walked Margie up her front walk.

At the door, Sean, the perfect gentleman, said, "I'll call you tomorrow, and I hope you'll want to see me again."

He took her hand in his and kissed it.

Margie, a bit flustered, responded, "Yes, that sounds wonderful," as she put the key in the lock, opened the door, and glided inside.

When Margie climbed into bed later, she couldn't sleep. She lay wide awake as the lovely night replayed in her mind. Once or twice she thought of Sean's odd reaction to Lara, but she pushed away the memory. *No one's perfect*, she told herself. *I won't let small, meaningless things spoil my happiness. Not this time.*

# CHAPTER THREE

## Of Mice and Women

THE next day Margie received yellow roses with a note from Sean. "Thank you for a night to remember."

Margie called Nila and told her Sean was not the stranger she'd been afraid he was. "In fact, he's a dream. First a perfect evening, and then roses," Margie exclaimed. "I can't believe how wonderful he is."

Sean called later that day. "How about a drive up the canyon tomorrow," he suggested.

"Guardsman Pass is a beautiful place to go," Margie said.

"A beautiful place for a beautiful lady," Sean responded.

"You're too sweet," Margie said as she blushed.

Sean picked up Margie right on time. They headed out for their Sunday drive with a bright lemon sun warming them. Their conversation flowed, and Margie felt relaxed as they drove toward the mountains once again.

"I had the car washed and polished for this special occasion," Sean said.

"I guess I didn't tell you, Guardsman Pass is a dirt road," she said.

"A little dirt won't hurt anything," Sean reassured her. "At least we'll start out clean. Where's a nice place to stop and eat lunch?"

"Park City," Margie suggested.

"Park City it is then," Sean said with a smile.

They laughed as they hit the bumps on the dirt road, and the jostling moved Margie closer to Sean.

"It's kismet," he said smiling.

Around them were green landscapes, from the deep dark

hunter of the pine trees to the yellow-green of the bushes and the peridot of the grass below, all set against an aquamarine sky.

For a while the scenery engulfed Margie, but then suddenly a strange sensation came over her as they drove along the dirt road. She thought about her vulnerable situation. Here she was, alone with a man she hardly knew, on an isolated dirt road high in the mountains. For a moment she felt afraid. Thoughts of rape, murder, and abandonment entered her mind.

*That darn Nila. Why did she have to fill my head with her paranoid ideas?* she thought.

Margie reassured herself. *He's wonderful. You are fine! Calm down!*

The fear inside Margie subsided but didn't completely go away until they reached Park City and civilization. She felt thankful to see people again. She tried to brush her worried thoughts aside and enjoy her lunch with Sean.

The afternoon was once again filled with Sean's admiring comments. When the day was over and she entered her home and closed the door, she told herself, *I deserve happiness. I have to trust myself and him. I don't have any reason not to.*

The next day the doorbell rang. When Margie opened the door, there on her front porch lay a beautiful bouquet of pink roses and a small wrapped gift. She looked around and, seeing no one, picked up her new-found treasures and brought them into the house.

The card on the flowers read, "Thank you, my beautiful lady, for a beautiful day. Love, Sean Paul Lanier."

Margie tore open the gift wrap on the small box and found a tiny Lalique bottle of Joy perfume.

Margie was overcome. *It's too expensive but so beautiful*, she mused.

When Sean called Margie later that day, her momentary uncertainty of yesterday in the mountains had almost evaporated.

"Thank you for the flowers and perfume," Margie said. "You are always so thoughtful."

"My pleasure, and I always will be," Sean answered.

When the conversation ended, Margie was left alone once again with her thoughts.

*I wish I could banish all my questions and just enjoy this new wonderful man in my life. Maybe it's just all I went through before. I have to start living in the present. I can't blame Sean for my past hurts*, she told herself firmly.

A few days later, Sean called and invited Margie to dinner. When he arrived to pick her up, he presented her with a dozen red roses, along with three red roses, each tied with silk ribbons for her daughters. A wondrous sensation crept over Margie as she realized that her daydream about the man on the postcard who brought roses to her girls as well as her had just become a reality!

Sean had already met June. That night, when he met Julie and Jessi for the first time, all Margie's prayers seemed about to be answered. He was so natural and gentle with the girls. Jessi talked on and on while Sean listened intently. Though Julie was a bit standoffish, he drew her out and seemed to enjoy the seventeen-year-old's stories of classes, friends, and school dances. All Margie's daughters, delighted, thanked Sean for their roses and ran to put them in water. Margie felt elated as she closed the front door behind her to go on their date.

This time, Sean took Margie to the Rosewood Restaurant where he worked as a chef-manager. They enjoyed a very pleasant dinner with preferential treatment from the staff.

"I think I'll nickname you Mouse," Sean told Margie over the chocolate mousse cake for dessert.

"Mouse?" Margie asked with surprise. "That's different. Why Mouse?"

"Because you remind me of a cute little mouse," Sean stated.

Margie smiled, "Okay, I guess mice can be cute. They are little. I'd never touch one though."

Sean laughed. "What about Mickey Mouse?" he asked.

"I'd rather be Minnie Mouse," Margie said.

Sean chuckled. "See how cute you are!"

The next day Margie received roses again with a card that read, "To my Mouse. Love, Sean Lanier."

When he called her later that day, Margie thanked him for the flowers. Then Sean asked if she'd like to try out a new restaurant the next night.

Margie said, "That sounds wonderful."

"Okay, see you then," Sean answered.

The next evening as Sean and Margie sat across from each other in a booth in an elegant Italian restaurant called Valentino's, relaxing and enjoying the atmosphere and each other's company, Margie asked Sean more about his childhood and his family.

"I grew up in a monastery in New Zealand where I learned karate," Sean informed her.

Margie pictured monks in robes who bowed and taught the ancient arts of Kung Fu and meditation.

*What an unusual life*, she thought.

Sean continued, "My children are college age. One's in school in Montana and the other in California."

"How nice," Margie said.

Margie wondered how his children could be older than her children. *Sean said he's younger than me*, she thought. *He must have married in his teens to have grown children.*

With sadness in his eyes, Sean revealed, "I raised the children myself, because my wife died in childbirth with Nickie, our daughter."

With compassion, Margie said, "Oh! I am so sorry! I'm impressed you raised the children alone. I know how hard it can be sometimes."

"You do what you have to do," Sean said.

Sean excused himself a few times during the meal to use the phone. Margie thought maybe he was really checking on the kitchen staff, to see how they were managing without him.

"Is everything okay?" she asked when he returned.

"I need to tell you something," Sean said with a serious look. "I can't keep this from you."

Margie turned anxious as she asked, "What, Sean? What do you need to tell me?"

"In addition to my job here, I work for the government. I deliver top secret documents," he said. "I'll be out of town the next few days."

Sean looked at Margie, whose mouth had dropped open. "Does that bother you?" he asked.

"I don't know what to think," she said, confused.

"I have top-secret clearance. I've worked for the government ever since I was released from the army," Sean explained.

Margie's heart quivered. "Do you have to carry a gun?" she asked with concern.

"Sometimes I do," he said. "It just depends on the situation."

Sean reached over to take Margie's hand. "You don't like this, do you?"

"No," she responded.

A look of worry crossed Sean's face. "You mean more to me than anything," he said. "I'll stop the government work."

Stunned, Margie managed to say, "Okay."

Concerned at Sean's revelations, Margie sat at the table in silence. *What is this all about?* she wondered. *How do I know for sure it's true? Maybe he thinks he's James Bond, or maybe this is a harmless ploy to impress me.*

She stared at him. A strange thought popped into her head. *Is this the man of my dreams or my nightmares?*

Sean started to talk, trying to ease Margie's mind. "Don't worry. I want to make you happy. I won't do anything to mar what we've found." As with the earlier incidents, some of Margie's fear began to drift away under Sean's reassurances. But then he got up from the table and walked out the front door. Margie's heart contracted again as she sat at the table alone.

*What is the matter with this man?* she asked herself.

As Margie's mind raced in confusion, Sean tapped her on the shoulder. He was carrying a big gift-wrapped box topped with a beautiful bow.

"Surprise!" he said.

Margie, overwhelmed by all of Sean's seeming contradictions, shook her head. "You left the table without a word! I thought you walked out on me!"

Sean laughed and said, "The atmosphere became a little too tense in here. I thought it was the right time to give you this gift."

"If you keep this up, I'll have a heart attack!" Margie exclaimed.

The present worked. Margie forgot about the secret government job and Sean's need to carry a gun.

Margie's hands shook as she opened the gift. She found two short tennis dresses made out of a fine cotton knit. One was a blue dress with the name "Mouse" embroidered across the front, and the other was a pink dress that said, "Margie."

Surprised, Margie said, "Thank you."

Margie didn't know whether to enjoy all this up-and-down excitement or scream and run the other way.

That night, Margie climbed into bed exhausted and with a lot on her mind. *This relationship is strange*, she thought. *Maybe I ought to just end it.*

She had to admit that the excitement and intrigue generated by Sean kept her involved though. As Margie tried to go to sleep, she wondered if she'd find roses the next day on her front porch.

*Do I want more flowers?* she thought. *Do I want this relationship? Maybe I need to think about all this.*

Although Margie didn't hear from Sean for a few days, she did receive more roses.

"My house is a flower shop," she laughed as she called Darrel.

"Is Sean on his top-secret mission?" Darrel asked.

"I don't know where he is," Margie said, "but at least I can catch my breath while he's away."

Sean stopped by the house on the next Saturday. Not a word was said about the government or top-secret papers, and Margie did not ask. He helped Margie work in the yard, and she felt more relaxed than the last time they were together. Julie, June, and Jessi were on a camping trip with their father for the weekend, so Sean and Margie enjoyed a quiet day together at her house.

"I'll fix us some lunch," Margie told Sean. "I'm a little intimidated though, because you're a chef."

"Whatever you fix will be great," Sean said.

The first meal Margie fixed for this talented chef consisted of a not-so-fancy tuna fish sandwich about which he teased her, and they both laughed.

But, while Margie cleaned up after lunch, Sean suddenly became quiet and withdrawn. He didn't answer when Margie spoke to him. She noticed his eyes darken as he just glared at her. Their splendid day together turned into an uncomfortable situation. Margie felt that same icy fear creep up inside her. She didn't know what to do or what to say. She just wanted Sean to leave as soon as possible. She didn't want to be alone with him anymore.

"Sean," Margie said.

He did not answer.

"Sean!" she called in a loud voice.

"What?" Sean asked with annoyance.

"I'm sorry. I don't feel well. Do you mind? I'd like to be alone," Margie stated.

"I don't mind. Are you okay?" Sean questioned.

"I'll be fine once I get some rest," she answered.

As soon as Sean left, Margie bolted the front door shut. She ran around the house in a panic, checking that all the doors and windows were locked. She tried to catch her breath as she picked up the phone and called Lara, the friend she'd seen at Henri's.

Margie explained to Lara what had just happened.

"Sometimes I feel like I'm in heaven. Other times I feel like I'm losing my mind," Margie said. "What is wrong with me?"

"Either you're falling in love or there's something weird about Sean. Remember the day I met him at the restaurant?" Lara asked. "He didn't meet my eyes when we spoke. I know you told me that he's shy. But," she hesitated and then confessed, "it's as though he has something to hide. Then again, maybe we're just looking for problems where there are none."

"I can't stay here alone! I'm too jumpy," Margie cried.

"Come over right now. You can spend the night here," Lara offered.

Margie felt relieved as she packed a few things and ran to her car. She cried all the way to Lara's house. Lara gave her hot cocoa and Margie calmed down. Later they laughed about the incident.

"I think I'm overreacting," Margie said. "Maybe it's an anxiety attack from all this romance."

"Yes, I suppose that could explain it." Lara laughed. "Too much of a good thing, I guess."

When the phone rang, Lara answered it while Margie sipped her cocoa. A surprised look came over Lara's face.

"It's Sean," she said, cupping the phone. "Do you want to talk to him?"

"No!" Margie yelled as all her anxiety returned.

"Margie is busy right now," Lara stated. She cupped the phone again. "He's insisting," she said and raised her eyebrows at Margie.

Margie took the telephone and said a meek, "Hello."

"What's the matter?" Sean said in an angry voice. "I thought you were sick."

"What do you mean?" Margie said. "How did you get Lara's phone number?"

Sean's voice grew calmer. "I called your place. There was no answer. Then I remembered I saw Lara's number next to your phone and remembered it," he answered. "I thought you didn't feel well and wanted to rest."

"I just needed to get away!" Margie explained.

"From me?" Sean asked.

"Maybe," Margie said softly. She hung up the phone.

Margie looked at Lara and said, "I don't know about him!"

"Maybe you need a break from him," Lara said.

"Maybe I do need a break," Margie said slowly. "Why does he scare me like this? Why do I feel great with him one moment and terrified the next? Maybe I just need some rest. I always get jumpy when I'm overtired."

"I agree," Lara said. "You'll feel better in the morning."

The next day, Margie did feel better and decided her anxiety was due to becoming committed to a new relationship after all she'd gone through. Lara and Margie chatted over a cup of morning coffee. "I'm not going to worry anymore about last night. I'll chalk it up to a bad case of nerves."

Several days later, Sean called. He was sweet, full of charm, and apologetic for his overreaction. Margie wanted to tell Sean of the fear she sometimes felt toward him, but she kept her thoughts to herself.

*He'll think I'm as crazy as I think I am*, she thought.

Sean and Margie let the incident drop.

On Tuesday, Sean introduced Margie to his roommate, Gerry Sue. To Margie this woman seemed to be another strange piece of the puzzle. Margie didn't know why though.

*My imagination is out of control again*, she thought. *Maybe I'm just a little jealous.*

Tall and dark haired, Gerry Sue worked as a teacher and appeared to be nice. Though Sean was solicitous of her, it was obvious there was nothing romantic between them and they were just good friends. She went by two names just as Sean did. Gerry Sue shared a two-bedroom apartment with Sean not far from where Margie lived. Soon Sean announced that he had become part owner of the White Horse Restaurant in town and that Gerry Sue had also invested in the restaurant.

As the weeks passed, Sean and Margie were growing more involved. Things seemed to be more comfortable. Margie didn't feel as threatened and afraid. Sean always sent flowers and little gifts and always knew the perfect thing to say and do to make her feel special. Her fear drifted away.

# CHAPTER FOUR

## *Summer Sun*

As Margie sat at her kitchen table looking out the window, she watched the pale blond, waning summer sun play on the leaves of her neighbor's maple tree.

Although her heart told her everything was wonderful, Margie's mind told her to be careful about her relationship with Sean. Something didn't seem quite right. Their relationship, like a roller-coaster ride, went up to a wonderful place and then down to one of confusion.

"Maybe I just need some sleep. Between Sean and the children, I'm running myself ragged twenty-four hours a day."

Suddenly, in the midst of her thoughts about him, Sean stood at Margie's kitchen window. Startled, Margie's heart ricocheted.

*I wonder why he came without calling and went through the backyard*, Margie wondered as she opened the back door and invited Sean inside.

They sat down at the table. Sean seemed different to Margie. He shook with nervous intensity, and his eyes looked blurry, as though he were drunk.

*What is wrong with him this time?* Margie reflected.

When Margie questioned Sean about his appearance, he responded with an abrupt, "I've got to leave," and, as quickly as he had appeared, he walked out.

"Here we go again," she said.

Later in the day, Sean called and apologized. "I'm sorry I acted so bizarrely. I'm a bit diabetic and I hadn't had anything to eat."

So there was a logical explanation. She shouldn't have

jumped to conclusions so fast. And he must be self-conscious about his illness. She had to make him feel more at ease.

"Sean," Margie said, "there's always plenty of food at my house, and you're welcome to whatever you want."

Sean answered, "That's okay. I feel fine now. Do you want to come over later to my place and listen to music, maybe get in the hot tub?"

"Yes," Margie agreed. "That sounds peaceful."

As they listened to soothing music and talked that night, Margie asked Sean what brought him to Utah.

A sad look overshadowed Sean's face as he said, "I managed a country club where I met my girlfriend, Stacy. Then when she died in a car accident, I wanted to get away as soon as possible."

Sean showed Margie a picture of Stacy. Margie was amazed at how much Stacy resembled her. Sean also showed Margie pictures of him with straight hair, and they both laughed.

With crystal stars shining down on them, they climbed into the hot tub, and all Margie's cares evaporated. In the quiet night, Sean spoke of love and romance. Margie liked this side of Sean. He was so kind and sweet. With him, she now felt safe and protected. "I want to devote myself to one woman forever," he said. "And I think you're that woman." She nestled into his arms. The evening was enchanting. She wished it could last forever.

The next day Margie's doorbell rang. There stood Sean.

"Do you have time to go somewhere with me?" he asked.

"Sure," Margie said. "Is it a surprise?"

"You'll see," he said.

They drove to a health club called Salt Lake Fitness.

"Do you need to work out?" Margie questioned. "Are you trying to tell me something?"

Sean just smiled as he took Margie's hand and led her through the front door. He took Margie on a tour of the spa and told her that he was a member. His friend, Steve, whom Margie met at the dance club that first night, was the manager of the club.

"The surprise is," Sean said, "you are now a member too."

"I am?" Margie asked, and she was surprised.

"I got a membership for you and the girls. We'll have fun working out together," Sean responded.

A little unsure, Margie agreed nevertheless. "It sounds like fun."

On the way home, Sean offered to buy workout clothes for Margie and her daughters. Margie refused his offer.

Sean persisted, "I won't take no for an answer."

Just as Margie stepped out of the car, Sean handed her five hundred dollars in cash.

"I can't accept this!" she exclaimed.

"You'll all look cute in workout clothes, and that will be my enjoyment," Sean insisted.

Sean hurried and shut the car door before Margie could refuse again. She stood in disbelief as he drove out of sight.

A few days later, Margie took her daughters to the mall, not to buy workout clothes though. She put the money Sean had given her in the bank to return to him later.

Arriving home with the girls late in the afternoon, Margie opened the front door and turned to walk down the hallway. She and her daughters stopped in their tracks as their eyes focused on jogging suits and shorts and shirts that hung from the doorways to each of the bedrooms. Margie walked toward the articles of clothing. Though she was astounded at the Santa Claus aspect of this gesture, a sudden sense of panic came over her.

"Who's been in my house?" she questioned.

She examined the shirts. The price tags still hung from them. The sizes for both the girls and her were correct.

"They must be from Sean!" Jessi exclaimed.

"But how did he get all this in here?" Margie asked.

Margie didn't know whether to feel grateful for his thoughtfulness or fearful that he had invaded her home and gone against her wishes about the clothes. Telling her daughters not to touch the new clothes, she called Sean, sounding upset.

"I am so sorry!" he apologized. "I meant to surprise you.

I knew by the look on your face you weren't going to keep the money I gave you, and I knew you couldn't afford those things because of the divorce. I got in through your unlocked bathroom window. I didn't mean any harm. Please forgive me!"

Not knowing what to say, Margie hung up the phone.

The next day Margie received more roses and a phone call.

"Please, let's make up!" Sean pleaded. "I didn't mean to scare you. How about lunch?"

"I can't go to lunch! I'm on my way to work and I have to work tonight too!" Margie said, still uncertain of her feelings.

"Then, let me take your daughters to the amusement park while you're at work," Sean begged.

"No!" Margie said firmly.

"Just tell me why you won't let me do that?" Sean asked.

"I don't trust strangers with my children!" Margie exclaimed. "We'll have to know each other a lot better for that."

Sean apologized again and hung up the phone. Margie sat down as uncertainty engulfed her.

*I don't know what to think*, she thought. *Is something wrong with him, or me? Is he just a wonderful guy, and I'm too scarred by the past to appreciate his caring ways, or is he an obsessive nut, from whom I should stay away?*

Margie went to work and felt the pit of her stomach churn all day.

After work, Margie felt exhausted as she drove home. The house was eerily quiet as she entered. She went to look for her daughters. No one was there. Her heart skipped several beats as she walked back to the kitchen. Then she saw the note on the kitchen table. "We've gone for ice cream with Sean. Love, Julie, June, Jessi."

Panic overtook Margie's entire body, and she started to cry. She was trying to get herself together to call the police when Sean drove up with her daughters. The girls laughed with delight as they ran into the house. Margie went outside to talk to Sean.

"You scared me half to death," she yelled. "You don't

know the meaning of the word no. I want out of this whirlwind relationship! When you took my children without my permission, that was the last straw!"

Margie stormed into the house as Sean walked away with his head down and got into his car. Margie felt relief, mingled with sadness, as she heard him drive away. In so many ways, Sean was the most wonderful man she'd ever met. There was just something about him that made her uneasy. Margie needed to be alone and get herself back together. She wanted to get off this roller-coaster ride!

# CHAPTER FIVE

## An Anguished Moment

ALTHOUGH Margie missed the excitement and romance, she felt a sense of relief now that Sean was gone. The busy days of early September dispelled Margie's fear and dismay. Though she felt lonely, she went on with her life, with work and the care of her three girls who were going back to school.

Several weeks later, Margie came home from work one evening and found an urgent note on her front door. She recognized Sean's handwriting. With trembling fingers, she opened it. "I need to talk to you. A terrible thing has happened. Love, Sean Paul." It was then she realized how much she missed him. The fact that something bad had befallen Sean made her feel bereft. Margie called Sean. His voice was a whisper, as though his whole body was drained.

Sean cried, "My daughter, Nickie, and her boyfriend, Jeff, visited Jeff's parents in Chicago. Nickie has been in a car accident caused by a drunk driver. She's in a coma in a hospital there."

"Oh my God! No!" Margie screamed. "I'll be right over!"

As quickly as she could, she explained the situation to Julie. "I have to go over there to Sean's apartment to comfort him right now." As she drove in the fading sunlight, the closer she got to his apartment the more her heart began to clutch. *What words can I say to make him feel better?* Margie thought.

Parking her car, she walked toward Sean's building. The sounds and sights of summer's end surrounded her: a man mowing his lawn, another man planting mums in a flower bed, the laughter of children drifting from a playground nearby. She tried to imagine the pain Sean felt, and it was almost like it was her own.

"Maybe I acted too quickly," Margie murmured. "Is this a sign to bring us back together? Sean needs me now. Maybe I need him too."

When Sean opened the door, Margie embraced him. He was pale and lifeless as he cried in Margie's arms. She helped him to the couch, where he fell in a slump.

Sean wept. "My daughter and her boyfriend planned a surprise visit here to Salt Lake for my birthday."

Margie's sympathy reached out to Sean as they cried together. She held Sean in her arms and listened as he spoke of love and devotion for his daughter. She stayed with Sean as long as possible and then left to go home to her daughters. Though she felt terrible, Margie was glad she'd been there to comfort Sean. The thought of one of her own daughters in a coma brought anguish to her heart. Margie pushed the tears away as she turned into her driveway.

She hugged each of her daughters as she told them what had happened. Margie thought of Sean and prayed for Nickie to come out of the coma soon and be okay.

"This is too much for a parent to bear!" she cried.

It was past midnight when Margie, too exhausted to call Sean, fell asleep.

She was awakened the next morning by the telephone. Sean was hysterical. "Nickie died!" he screamed.

Margie didn't want to believe this terrible tragedy as she cried in shock. They discussed drunk drivers and their innocent victims through their tears.

Sean sobbed, "I can't live without my child!"

"Yes, you can!" Margie pleaded. "I will help you."

"Will you?" Sean asked.

"Of course I will," Margie said.

Sean calmed down and said, "I want to ship Nickie's body back to New Zealand. I'd better hang up the phone to make the arrangements. Thank you for your kind words. You mean so much to me."

"Call me any time of the night or day if you need to talk," Margie said.

Sean, his voice drained and weak, asked, "Do you still have the five hundred dollars I gave you? I may need some cash. Tomorrow's Sunday and I'm in no shape to go out now."

"Yes, I'll bring it right over. I know you will need it," Margie said.

Margie ran to her car as a late summer rain, thick and filled with humidity and fog, began to fall. The weather was as dismal as the situation. She drove in the rain toward the bank as tears flowed down her face once more.

*Why did this happen?* Margie thought. *It's not fair! What do you say to a man for whom you care who has just lost his only daughter?*

Margie felt pain and sadness for Sean. She wanted to be there for him. She wanted to help him with his grief. With her heart full of compassion for Sean, she stopped at the bank, withdrew the money he had given her and quickly drove to his apartment complex.

Margie ran up to Sean's apartment and rang the doorbell. Though he had sounded hysterical on the telephone, she was not prepared for the look on Sean's face when he opened the door. The man she saw before her was not the Sean she knew, but someone else. His blue eyes were cold and eery as though he were possessed by a demon. Margie was filled with terror. She saw the anger in Sean's flushed face as he demanded she come inside. Though she told herself that people often act strangely when grief-stricken by the loss of a loved one, there was something about that look that terrified her. All compassion drained out of Margie. Quickly, she handed Sean the money, made an excuse, and left. She ran to the parking lot, her heart beating as fast as the pouring rain. Opening the car door, Margie jumped inside, inserted the key, and turned on the motor. She sped away and could not suppress a feeling of elation. She'd escaped! What she had escaped, she did not know. Margie both cried and laughed as she drove home. So many emotions were jumbled together inside her: fear, compassion, confusion, love, hate, anxiety, anger, sadness. She didn't know what she felt anymore.

# CHAPTER SIX

## The Return of Prince Charming

DURING the next few weeks, Margie didn't call Sean, nor did she hear from him. Although she thought a lot about him, Margie tried to stay busy at her job and with her daughters. She wondered if Nickie was laid to rest in New Zealand and how Sean was surviving the death of his beloved daughter. Yet, after her last meeting with him she felt she, and perhaps he, needed space.

And, as fortune would have it, another traumatic event captured her attention. Margie's friend, Darrel, worked the graveyard shift at the copper mine. Late one night, Darrel's teenaged son, Tim, called to inform Margie that his mother had been in a serious car accident.

Tim's voice was hysterical. "Mom took the freeway. She took the airport exit and the street was quite dark. Mom told me the darkness frightened her. She was turning the corner in second gear, when out of nowhere, a horse tried to jump her car."

"A horse?" Margie asked, surprised.

"Yeah, can you believe it?"

Margie wondered if the horse cleared the small Toyota Darrel drove. Otherwise, she imagined the damage to the car and Darrel.

Tim calmed down and continued. "The horse hit the top of the car and slid off. I guess other horses wandered around. The horse was dark, chestnut in color, so Mom didn't see it."

"How's your mom?" Margie blurted out, interrupting him.

"The horse flattened the car and pinned Mom inside," Tim continued. "She couldn't move or open the door. When the paramedics arrived, she complained that her back hurt. They used the Jaws of Life to get her out. The car was smashed in like a sardine can! I saw the car when I arrived at the accident with my dad. They put a brace on her neck and carried her on a board. I don't think she remembers much."

"Tim, where is she?" Margie asked. "I need to know!"

"She's in intensive care at Avenue Hospital," he said. "They tried to round up the other horses when the police got there."

"I'll go to the hospital right now, Tim," Margie said.

"They won't let you in to see her if you're not family," Tim cautioned.

"I am family!" Margie said. "I've got to go to her! Thanks, Tim. Goodbye."

Tim wanted to tell Margie more, but Margie just wanted to go and see how her friend was. By now, it was almost midnight.

When Margie arrived at the hospital, she told the nurse in the intensive care unit that she was Darrel's sister. In a sterile, stark room, Darrel lay hooked up to machines. Tubes protruded everywhere. She was sleeping, her face a pasty white. Margie held Darrel's hand and wept.

Hearing the sound, Darrel awoke and looked at Margie. "I don't remember anything," she said. "All I remember is the pain. I yelled, 'My back hurts!' over and over."

"The nurse says you have a serious back injury," Margie confirmed. "But you'll be fine."

"How did you get in here to see me?" Darrel asked.

"I told them I was your sister," Margie said.

"You are!" Darrel said as she tried to smile. "They asked me if I was drunk or on drugs. Hell, I was on my way to work! I didn't jump in the horse's way! He jumped in mine. Poor horse."

"The horse must have been drunk," Margie said to lighten things up. They both laughed.

Darrel remained in intensive care and on the critical list for three days. Margie was there as much as she could be. Darrel's first day in a regular room, a visitor appeared.

A smiling, somewhat familiar man offered the flowers in his hand. "Darrel, how are you?" he asked. "Margie told me about the accident and I was concerned."

When he mentioned Margie's name, Darrel realized who he was. She was surprised but touched by his thoughtfulness.

"Where's Margie?" Darrel asked, confused at seeing Sean alone. The last Darrel knew about Sean was what Margie told her when she last visited: that she and Sean were estranged.

"I'm right here," Margie said, walking into the room.

After their visit, Sean walked Margie outside. He was full of apologies for the way he had acted when she brought the money to his apartment. "I took the pain of the loss of my daughter out on you."

Sean voiced his regrets over and over and reached Margie's heart with words of love and affection. He asked if they could start over.

"Start over?" Margie asked. "How?"

"Let me just call you on the phone. I won't push or go too fast," he promised.

To talk on the phone seemed innocent enough, so Margie said, "Yes, I guess that's okay."

No more flowers or gifts were left on Margie's front porch. She and Sean just talked for hours on the phone as they had in the week before their first date. Margie expressed her anxieties and Sean kept reassuring her of his love. Sean laid Margie's fears to rest. He seemed sincere about doing anything to make this relationship work.

Sean began coming over and helping with the yard work. He even trimmed the hedges by hand when the electric hedge trimmer broke. He tried so hard to win Margie over and impress her. They danced together, barbecued, went to the pool, bowled, and did child-centered activities with Margie's daughters. Margie felt relieved that her fear and confusion no longer existed.

One night, Sean took Margie to a movie. In the movie, a married man cheated on his wife with a woman he'd just met. The mistress did not want the affair to end. She began to stalk the man. When the man rebuffed her advances, the woman damaged his car with acid, killed their family pet, and kidnapped his daughter. The police didn't help, because there was no proof the woman was guilty. In the end, the man killed the obsessed woman when she tried to kill him and his wife with a knife.

Sean sat next to Margie in the movie holding her hand. He patted her when Margie covered her eyes during the intense parts and reassured her. She was glad he sat next to her. Margie felt safe with him now.

Sean and Margie had been working out at the health club together. They invited Darrel, now recovering, and her boyfriend, Ted, to join them. By this time, the doctor had okayed light weight training and exercise to strengthen Darrel's back. Sean paid for their membership. "No one's ever been so wonderful to me or cared so much about my friends," Margie said, entranced with Sean's good deeds. Sean and Ted lifted weights while Darrel and Margie took a Jazzercise class. Sean began to look even more like the muscle-bound hunk on her postcard. Gray streaked his blond hair, making him even more distinguished looking.

"My hair's turning gray because of you," Sean said with a laugh. "See what you do to me."

The strange personality quirks from before seemed to be gone, and Margie was pacified. Sean tried so hard to do everything right.

As the months went by, Sean persuaded Margie to let him upgrade her house. "I can finish your basement and put a hot tub in the backyard for you," he said with excitement in his voice. "If you take out a loan, I'll help you with the payments." At his bequest, she took out a large second mortgage. By this time, Sean had suggested a pool, too. And Margie gave him all her money.

Ted helped Sean work on the basement. Together they put sheet rock on the walls, sawed wood, and bonded as friends. One day, however, another strange event occurred.

"Sean!" Ted yelled while they worked.

Sean did not respond.

*Maybe the music on the radio is too loud*, Ted thought.

"Sean!" Ted yelled again.

Still no response.

Ted hesitated and yelled, "Sean Paul!"

Sean answered.

When Ted questioned Sean, Sean said, "I'm just used to Sean Paul. Most people call me by both names."

So Ted called him Sean Paul from then on, and Sean answered.

Margie explained to Ted, "Sometimes it's hard for me to get Sean to answer too. I'm determined not to call him Sean Paul though. It's too stilted. Just give Sean time."

Margie's house payment doubled. Sean helped her with the payments as he promised. He also bought a new black Toyota truck. Sean explained to Margie that he needed her signature to buy the truck, because in New Zealand he always paid for everything in cash. Therefore, he needed her help to build his credit.

"The truck will be in both our names," Sean said. "You can drive it too and I'll make all the payments myself."

In early November, Sean bought Margie a blue sapphire and diamond ring. "It's a promise ring," he said. "That's my true-blue heart." He laughed. Sean slowed down when she asked him to slow down. He reassured Margie often. Sean's reassurance, love, and devotion helped Margie to forget whatever fear she had felt before. Love and trust replaced the fear. Sean became the fantasy man of whom Margie had dreamed, and this helped Margie to forget the traumas of the past.

The leaves on the trees were turning a rusty, burnt orange. Just before Thanksgiving, Sean took Margie and her daughters for a ride up the canyon to enjoy the last of the autumn colors. Margie felt no fear this time as they traveled on the canyon road. When they arrived at the scenic lookout, Margie's girls jumped out of the car and gathered brightly colored leaves to take home and press.

Time passed swiftly. The trees were soon frosted with glistening white snow. Everyone looked forward to Christmas. Sean and Margie built a huge snowman in the front yard with Julie, June, and Jessi. They enjoyed playful snowball fights.

Sean shoveled snow from the driveway and sidewalks while Margie's daughters played in the snow nearby. The house was a winter wonderland adorned with Christmas lights. Everything turned around, and Margie enjoyed every minute of her new life with Sean.

Sean always wore a heavy gold necklace around his neck. One day he came to pick Margie up to shop for Christmas presents. She noticed he didn't have the necklace on.

"Where's your necklace?" Margie asked.

"Lost. I can't find it anywhere," Sean said.

"Oh no, that's too bad. I wonder where it is." she said.

"It'll show up somewhere, I'm sure," he said.

"Maybe you'll get a new one for Christmas," Margie said as she smiled and winked.

Sean smiled back. "Let's get on our way. I want to get this over with. I'm not much of a shopper."

Sean decided to sit on a bench in the mall with all the other men who waited for their wives and girlfriends.

Sean handed Margie his wallet and said, "Pick out something spectacular for you and the girls. I want my presents to be special. I'll just get some ice cream and wait out here."

"Okay, you chicken," Margie said as she kissed Sean on the cheek.

Margie walked into a clothing store and browsed around. A beautiful red cashmere sweater caught her eye. Carefully, Margie took the sweater off the table and went into a room to try it on. She placed Sean's wallet on the bench inside the room. As Margie started to take off her blouse to try on the sweater, she glanced down at Sean's wallet. She sat down next to it. She picked the wallet up and held it in her hand. She wanted to look inside. Margie felt too guilty to snoop though, so she set the wallet back down on the bench. She tried the sweater on and loved it. She went to the cash register and paid.

As she walked away, a piece of yellow paper fluttered down from Sean's wallet. As she picked it up to replace it, she idly flipped through the papers inside the wallet: driver's license, Utah identification, Social Security card, business cards, wallet-sized pictures of Margie and her daughters. Not able to stop herself, Margie unfolded the yellow piece of paper. It was a slip from a pawn shop for Sean's gold necklace!

Margie trembled. *He didn't lose his necklace! Sean pawned the necklace for money! My God, he's been spending so much on us—the house, the truck, the gym—I bet Sean pawned his necklace to buy Christmas presents for us!*

She wished she'd picked out something less expensive as she quickly closed the wallet. It might embarrass Sean. Margie located Sean in the center of the mall and hugged him tightly.

"You must have found something great!" he exclaimed.

"You're a very caring man," she said.

After Sean's next paycheck from the White Horse Restaurant, Margie noticed the gold necklace back around Sean's neck. "Where did you find the necklace?" she asked.

"Under the couch cushion," Sean answered with his eyes focused on the floor.

"I'm glad you found your necklace," Margie said. She knew the real truth and loved him the more for it.

Sean, Margie, and her daughters shared their first Christmas day together. Sean spoiled them with more presents.

That afternoon, Margie noticed that Julie seemed a little closer to Sean. After all, Julie was seventeen, emotional, and hurt about her separated family because of the divorce. She always treated Sean nicely within reason but kept her distance. June and Jessi adjusted faster and accepted Sean more easily. Margie was glad to see Julie come around. Margie found out why when Sean presented her with a small, white Maltese puppy.

"He's a gift of love for the four of you."

Margie squealed, "What a surprise! He's the cutest thing I've ever seen, so soft and furry like a cloud!"

Julie beamed as she exclaimed, "I helped pick him out!"

Margie smiled at Sean. He had included Julie in his little adventure and won her trust. He was so terrific. Margie wanted everyone to get along and be happy, and Sean had made that a reality. Margie was proud of Sean taking the time to make Julie feel special. It meant a lot to Margie.

"Let's name him Socker!" Julie said, and everyone agreed.

Christmas that year was the holiday Margie had always wished for. Christmas brought them closer to being the family for which she had so long dreamed.

# CHAPTER SEVEN

# A True Friend

Now, even if they didn't see each other every day, Sean and Margie communicated for hours on the phone. As time passed by, they became closer and closer. Their relationship was full of love, romance, and tenderness. It was the first real happiness Margie had ever known.

It was late January when Sean convinced Margie to marry him and presented her with a beautiful diamond engagement ring. When she protested, "It must have cost a fortune," he countered, "Business at the restaurant has really picked up. I can feel it. We're on our way to a real success."

He whirled her in his arms. "We'll be married soon," he said. "I can't wait to start our life together. I'd really like us to move in together."

Though intensely in love, Margie felt doubtful about such a move. "What about the children? If anything happens, they'll be devastated."

Sean reassured her. Smiling, he embraced her. "Nothing bad is going to happen. Our future is built on a rock." He pounded his chest and jokingly coughed, making her laugh and whisking her doubts away.

In his only ownership claim, Sean hung a picture of New Zealand, his homeland, in the front room. Other than that one item, he tried to change nothing. Never intruding or being possessive, he made Margie and her daughters feel comfortable with his presence in their home. Sean was gentle, pleasant, and devoted to all of them. Their lives meshed together in comfort. Margie felt they were becoming a family.

Sean sometimes took Jessi to work with him on Saturday

mornings. Jessi loved having the run of the restaurant. Sean gave her bread and crackers to feed to the ducks who made their home nearby. He took the time to explain to her the different breeds of ducks and where they came from. Sean tried to befriend each one of Margie's daughters. He tried hard to be there for them and for many others in his life.

One day, he came home with the truck filled with pans and supplies from the restaurant of which he was part owner. A co-owner and the restaurant manager, Hal, a tall man with black hair and brown eyes, had been over to Margie's house several times for dinner with his wife, Evelyn. The couple might have been brother and sister. She was tall like her husband with the same black hair and brown eyes. Evelyn suffered from serious health problems, and her husband doted on her. "Hal told me," Sean explained, "they needed some extra money for medical supplies, and he asked me to clean out the storage shed and sell the extra restaurant equipment. He said he'd give me a percentage of the profits, which, of course, I won't take."

The next day Sean set up tables filled with the supplies from the restaurant in Margie's driveway. He advertised with posted signs on all the streets. By the end of the day, Sean had sold everything. Sean said that when he told him, Hal insisted Sean take half. Sean told Margie he felt wrong taking it and instead gave his share to her. "Spend it on the girls and yourself," he said.

Life was good. Margie had never been so happy. She still wondered why she had felt so cautious and suspicious at first, but she attributed it now to her own demons and let it go.

"I guess I built the fear inside me into a volcano," she speculated in her letters to a friend. "I made something out of nothing. At least now I feel great. I don't have to worry anymore."

Time flew by, and the first of February arrived along with Margie's birthday. Sean worked late the night of Margie's special day.

"Meet me at the restaurant," Sean suggested. "We'll go out and celebrate your birthday from there."

Margie dressed up in a new long, black silk dress. Margie had just slipped on her black heels when the phone rang.

"Hi, beautiful," Sean said. "Are you about ready?"

"I'm just about to leave," Margie answered.

"Will you do me a favor?" he asked. "Stop by my old apartment and pick up a jacket I left there. I called Gerry Sue, and she'll be there."

"Oh, if I have to. She's kind of weird," Margie said.

"Come on, be nice," Sean said.

"Okay," Margie said, "if I have to."

"I love you, and I'll see you soon," Sean said as he blew Margie a kiss through the phone.

Margie smiled and said, "I love you too."

Margie drove over to Sean's old apartment. The place filled her with haunted memories of the escape in the rain from her own imagination, and she felt a bit nervous as she walked up to the front door. Margie reminded herself of the good times she and Sean now shared. She thought of how safe she felt in Sean's arms these days. Margie felt better when she rang the doorbell.

Gerry Sue answered the door with a smile. She was nice enough. There was just something peculiar about her that Margie couldn't quite put her finger on. "Come inside," she said. "It's so good to see you again."

Margie's uneasiness returned. She wanted to run as she had once before. Instead, Margie held her head up high. Determined not to let her imagination get the best of her again, she walked through the door.

"The jacket's in the other bedroom," Gerry Sue said. "I'll get it for you."

Margie peered through the open bedroom door. She saw an open briefcase on Gerry Sue's bed. Inside it, Margie saw what looked like pills—so many of them!

*She's a drug dealer!* Margie thought, looking away just as Gerry Sue came back with the jacket. Margie fought the urge to run out the front door.

"Are you okay?" Margie asked, looking quizzically at the briefcase. "Are you ill?"

Gerry Sue looked in the direction of the open briefcase and said, "Oh, I see. You saw all the pills. Let me explain so you don't get the wrong idea."

Margie awaited her explanation.

Gerry Sue looked at Margie and said, "I was born a man."

Margie stood for a moment bewildered and then realized what Gerry Sue meant.

*She's a transvestite*, Margie thought. *She's a man dressed up as a woman!*

"The pills are to help me change my body to go with my true identity."

Nodding, Margie tried to remain calm and not act surprised. She mumbled something senseless and, stuttering a quick goodbye, stumbled out the door.

Margie drove to the restaurant wondering about Gerry Sue. *Does Sean know? Of course he knows! Why didn't he tell me?* Although the mystery of Gerry Sue had just been solved, Margie didn't have time to dwell on it. Late, she drove quickly but safely through the moonlight.

When Margie arrived at Sean's restaurant, the hostess greeted her and rushed her upstairs. Outside a set of closed double doors in the upper hallway stood two muscular men dressed in almost identical white robes. "We're friends of Sean Paul's and work with him sometimes," one of the them said to Margie.

"For the government?" Margie asked. There was something about them Margie didn't like. She thought back to the night Sean had spoken of his secret work with government agents.

"Of course not," the one said, smirking and elbowing his companion. "Do we look like government agents?"

The hostess spoke up. "He's in that room." She pointed to the double doors and the men, grabbing her, half carried her into the room. As the doors opened, lights went on in the room and voices yelled, "Surprise!" Her first reaction after the two men released her from their grips was to back out the door, but Sean came up and steadied her. Margie looked into familiar faces there to celebrate her birthday, and she embraced the man she loved. There stood Margie's identical twin brothers, Brian and Brent. They laughed at Margie's surprised response. Her neighbors, Robin and Dave, smiled. "We sure fooled you," Margie's good friend Nila and her husband, Tom, chuckled as they wished her happy birthday. Margie's older sister, Donna, and her husband, Alex, were also in attendance as was Margie's friend Lara and her boyfriend. Of course, Darrel and her boyfriend, Ted, were there too. Margie felt overwhelmed and touched to see all the wonderful faces of the people she loved.

She found out Sean had worked hard to plan the celebration and surprise her. The ceiling was alive with bobbing jewel-colored balloons and bouquets decorated with balloons adorned the tables. The food was special and spectacular. A band played and there was a singer who sang their favorite love song. Margie had never felt so loved and cherished.

It was not until the party was over that Margie noticed that the two men in white robes who had carried her through the doorway had since disappeared. Sean laughed when she mentioned them.

Then she asked him about Gerry Sue.

Sean explained, "Gerry Sue is indeed a man. He's the father of two sons. Gerry Sue is also a woman trapped inside a man's body. Now he is free to be who he wants to be. The pills will give Gerry Sue this freedom by changing his body. He plans to get an operation to make him a complete woman soon."

"Won't that be awful to go through so much?" Margie asked.

"What he suffers through now is much worse," Sean stated. "He'll be much happier as a woman."

Margie's heart warmed at Sean's sensitivity, at his lack of male ego and insecurity. So many men would have felt threatened. He understood Gerry Sue. Margie wanted to understand, too. Margie looked at Sean in a new way that night because of his compassion for another human being who was looked down upon by society.

"How courageous of you to stand by Gerry Sue," Margie murmured.

"That's what friends are for," Sean said quietly.

Margie's heart filled with love for this kind and compassionate man. She felt proud of her future husband. Margie was delighted at the prospect of being married to a man with such a magnanimous heart.

# CHAPTER EIGHT

## Hearts and Flowers

SEAN and Margie married on Valentine's Day, in a quaint little chapel in Salt Lake City. Margie's family, plus Nila and her husband, Darrel and Ted, and Sean's friend Steve and his wife, Lynn, as well as Hal and Evelyn, joined in the celebration. It was a beautiful ceremony. Red and white roses and hearts made of lace decorated the chapel. Margie smiled with happiness as she looked into the eyes of her prince. Sean smiled with pride as he held the marriage license tightly in his hands. He stared at the paper often. "I can't believe my good fortune," he kept saying. Jessi squealed with delight when she caught the bridal bouquet, and the other two girls had rarely been in such happy spirits. "We're a family again," they told one and all. The day was glorious.

Sean rented the top floor of the Imperial Hotel for the party. Margie and Sean danced the night away. The next day, shiny, white limousines drove them and their closest friends to Wendover, Nevada, for the day. Margie was so excited to leave her home state for the first time and although she didn't gamble, the thoughtfulness of Sean's extravagant excursion meant a lot to her. Back at the hotel in Salt Lake City, she and Sean spent one more romantic night alone.

Margie arose early the next day full of joyfulness and satisfaction. Peering out the window of the hotel, she saw a peach-colored sunrise. Margie sighed as she said a little prayer. "Let this new life be a good one." She looked forward to a long and happy future with her new husband and her children.

Sean walked up behind Margie and put his arms around her. "Good morning, Mrs. Lanier," he said.

Sean kissed Margie's cheek and held her close as Margie smiled.

"I don't want this wonderful day to go away," she said to him. "You're spoiling me!"

"I promise you will always feel this way, because I will love you forever," he proclaimed. "Now, let's get home to our children."

They gathered their things and checked out of the hotel. When they arrived home, Sean picked Margie up in his arms and carried her through the front door as she laughed with delight.

Sean put Margie down and said, "Now it's all said and done, get to work, woman."

Margie responded, "You get to work!" They both laughed.

A new husband, a new start. Margie wanted to do things right for a change and have a normal family like she thought everyone else had. Margie sold her half of her cleaning business to the other owner so all her devotion and time could go to her wonderful husband and beautiful children.

A few days later, Margie was excited to hear about Sean's upcoming appearance on a midday television show. He was asked to cook a flaming dessert from his restaurant's new menu. Margie called everyone to tell them to be sure and watch the program. Sean stated he was too nervous and tried to get his assistant chef to do the show. The television producer insisted that Sean make the appearance. Margie felt proud of Sean and excited about his debut.

Margie watched with eagerness as Sean appeared before her eyes on her television set with his face half-hidden by a tall chef's hat and glasses which she'd never seen him wear. She hardly recognized him. As he prepared the crepe Suzette, the hostess of the show stood next to him and asked him questions about being a chef which, Margie noticed, he answered tensely and while looking down at the floor a lot. She attributed this to nerves.

"Do you cook much at home?" the interviewer asked.

His head down and his voice quivering, Sean said, "No. One shouldn't take their job home with them if they want their relationship to be happy, and I do. I let my wife cook at home," he answered, which was true.

"I understand," she said, "since you cook all day at work."

Despite the nervous moments, the show seemed to be a success. Margie thought Sean did a wonderful job, except for his strange behavior. Lots of people called afterwards to commend him. Business at the restaurant continued to boom.

"I'll be able to give you the life you so much deserve," he said that night, pulling her into his arms.

After Sean's brief moment in the spotlight they went back to their normal lives. They continued to go out with friends and family. They took the children on all kinds of outings and even found time to work out at the health club. Sean took over the household finances and was generous with them all. Everything seemed perfect.

Soon Sean started to bring legal documents home for Margie to sign. He put Margie and her daughters on his life insurance policy, so in case of his death Margie would get his benefits. Trusting Sean completely at this point, Margie didn't read the long, dull documents. Even so, Sean insisted on explaining them in detail.

"I want you to understand everything, just in case."

Sean seemed so knowledgeable in the business world. "I feel confident about your decisions," Margie told him.

He smiled. "I'll try to deserve that confidence."

More and more, Margie felt an increasing sense of security. *Sean seems to accomplish everything he puts his mind to*, she thought. *I'm sure he'll be successful. How lucky I am to have such an enterprising husband!*

Six weeks after their Valentine's Day wedding, Margie was sitting at the kitchen table smiling to herself as she sipped a second cup of dinner coffee. Her new husband had taken the children out for ice cream. She was enjoying the time alone before she did the dishes. "Yes, life is good," she murmured, thinking out loud about how caring her new husband was and how good he was to her children. She felt lucky, very lucky, to have found him. It made up for all the earlier heartbreak she had suffered. Now, finally, she and the children had the family life she'd always envisioned.

She was still half enveloped in her thoughts when the telephone rang and Margie heard Nila's voice. She thought at first her friend's words rushing together were further congratulations, and in her rose-colored haze she was about to reply her thanks when she heard Nila saying, "Margie, you'd better turn your television on to *America's Most Wanted*. They're showing a murderer's picture." Nila paused and there was a catch in her voice when she rushed on. "And, Margie, it's either Sean Paul or his double."

Trembling as she stumbled over to the counter as if on automatic pilot, Margie flipped on the small kitchen television set and found the right channel. A moment later in front of her eyes on the screen, with the voice of John Walsh, the announcer, in the background, she saw one of America's most wanted criminals, a man who bore a striking resemblance to her husband.

"If we are able to capture this fugitive, we may be able to solve two murders. Paul Steven Mack," Walsh continued as Margie's eyes widened, "has been in and out of prison his whole life for fraud, forgery, and embezzlement, the crimes of a con artist. Paul Steven Mack is a dangerous man."

"Oh my God," Margie exclaimed as Walsh continued.

"Two women are dead, and Paul Steven Mack is wanted for murder."

"No. It can't be," she cried out in the empty house. "It can't be."

She listened to John Walsh's words transported now. *Could it be someone else? Someone who looked like Sean Paul? It had to be.* She scrutinized the man on the screen. He had a different name, his hair was a different style and color, his features were gaunt, and he was about thirty pounds lighter. "It has to be someone else!" she cried out. "Just a crazy coincidence."

# CHAPTER NINE

## *Puzzling Pieces*

FRANTIC to learn the truth, Margie, alone in the house, ran to the bedroom and took out some papers Sean had put in the dresser. "He certainly didn't hide them," she said, trying to reassure herself. There was a letter on the governor's stationery stating that Sean had been in the army, and there were copies of his birth certificate and death certificates for his parents, brother, and sister who had all died in a plane crash. The name Sean Paul Lanier appeared on all the documents, and this made Margie feel a little better. "The television program must just be some strange coincidence," she murmured.

*We've been through a lot,* she thought as she began to relax.

The next form she came upon was Sean's daughter Nickie's death certificate. Something caught her eye, and a sick sensation crept over her. The date on the death certificate was wrong. Nickie had died in September. The date on the death certificate said August 10. Margie stared in disbelief.

Margie remembered how Sean commented to her that he would be taking Nickie back to college. She did not die in August as the certificate stated! Nickie died in September! Then Margie noticed something else. There was no State seal on the certificate to authenticate it as a legal document.

Images from the *America's Most Wanted* program flashed through her mind. But she told herself she was just letting her imagination work overtime. Still, when Sean walked through the front door, she could not hide her confusion.

Sean looked concerned and asked, "Honey, what's wrong?"

She did not want to tell him about the television show, but

she showed him Nickie's death certificate and pointed out the mistake she found.

"It's just a clerical error," Sean said. "I will call the hospital in Chicago right now and straighten this out."

Sean strode into the bedroom and called information for the number. He told Margie to go into the kitchen and listen in on the phone in there. Sean dialed the number to the hospital in Chicago as Margie listened. After being transferred to several departments, he was finally connected to a woman administrator.

The administrator said, "I can't give out death certificate information over the phone. You can write a letter and request the information if you send a form of identification to prove you are this girl's father."

Margie hung up the phone. She felt somewhat better. At least Sean didn't hesitate to make the call.

Sean came into the kitchen and reassured Margie, saying, "I'll write a letter and get everything straightened out. I don't want you to worry."

Margie put the death certificates and other documents away and started washing the dinner dishes. Despite Sean's denial, the pictures of Sean's look-alike on television haunted her, and she spent the night vacillating back and forth. As she tried to sleep, her mind wandered from the man on the show to the discrepancies in the death certificate. Did any of it mean something? Did it mean nothing at all? Margie tossed and turned all night until the morning sun prompted her to get out of bed.

When Sean left for work and Margie's daughters went off to school, Margie thought about the piece of paper that haunted her. She reached for the phone and called her friend Darrel. Margie poured out to Darrel her fears, doubts, and concerns.

"Has it started again?" Darrel asked. She was sympathetic and concerned. "It all could be nothing, but I'll call around town and see if anyone has noticed anything suspicious," she offered. "I'll call you back."

Darrel called later that day. "No luck. I didn't find a thing," she said.

"Darrel, I'm probably crazy, but I can't help it. I'm going to hire a private investigator."

With Darrel still on the phone, Margie looked in the phone book and selected an investigator named Jed McCall.

"I feel awful doing this," Margie said, beginning to weep.

"I'll call for you," Darrel suggested. "I know you're too upset to call and make an appointment."

Margie hung up the phone as she fought back her tears. "This can't be happening again!" she said aloud.

The minutes it took Darrel to call Margie back seemed like hours to her. When the phone rang, she ran to answer it.

"We have an appointment with him tomorrow morning at ten o'clock at the Main Street Diner," Darrel said. "I thought it would be easier on you if you didn't have to go to his office."

"We? You'll be with me?" Margie asked pleadingly.

"Of course. I won't let you down," Darrel responded.

Margie dreaded Sean's arrival home from work. She knew she needed to act normal. Margie retrieved the papers from the dresser drawer and looked more closely at the other death certificates and documents. To her dismay, she now noticed words misspelled, wrong dates, and the absence of State seals on many of the papers. One by one, she discovered more mistakes on Sean's personal credentials. But she still understood none of it. She put them back carefully in case Sean looked for them.

Margie's daughters arrived home from school and Sean drove into the driveway. Margie took slow deep breaths as he walked through front door. They all sat down for dinner and Margie pretended everything was fine.

The night wore on. Margie did not sleep. Over and over, her mind reviewed the fugitive she saw on television and the documents she'd looked at.

*Was it Sean on television? Maybe not, but then, what about the documents? Maybe one death certificate is a mistake*, she thought, *but not all of them!*

The next morning Margie rushed everyone out the door and got ready for the appointment with the private investigator.

The clock seemed to tick in slow motion. Her heart beat with trepidation as she ran out the door. She tried to drive within the speed limit on her way to pick up Darrel.

They arrived at the restaurant to meet Jed McCall. The private investigator was a small, compact man with red hair and a mustache. He was sitting in a booth drinking a cup of coffee while he waited for them. Nervously, Margie sat down in the booth next to Darrel and was thankful when Darrel began the conversation.

"I'll need a thousand dollar retainer," Jed McCall explained, "so I can start researching information. By the way, I'll also need his social security number."

Margie assured Jed, "I'll get the number and have the money to you tomorrow."

*Where will I come up with the money?* she wondered. *I'll have to make up an excuse so Sean won't get suspicious. I have to know what secrets Sean is hiding!*

She and Darrel spoke of the problem on the way home.

"I wish I could help you, but all my medical bills have practically bankrupted me. I don't have a cent to spare." Darrel stopped. "Hey, that's it. Why don't you tell Sean I came to you for a loan?"

"That's a good idea," Margie said.

"I'm sure there's a logical explanation for all of this," Darrel reassured her. "Nevertheless, you need to find out so you won't worry."

"Thanks, Darrel. You've been a great help," Margie said as she pulled up to Darrel's house. "I feel better."

At home, Margie thought about what she had done that morning. As she went about her daily activities, Darrel's pep talk faded and was replaced by thoughts of being married to a wanted criminal. By that night, her imagination overwhelmed her. Despite knowing that she needed to be careful, after dinner Margie mentioned some of her doubts to Sean.

"There are mistakes on the other death certificates too," she told him.

"This happens all the time. I promise I will straighten this all out," Sean pledged.

Margie was not consoled or relieved this time. Something was not right, and she had to find out.

"Sean," Margie said. "I want to loan Darrel a thousand dollars. She's choking on her medical bills, and she can't even make her house payment this month."

"Sure," Sean said without hesitation, in his usual generous way. "I'll write you a check and you can cash it tomorrow."

"Thanks," Margie said, feeling ashamed for a moment. *It couldn't be true. It couldn't.* Still, she had to know.

"Always glad to help out," Sean said with a smile.

After Sean was asleep that night, Margie crept out of bed in silence. She took Sean's wallet off his dresser. She went into the bathroom, locked the door, and searched the wallet for Sean's social security card. She was surprised to find two cards with different numbers, so she wrote both numbers down. Ever so quietly, Margie eased out of the bathroom, put the wallet back on the dresser and slipped back into bed.

The next day, Margie drove with Darrel to the bank and cashed the check for a thousand dollars. They took the money and the social security numbers to Jed McCall's office. "I'll call you as soon as I find any information," the private investigator said.

Once home, Margie sat at the kitchen table for awhile. She tried to slow down her overworked mind. Suddenly, she remembered something Sean had told her: he had once worked in Ohio at a country club!

She phoned Jed McCall and told him about this newly-remembered clue.

"I'll make some calls to my contacts in Ohio and see what I can find out," he said.

Margie tried to keep busy while she waited for his report, but the hours dragged by. When the phone rang later that day, Margie grabbed it, full of anticipation.

"Sweetheart," Sean's voice echoed from his cellular phone, "I've been in a slight car accident. Just a small dent. I'm fine."

"Oh, I'm glad you're okay," Margie replied distantly. Her thoughts were somewhere else.

An hour later, Jed McCall called back. "I found a country

club in Marion, Ohio, that I thought Sean might have a connection to," he relayed. "I pretended to be an employer checking on Sean's references as a chef. I told the lady I spoke with that Sean's application gave their country club as a former place of employment. Unfortunately, the lady said she never heard of Sean Paul Lanier, and no one by that name has ever worked there."

After Margie talked to Jed, she called Darrel to update her.

"Nothing yet? Maybe Sean is covering up that he was in prison," Darrel said speculatively. "Then again, maybe it's all just a mistake," she said, trying to reassure Margie. "But, still, you have to find out the truth."

In frustration, Margie called Jed McCall again, and they went over the information.

"If he has been in prison," Jed told her, "I'll find out, but meanwhile you be careful."

Margie didn't know what to think.

The children and Sean came home by six that night and Margie rushed them through dinner. Sean and Margie left to pick up Darrel and her boyfriend to go work out. Margie was quiet on the ride.

"Are you okay?" Sean asked.

"Yes," Margie said. "Just a little tired." But she could not stop the agonizing visions passing through her mind.

Once they arrived at the health club, Margie pulled Darrel to the side. "I can't seem to put it out of my mind. I have to know about his past."

"Maybe he learned to cook in prison instead of in Paris!" Darrel joked, trying to make her friend laugh, but Margie was taut and serious.

"The prison speculation sure comes up a lot," Margie stated. "I hope that's not true!"

That night as they drove home she watched Sean glancing in the truck's rearview mirror every few minutes.

"What's wrong?" she asked as she turned to observe what was behind them. Maybe Sean was afraid of the police following them. Maybe. . . .

"I'm just careful," Sean—or was it someone else?—answered.

*Oh God*, Margie thought, *what is he afraid of? What am I afraid of?*

The next morning when the kids and Sean had left, Margie sat in the kitchen waiting for the phone to ring. When it finally did, she expected Jed to be on the other end with some news. Instead, the voice belonged to an insurance agent.

"I called because of Sean Paul Lanier's automobile accident," the agent explained. "I can't seem to find a driving record for him."

"Sean told me he lived in Ohio before he moved here," Margie said tentatively.

"Okay, I'll call the Ohio D.M.V. and see what I can find," the agent said. "Thank you."

*Oh great! No driving record! This just adds to the whole mess!* Margie thought. *Not one thing makes sense!*

Jed finally telephoned. "Both social security numbers belong to people who are dead," he said.

Frustrated, Margie yelled, "Great! What does that mean?"

"Try to keep calm, Mrs. Lanier. It means that at the moment, your husband is not using his own social security number. We will find out why. Don't worry," Jed said.

"Don't worry? This is driving me crazy!" Margie yelled again. "I'm afraid for myself and most of all for my children. What if he is that murderer?"

"We will find out," Jed repeated.

After she hung up the phone, Margie sat down and cried until there were no more tears left for her to cry. She fell asleep on the couch with her head throbbing.

That evening, Margie questioned Sean about the two social security numbers. She made the excuse that Sean's work had called about which one to use.

"I always mix my son's social security number up with mine," he clarified.

Sean was so genuine about his explanation that Margie sincerely wanted to believe him.

She was trapped between his sincerity and her suspicions.

When Margie, trying not to appear desperate, started to question Sean again about the death certificates, his mood changed.

"Give me the papers!" Sean snapped. "Enough is enough! I'll lock them in my briefcase! I told you I'd straighten things out!"

Frightened now, Margie backed off. She sat, fearfully quiet. The night dragged on in silence.

The next morning came, and things were no clearer. Her head ached as agonizing questions whirled around her brain.

The automobile insurance agent called again. "I still cannot find a driving record for Sean Lanier. Do you have any other information that might help—a previous address, for example?"

"I'm sorry, I don't know what else to tell you," Margie told her apologetically.

"It's so strange, like he never existed. I've never run across this problem before. Well, thank you for your help. I'll keep up the search."

Margie wasn't about to give up either. She called Jed.

"I was just about to call you." he told her. "The man on television who looks like your husband has been married before. I've been checking marriage and death records and have found that if the man is Sean he's had seven other wives."

"Are you sure?" Margie said in a choked voice. "Are you sure there isn't some mistake?"

"We can't be completely sure it's him but it looks suspicious. I'll keep checking. Don't say anything to him about this."

"Of course, I won't, but I don't know how I can keep pretending much longer."

It was another day of confusion. It was hard to concentrate on anything else. After dinner, Margie asked Sean, "Do you mind if I take the truck to go shopping for an hour or so? I don't have much gas in my car, and the truck is fun to drive."

Sean tossed Margie the keys, obviously happy to see her leave. He didn't want to answer any more questions from his snoopy wife.

Margie drove toward the mall. Looking in the rearview mirror, she noticed Sean's briefcase in the back seat. She pulled up to the curb. Sean didn't know she knew the combination, but Margie had watched him open the briefcase enough times when he didn't think she paid attention. Three sevens and click. She tried it. The briefcase opened, and all the certificates and documents were there. Margie drove to a copy center and made copies. She put the documents back in the right place with care and turned the numbers on the lock back the way they were before she opened the case. Margie drove around for a while thinking about her up-and-down life with Sean. What was the truth? She had to know. *I wonder if his finger-prints would help? I'm sure I could get them.* She drove aimlessly, waiting for enough time to pass before she drove home. She hid the copies of the papers in the garage and went into the house with the fingerprint plan on her mind.

"Did you find anything fun to buy?" Sean asked.

Caught off-guard, Margie said, "No. I guess I wasn't in the mood to shop after all."

He looked at her warily but said nothing.

At breakfast the next day, they all chatted about the weather, school, and work. When everyone left, Margie put on rubber dishwashing gloves and carefully picked up Sean's orange juice glass. She placed the glass in a plastic bag like they do on television and hid it in the back of her closet in case she needed the evidence later.

Dressing quickly, Margie went to Jed's office. She showed him the copies of the death certificates and other documents.

"You're making my job a lot easier," Jed said.

That afternoon, Margie went to lunch with Darrel. "Let's go over every detail to try and figure out this bizarre situation," Margie said. Again, the prison explanation seemed to be the most logical answer. "What could he have gone to prison for?" Margie asked.

"Maybe he beat someone up," Darrel speculated. "He's pretty strong with those big muscles."

"I need to do this searching myself. I'm going crazy waiting," Margie said. She called Jed and he agreed to let her help him.

For the next two days, Jed and Margie continued their search for information on Sean. They talked to everyone they could who might have known him. They researched every detail. Margie spent a lot of time in Jed's office. She was consumed with finding out the truth.

Late Wednesday afternoon, McCall again called the country club in Marion, Ohio. When Jed didn't get anywhere, Margie tried. She talked to the same woman Jed had. Margie explained she wanted to locate Sean Paul Lanier.

"A lot of people are curious about this man. I've never heard of him, and he has never worked here," the woman said.

Margie sat there listening in while Jed called the restaurant where Sean worked and, as he told Margie, had become part owner. "According to the man who answered," Jed explained after he hung up, "the restaurant's owner is on vacation. The man was adamant that he knows for a fact that the woman he works for is the sole owner and does not have a partner."

The lies were suffocating her.

The children. All she could think of now was that her girls might be in danger. "I feel like my life is breaking into small jagged pieces," she said. "I have to go home right away."

She looked at Jed searchingly. "I don't want the children to be alone with him anymore until we find out the truth. I want to get there before my kids come home from school," she explained to Jed.

"Listen," Jed said quietly. "I have a friend down at the police station who is very discreet. Maybe the time is right to get the police. . . ."

"No," she interrupted him. "Not yet. First, we have to find out who Sean Paul Lanier really is."

# CHAPTER TEN

## Suspicions

DAY after day, the tension mounted. Margie feared there was no escape. "I won't stop until I find out the truth!" she told herself. "I need to know!"

Finally, the next Saturday, Margie decided she had to talk to Sean. She asked him to take her for a drive to talk to him in private.

After they drove for awhile, Sean parked the truck in a parking lot and asked, "What did you want to talk to me about, honey?"

Margie explained her investigation as if she were doing it all herself. She did not mention Darrel or the private investigator.

Margie looked at Sean in desperation and said, "How do I know who you are? You might be a murderer!"

Sean sat in silence for what seemed like an eternity and then said, "You've got a great imagination! I need to tell you the truth, I guess. I was afraid to say something before, because I didn't think you'd have a thing to do with me."

Margie's heart beat faster as she thought about the possibility that Sean had been in prison. She waited for the words to come out of his mouth as she tried to breathe. Margie was stunned at what Sean said next.

"In reality, I'm with the Federal Witness Protection Program," Sean said. He looked at Margie for a reaction.

Margie looked at him in shock. "What?"

Sean continued. "My parents were in the mafia in New Zealand. I testified against them. As I grew up, my family was wealthy. I always knew the money was from drugs and illegal activities. I grew up with shady characters who invaded our home. They carried guns. My father even brought a gun to the dinner table! They put me and my brother and sister in a boarding school to protect us. We grew up with no parental love. I saw more and more crimes as I grew older. My father tried to hide the transgressions from me. My brother and sister turned away and ignored the situation. I was ashamed. I was frightened by the experience of betraying my own parents, but I saw too much that was wrong."

His stories and the way he told them were so believable that she truly wanted to believe them herself. Sean cried in Margie's arms while she tried to convince herself this new story could be true. Hours later they drove home.

The next morning, Margie arose determined to make some headway in her search for the truth. Sean had said he was in the Witness Protection Program. Margie decided to call the FBI and try to find out.

The man who answered paused for a few minutes as he sensed the urgency in Margie's question and then said, "I cannot confirm or deny that the man with this name is in the Witness Protection Program."

He hesitated and spoke again. "I will say that this name does not sound familiar."

Margie knew what he was trying to tell her. Sean was not in the Witness Protection Program. She thanked the man for his kindness and said goodbye.

*Who is this man, my husband?* Margie asked herself.

Visions of a spy, a murderer, and a sociopath with multiple personalities entered her mind. Margie sat next to the phone for several minutes. She tried to figure out her next move.

"Whom do I contact?" Margie murmured. "What do I do next?"

The strain of pretending her life with Sean was fine and of worrying about her children was getting to her. She tried to keep busy with housework to keep her mind occupied with minor things. But her anxiety intensified. She had noticed Sean watching her when he thought she wasn't looking. She knew he was becoming suspicious. Margie's mind fought with her all day until she lay down on the couch, exhausted from the emotional tumult, and fell asleep.

At four o'clock, Margie's daughters rushed in the front door from school. As she heard their chattering voiçes, Margie felt even more anxious. She jumped up and asked if they were okay.

They looked at Margie in confusion and said, "We're fine, Mom. Are you okay?"

"I'm fine," she mumbled.

Margie went to the kitchen to start dinner and then get ready to go to the health club.

Sean came home early and they all ate dinner together. The girls left after dinner to spend the weekend with their father. Margie was tired and withdrawn. Sean sensed something was wrong and he helped with the dishes. He patted Margie on her back and kissed her forehead, but she could not help herself. She shrank from his touch.

Watching her, Sean said nothing, but she knew he was becoming more and more wary of her. Had he figured out what she knew? If so, the danger to her and the girls was increasing.

Sean went to change into his workout clothes. Margie walked out the front door and sat down on the front porch to wait for him. She wanted to give up. Margie looked up to the heavens and asked for help.

"I'm so tired. I can't do this anymore," she murmured. "The uncertainty is more agonizing than knowing the worst is true."

At the gym that night she could hardly make conversation.

Later, as they lay in bed, Sean wanted to make love to her, but she broke away. There was silence for awhile. Sean was the one to break the quiet.

"Margie, you seem different towards me. Is anything wrong?"

"I'm just tired." She looked at him with blank eyes, the word *anything* echoing. Terrible thoughts ricocheted through her mind. *Could he be a sociopath? Could he feel nothing for others? Could he commit the most heinous crimes without guilt or remorse? The murdered girls mentioned on television—they had been sexually abused. Raped.* She thought of herself, her daughters, and her fear grew. She tried to calm down. *But he was always so gentle, so giving.*

"What do you want from me, Margie? I've tried to give you everything I could. What else do you want me to do?"

"I don't want anything but the truth," she said. "You say all the right things, but the facts always seem to contradict your words."

"What facts, Margie?" he said, his voice suddenly icy.

"I don't know. I don't know, that's the problem," she replied, tears falling down her cheeks. "I just don't want you to lie to me."

His voice grew icier. "I haven't lied to you. Are you still checking up on me?"

Margie looked away. Chills ran through her body. *Does he know about the private detective?*

"Look at me." His voice was stern. "Can't you see I'm telling you the truth? That I always have?" He was leaning over her, his steely blue eyes boring into her.

She looked into his eyes and shuddered. Was that evil she saw, or a mirage? Margie sighed. "I'm so tired," she said, her breathing labored and painful.

"Come on, Margie." He tried to take her in his arms, to coax her into passion, but she was beyond that now.

"I just can't," she said. Was she imagining these lies? He was always so good, so giving in his lovemaking. Still, she had never refused him, always desired him until now. "I'm just exhausted."

She could keep still no longer. Desperately, knowing she was doing the wrong thing, Margie began to question Sean again. He responded with a smoothly reasonable answer to every question she asked, which confused Margie even more. She gave up and said dully, "Never mind. I just want to go to sleep."

"No. I don't think so," he said appraisingly, and there was a look in his eyes, a razor-edged look she'd seen only a few frightening times before. Margie shuddered and turned away.

"Don't turn your back on me," he yelled out.

Trembling, Margie turned to face him. "I'm going to sleep," she said, defying him.

"No, you are not," he yelled, only inches from her ear. His piercing gray-blue eyes stabbed her, searing into her heart.

"But—"

"But nothing," he said.

She lay frozen in silence, unable to say another word. His body was rigid against her. Then, just as quickly, he was okay again and got up from the bed, coming back with a glass of water and a pill.

"This will help," he said. "It will calm your stomach down."

"I don't want a pill," Margie cried. "I'll be fine if I just get some sleep."

"Just take the pill," Sean insisted. "It's harmless, and you'll be able to sleep."

She opened her mouth to protest, then the thought occurred to her that she was trapped. Margie took the pill with reluctance. Instead of making her feel better, a few minutes later she felt sick to her stomach. She ran and locked herself in the bathroom and threw up violently. Sean came to the door and demanded to be let in. Weakly, Margie opened the door. Sean picked Margie up in his arms and carried her to bed.

"Just lie here and get some sleep. You'll feel better soon," he said.

Margie begged Sean to take her to the hospital. "I feel like I'm about to die!" she sobbed.

"You are fine! You're not about to die! I'm here with you," he insisted.

The hours that followed were filled with images fading in and out of her mind in bits and pieces. Was she dreaming? She wasn't sure. Over her, she saw those piercing eyes narrowed with hatred. Manicured fingers with fists clenched. She felt herself trying to scream into the darkness of the night. The screams died in her throat. Then she lapsed into merciful unconsciousness again, only to later feel more of the scene unfolding like a nightmare from which there was no escape. At some point she felt her own tears falling into her open mouth, her head slammed back. She thought she saw blood on the hands of the shadowy figure looming above her, parting her legs. And then there was pain, pain which blotted out everything else.

Margie felt dizzy and disoriented as if she had fallen off the edge of the world. At times she drifted into semiconsciousness. She tried to scream. Nothing came out of her mouth. Her voice had vanished. She fought to wake up, but she could not. When Margie did wake up the next day, she was soaked in perspiration. She was naked, and she shook with weakness.

"What happened to me?" she asked herself.

Getting up, she could hardly walk. Her thighs burned in agony. Looking down, she saw black and blue marks all over her legs and arms. When she looked in the mirror there were bruises on her throat and near her mouth as if it had been pried open.

"Oh my God," she whispered.

*Did Sean drug and rape me?* she agonized. *Did I fall when I blacked out last night? What happened? There are never any answers, only questions!*

She dragged herself to the kitchen. Sean had left for work before she awoke.

She thanked God the children were with their father.

*Maybe I'm going mad*, she thought.

When Sean came home, she could stand it no longer. She asked him what happened the previous night.

"Did you rape me?" Margie asked in a choked voice.

"What?" Sean said. "Good hell! No! I love you! I think you were allergic to the pill I gave you because you were delirious. You fell on the dresser when you tried to get out of bed," he explained.

"Why didn't you take me to the hospital?" Margie asked.

Sean responded, "Do you think I'd ever let anything happen to you? I knew you were fine. It was just one little pill. Trust me. Honey, I love you." He was playing down Margie's horrifying experience as though it didn't mean a thing.

That night, she went through Sean's briefcase and came

upon a bottle of Percodan pills prescribed by his dentist.

*Have I lost my mind?* she kept thinking. *Isn't that the drug that killed one of those girls? Am I making something out of nothing? Was I poisoned? Was I raped? I have to find out what is going on!*

## CHAPTER ELEVEN

# *Jeopardy*

DURING the next weeks, Sean told Margie over and over in the most charming ways possible, "I'll never let you and the girls go. You must never try to leave me. I love you all too much." His voice was always quiet and almost too gentle, but his eyes went straight through her, like daggers of cruelty.

Now it became a deadly game of cat and mouse. Margie had learned during her sad childhood to keep her emotions hidden, and she called upon that skill in the days to follow.

But inside she was afraid. At night she could not sleep. She would lie awake with the covers pulled up to her chin, ears straining to hear Sean's every breath, her eyes wide open, and her heart pounding. Every hour or so, she would creep out of bed as surreptitiously as possible to check on her daughters to be sure they were in their rooms and safe. Standing at their beds, she would lean over to watch their breathing, brushing their foreheads with her lips. She was so grateful to have them there and yet so afraid for them.

She didn't fight having sex with Sean again, but she prayed as he curved his hand almost lovingly around her throat, lingering there and silently staring into her eyes, that he would not kill her. For she was almost sure by then that her life, her world, was in jeopardy.

"You won't try to go, will you?" he often said in the midst of their intimacy. She no longer called it lovemaking.

"Of course not," she'd say flatly. "I won't."

"Never. Promise," he'd say, laughing. A laugh she would never forget.

Sometimes he would squeeze her wrist until her eyes filled

with tears. "I promise." She didn't dare try to budge his hand.

When Sean was gone or she was out shopping or running errands, she often thought she saw two men watching and following her. Their faces looked vaguely familiar. She thought of the white-robed men who had been standing outside the room at the surprise birthday party Sean had given her. She thought they looked like those same men but couldn't be sure. The children mentioned seeing them too.

That year, when spring buds peeked through the earth, Margie could not enjoy her favorite season. She had forgotten its meaning. She had forgotten how to feel anything but fear.

And then, one weekday afternoon, the thing she dreaded most, the unthinkable, happened. She had rushed home later than usual from shopping, but the girls were not home from school when she dashed into the house calling their names. At first, she was calm, thinking up reasons why all three should be late, but by six o'clock, panic had crept up Margie's throat, threatening to cut off her air supply. Margie closed her eyes and let out a mournful sigh.

"God help me," she whispered. She wondered if she should call the police and report them missing. "They will probably think me crazy," she murmured, and dialed the number anyway.

"Call us again after they're gone twenty-four hours," the desk clerk who answered said. "They've probably gone for ice cream and a movie. These things happen all the time with kids their age."

They were still not home at seven, and, frantic, not knowing what she expected to hear, she called Sean at the restaurant.

"Oh, they'll be along," he said very pleasantly. "Stop worrying. I'll be late tonight."

By seven-thirty, Margie was fighting to control herself, taking deep breaths. "He's right. They must be at some after-school function they forgot to tell me about," she said unconvincingly to the empty house. She sat down at the kitchen table. A minute later she decided to make a pot of tea to calm herself.

The burner on the stove glowed red as she wiped excess

water from the kettle and placed it on the hot surface. She peered out the window between the vertical blinds. "It's still light. They probably don't realize the time."

She called Sean again an hour later. "They're still not home," she said.

He sounded annoyed. "They're fine. I told you that."

"They called you?" she asked, not feeling as relieved as she wanted to.

"Let's just say I know they're fine. They're probably at some school shindig or another adventure. You overprotect them."

"Please, Sean, tell me where they are."

"I'm coming home. You just wait there and don't call here anymore. Everyone has begun to think you're nuts."

Margie heard the phone click off in her ear. When she called back, the woman who answered said Sean had left but, to Margie, her voice sounded strange.

She waited.

Neither Sean nor the girls appeared.

It was dark now. She had turned the outside lights on. She was sitting near the telephone, her eyes riveted on the window so she could see the driveway and the path to the front door.

It was almost eleven when Sean walked in.

Her eyes burned into him. "They're still not here," she said hoarsely, almost in a whisper. She had been crying for hours. "I think I should call the police again."

"Again? What the hell do you mean, again?" he said. He was standing over her now, glowering. "Didn't I tell you they'd come home?"

She swallowed and forced herself not to sound hysterical.

"Sean." She looked at him, studying his face. He seemed steady and fidgety at the same time. "Do you know where the children are?"

He leaned over, bringing his face close to hers. "Honey," he said, smiling and revealing his perfect teeth, "I'm disappointed in you. I told you they were safe."

Margie started to cry. She could not help herself. "If you've hurt my children, I'll kill you," she cried out.

His eyes were void of emotion. There was a look of surprise on his face. "Margie, I'm amazed at you. No one would hurt those girls. Now, you just keep sitting there like a good girl. Don't move, and they'll come home." Sean smiled, obviously pleased with himself.

She could not have moved. She was frozen with fear. *He wouldn't hurt the children*, she kept saying to herself, but she felt as if she'd been slugged in the chest.

The night wore on. Her body ached, and still she sat. Fear filled her heart. It had begun to rain. She thought of the girls out in the torrent, rain soaking them. Tears streamed down her face.

1:00 A.M. . . .

2:00 A.M. . . .

Intermittently, Sean came and sat across from her. He seemed to be playing a psychological game with her. "Remember," he instructed, "just sit there and wait."

She wanted to plead with him, but something told her to remain quiet and do as he said. She had never seen him really angry, and she did not want to set him off. Not now. *He really knows where the girls are, as he said. They have to be safe.* She would not permit herself to think anything else.

And then, near dawn, she heard her daughters streaming into the house followed by two men, the same two men, she saw with a shock, who had been at her party and whom she'd seen watching her when Sean was not around. The men wore the same white robes they had on at Margie's surprise party and were holding multitudes of red, purple, yellow, and blue balloons. They acted happy, as if they'd taken the girls to a party.

"June, Jessi, Julie!" Margie screamed in agony and relief.

"See, I told you," Sean said. "It was a big joke. You know what a practical joker I am."

She gathered the girls in her arms, covering them with kisses. For the moment, they were like rag dolls, silent, inscrutable. It was only later as she tucked all three of them into their beds that they each told her how terrified they'd been.

"They picked each of us up at our schools and took us to

an amusement park. They said Sean sent them and let us speak to him on the car phone," Julie explained.

"But it got so late, we thought they'd never bring us home," Jessi cried.

June said, "We had to keep quiet and not act scared."

Margie did not want to tell the girls the real extent of their danger, but she knew she had to build up and keep their confidence if they were all to gain their freedom.

"It has to be a secret and you will have to act like things are just the same," she explained. "But we have to get away from Sean as soon as we can."

For the next several days, the girls managed to do as Margie asked. They were good little actresses, but with her mother's instinct, she could see how afraid they were of Sean underneath their smiles. She worried about the trauma to them, but knew she had to keep her mind focused on gaining their and her freedom.

# CHAPTER TWELVE

## *Unvarnished Truth*

EARLY one evening, just after dark, when the sky was highlighted by a full, lemon colored moon, an old white car with two men in it drove by Margie's house. They stopped for several moments in front of the entrance before they drove on. Sean asked Margie, "Do you know who they are?"

"No," she responded.

Later, Sean, Margie, Darrel, and Ted arrived at the health club. Margie and Darrel headed for their Jazzercise class.

"How are you?" Darrel asked with concern.

"Not my best."

Margie worked out harder than she ever had. She felt better after the intense workout. Sean and Ted met Darrel and Margie at the door of the Jazzercise room. They all walked out of the health club together into the cool evening.

"Let's go get something to eat," Sean said. "I've built up an appetite."

"How about ice cream," Ted suggested. Margie heard her own hollow laugh as they got into the car.

As they drove down the street, Ted told the two women that Sean had seen two undercover police officers at the health club.

Sean spoke up and said, "I can spot them anywhere."

"Oh! How mysterious!" Darrel said as they snickered. All but Margie, who was silent.

Sean and Margie dropped Darrel and Ted off. As they drove home, Margie watched Sean look in the rearview mirror every few minutes.

It was late as they drove down their street, but the moon

shone. Sean again pointed out the same old white car with the two men inside parked across the street from their house. Sean pulled into the driveway and they went inside.

Sean was unnerved and followed Margie around the house that night. Until they went to bed, he never let her out of his sight.

Finding out in this way that the police might be watching Sean, Margie finally decided what she needed to do. She had to go to the police right away. Danger or not, it was the only path out of this hell.

Margie knew Sean was not the only one who was under surveillance. She herself was being watched, both by Sean and by his friends, the very same men who had taken the children that night. Whenever Sean wasn't home, she saw them outside in their car. To go to the police station, she knew she would have to elude them. Margie began to think out a plan. She decided to include Darrel who she knew would be discreet. Darrel would go with her to the police, Margie was sure.

However, when she attempted to call Darrel, Margie heard a strange bleep on her telephone. Could the phone be tapped? Margie couldn't take the chance. She would have to go to the police alone.

The next morning, as soon as the children had left for school and Sean for work, Margie put her plan into motion. She took out the glass with Sean's fingerprints from its hiding place in the closet to take with her.

Driving to the mall, Margie ambled around the stores, moving closer to the multiplex movie theater all the while. She was sure she caught glimpses of the two men behind her, but they apparently grew bored with her dawdling and she saw them take a seat in the food court. Quickly, she ducked around the theater and got into a cab.

Those old familiar feelings of fear, anxiety, and turmoil flooded through Margie again as she walked through the automatic doors of the police station. But she felt better when she saw Hank Conrad, a detective from Salt Lake City who happened to be her neighbor, talking to the policeman at the front desk.

"Margie, what are you doing here?" Conrad asked in surprise.

"It's my husband," she began in a shaky voice.

"What about him?" Conrad said. "Come into my office where we can talk privately."

Margie followed the detective and took the seat he offered. "I don't think he's who he appears to be," she said.

Conrad's eyebrows raised. "What do you mean?"

Margie spilled her story out. "It's the inconsistencies. He's the most charming, wonderful man on the one hand, but, on the other, nothing about him checks out. He always has an explanation, but. . . ." She paused, looking at the detective.

Hank Conrad was an attractive man whose dark skin matched his deep dark eyes and hair. "Tell me about it," he said.

"A few weeks ago, my girlfriend alerted me to watch *America's Most Wanted*. The wanted man's name was Paul Steven Mack, but the man could have been my husband's twin, though Sean's heavier and more muscular. Before that, Sean had told me stories and done things that made me uneasy, so, soon after the show, I hired a private detective and we've been uncovering things. Things like the wrong date of death on his daughter's death certificate and the two social security numbers he uses that belong to dead people."

Pausing to catch her breath, she took the wrapped glass with Sean's fingerprints from her pocketbook. "I also have these." She gave Conrad the plastic-wrapped glass, the documents she'd photocopied, the pawn ticket from the time Sean had pawned his necklace and Jed McCall's name and address.

"How did you accomplish all this without your husband's knowledge?"

"I think he does suspect." She told Hank about being followed and the overnight ordeal with the girls. "But he thinks I'm too scared to do anything, I suppose, or he's explaining it all away to himself."

"Let me give this to our forensic department. I'll be right back," he said.

Margie sat tensely in the chair, gripping the armrest while

Hank was out of the room. It was almost a half hour before he returned with another man.

"Margie, this is Detective Jay Frank from California. He's been following the case of an alleged murderer called Paul Steven Mack and is here conferring with our department."

"The thing is, Margie, the fingerprints you brought us are a perfect match," Detective Frank said. "Also, we're checking out the pawn ticket. In this state, you have to record your thumb print when you pawn something." He paused, watched her intently, then went on. "I can't make this any easier for you. We're almost sure that your husband is the man you saw on *America's Most Wanted*."

Blankly, Margie looked at the older man. His receding hairline showed drops of perspiration. His mustache showed streaks of gray. He looked weary.

"You remember the woman you spoke to in Ohio?" Conrad asked. "The one from the country club?"

"Jed and I both spoke to her," Margie said, still staring, zombie-like. She felt numb all over as she tried to grapple with the fact that her worst fears were true.

"Well, she remembered all the phone calls from Salt Lake City about Sean Paul Lanier. She remembered the name, because Jed apparently called back about him. She never worked with or knew Lanier, as she told you. But she did work with and know a Paul Steven Mack whose description sounded like Lanier's. She wondered if Sean Paul Lanier could be Paul Steven Mack. She had also been watching *America's Most Wanted* that night, and she put the pieces together and called the police, who in turn called the producers of the show and then called us.

"With the lead about Salt Lake City, another detective and I flew here from California to check out your husband. We couldn't be sure until today that Mack and Lanier were one and the same. We've been searching for Mack for over a year."

And then Detective Frank told Margie the truth about the husband she hardly knew.

# CHAPTER THIRTEEN

## *Floating in the River*

THE County of Marion in the middle of Ohio is a secluded farming community, about an hour's drive from Columbus. It is a typical, small country town. To big city mentalities it could be perceived as hackneyed, but to those who enjoy living there it has an idyllic feel to it, with its white picket fences and everybody waving hello to each other. Marion is bordered on the east by the Olentangy River, a calm, fairly shallow body of water, around which nearly every local man, woman, and child spent some warm summer days lazily wading, swimming, or canoeing. However, it was in this river that a local girl's dead body was found. One summer, a stranger, Paul Steven Mack, drifted into town. No one knew where he came from or who he was, but he was handsome and seemed educated, and people instinctively trusted him.

In truth, Paul Steven Mack had been arrested elsewhere in Ohio on sixteen counts of theft. When he was released from Ohio State Prison, he met and married wife number six, Nancy. After this passionless and short-lived marriage, early that summer Mack moved to Marion, into a small house on tranquil Oak Avenue. Why he picked Marion was a mystery, but perhaps his reasoning was related to the fact that people there believed in other people and didn't lock their doors at night. Lying about his background references to his employer, Mack was able to wheedle his way into the prestigious position of manager at the scenic and secluded Marion County Country Club that lies next to the Olentangy River.

About fifteen minutes from the club, in the town of Harpster, brunette and winsome nineteen-year-old Annette Huddle lived with her father and younger sister in a two-bedroom ranch house off Delaney Street. She began working as Mack's secretary. On break from college classes for the summer, she was a popular, straight-A student.

On the morning of July 8, Annette's grandmother came over to the Huddle home to drive the young woman to work. Annette jumped into the car with her usual exuberance.

"Have you had breakfast yet?" her grandmother asked. "I have some bagels in the back seat that I just picked up at Mr. Kelly's bakery for the picnic your sister and I planned this afternoon, but you can have some now if you'd like."

"Thanks, Nana, but I ate already. I try to get up early to help with the housework. You know Dad's got his job, and since he and Mom split up and we decided to stay with him, he has to take care of the house and Cassie and me too."

Her grandmother smiled at her. "Annette, you're a terrific kid. Maybe you can teach Cassie how to dust or how to set and clear the table so she can help you both. Cassie isn't too young to be part of the team effort."

Annette smiled and then frowned. "I know, but I hardly feel like her responsible older sister since I got into that stupid accident on Monday. With my car in the body shop, I have to get rides everywhere. It's so inconvenient and I feel like I'm in grade school again, waiting for my mother to pick me up."

"At least the good side of not having your car is that you get to spend time with your hip grandmother, right?" the older woman said.

"Actually, Nana, I do like spending time with you. I feel like I can tell you anything."

Her grandmother readily responded, "Good. So why don't you tell me all about this new boyfriend of yours? I was starting to worry about you ever since you came back from Tennessee after breaking up with that other fellow—what was his name again?"

"Oh, I've forgotten him already. I've been dating this new guy, Joe, ever since May, and he is so sweet, funny, and really good to me. I like him a lot, Nana, but don't get how you get about these things and think that I'm going to marry him, because I'm only nineteen, and I still want to finish college and be a flight attendant before I settle down with someone."

Her grandmother smiled. "I love that you're happy, because that makes your Nana feel happy. But I was just wondering, why are you working at the country club as a secretary if what you want is to be a flight attendant? Maybe you should get another job somewhere that's related to flying."

Annette huffed and said, "Nana, this is Marion. We are smack-dab in the middle of Ohio, and the nearest commercial airport I would want to work at is about a million hours—and dollars—away. This is the closest thing I could find to being a flight attendant, since it's in the service industry. And anyway, I have to get my college diploma before anyone will even look at my resume. Also, don't you think that it will help that I work directly under the manager? I have an important position there, Nana, and I'm sure the airlines will appreciate my experience working at the country club. Maybe my boss will write a great recommendation for me." Annette stopped and sighed.

"What's wrong this time?" Nana asked.

"Well," Annette said, coloring, "my boss is pretty old—he must be nearly forty—but sometimes I think he's after me."

"What did you say?" Her grandmother's voice rose. "I want you to quit that job right away if he lays a finger on you."

Annette started to laugh, put her hand on Nana's arm to calm her down, and said, "Nana, he can be a pain, but I'm sure he's not serious about making a pass at me. After all, he's a sophisticated city guy and lots of the women at the club are dying to be with him. He knows I'm just a kid. In fact, he calls me 'Kiddo' sometimes. He's just that way. In fact, he's trying to help me. You worry too much, Nana."

Her grandmother pulled up to the club's side entrance for employees and Annette kissed her goodbye on the cheek, still laughing. Before Annette shut the door, the older woman called out, "Darling, you forgot to tell me what time I have to come and pick you up. Last time, I sat here and waited half an hour for you, and before that, you were mad because you had to wait for me. So what time should I be here this evening?"

Annette told her, "Oh, it's okay, Nana. You can have the night off. I'm getting a ride home. I'll be fine. I love you. Goodbye!" She blew her grandmother a kiss, and with that, she shut the car door and happily walked into the office. It was a goodbye her grandmother would never forget.

In the office, Annette was met by her coworker, Cora, the bookkeeper. Cora was blond, in her mid-twenties and recently divorced. The two went outside to the coffee machine to fill it. When the pot of coffee was full, Annette's boss, Paul Mack, strode into the office. He wore a well-pressed gray wool sport jacket and slacks. A heavy gold chain hung around his neck. His dark hair was short and impeccably styled, and the fingernails of the hand he raised in greeting were freshly manicured.

"Hello, ladies." He looked over at the younger woman. "Well, Annette. You look very beautiful and professional today. Maybe one day you'll be *my* boss. I hope you haven't forgotten about our very important meeting later on," Mack said.

"Good morning, Mr. Mack, and no, I haven't forgotten," responded Annette. After pouring himself a cup of coffee, Paul walked into his office and turned around to smile at the two women before shutting the door.

"I can't believe he got a haircut and manicure again," said Cora, ripping three sugar packets for her coffee. "It's only been a week!"

Annette took a sip of her tea, felt that it was too hot, stirred it with a stick, and replied, "I'm not surprised. That man could be a movie star with the expensive clothes he wears. I've never seen him without a roll of Certs, either."

Cora nodded. "He's obsessed with his breath and his looks. But he does have great manners though. Anyway, in other news, want to go out on a double date tonight? My boyfriend's in town."

Annette smiled thoughtfully. Her dad and Nana probably wouldn't like her going out with Cora because of her divorce.

Then Annette's face became serious as she replied, "I can't. After work I have to meet Mr. Mack to talk about my future. He didn't tell me exactly what time, so I can't make other plans just yet."

Cora grimaced. "If I were you I'd watch out for him. I don't like the way he looks at you sometimes."

Annette looked searchingly at Cora for a moment, then shrugged. "He's twice my age, silly. I could almost be his daughter, although I've caught him eyeing me when I bend over. But what's to say? He's a man."

The two of them laughed but stifled the sound for fear that Mack might hear them. Cora nudged Annette. "Well, watch out anyway."

Annette nudged her friend back. "I'd better get to work now. Talk to you later."

Cora noticed nothing different that day between Mack and Annette. At about five o'clock in the afternoon, Mack walked past Cora and Annette, who were now cleaning the coffee machine and washing their cups in the sink, and said, "Good-night, ladies. Annette, I guess I'll see you tomorrow." He winked at her and walked out the door.

Cora lightly pushed Annette against the counter and said, "Okay. I saw that wink he gave you. Remember what I said about the way he looks at you."

Annette laughed. "You're too smart for us, Cora. You've got the two of us figured out. I should tell Mr. Mack to stop his winking because our relationship is too obvious to everyone in the office now. No, seriously, I don't think he really is leaving the office for the night, because he told me that he wanted to meet with me later about something I mentioned to him earlier." She paused and then confided in Cora, "I told him I wanted to join the airlines. He's offered to help me with my plan to become a flight attendant. He says he knows one of the executives at a major airline."

Cora and Annette dried their hands and walked towards their desks. Cora packed up her things while Annette leafed through some papers and then through her purse. Cora said, "So you really are meeting with Mr. Mack later? I thought the whole thing was just a joke when he walked out."

Annette smiled furtively and said, "You just believe what you want to believe, Cora. I'll see you tomorrow."

Walking over to the door, Cora opened it to leave and said, "Have a good night, Annette," and gave Annette a wink, laughing as the door shut behind her.

That was the last time anybody saw Annette Huddle alive, because she didn't arrive home that night or report for work on Thursday or Friday.

That Saturday, July 11, a warm, sunny day, the Grogart family went out for a relaxing canoe ride along the Olentangy River. Their eldest son, Leo, sat in the front and steered the boat. He was the first one to see something bobbing up and down in a shallow part of the river. Instead of steering towards it, he jumped out of the canoe and trudged towards it. The water was barely up to his waist. As his father called for him to come back, Leo poked the floating mass, turned it over and ran back to his family, screaming, "It's the body of a dead woman!" The Grogarts calmed Leo down, distracted the younger children, and pulled their canoe up to the shore. The screams were heard by everyone around the river, and some-one made a phone call to the police. Soon, sirens sounded and a squad car approached. The story of the badly decomposed woman's body found in the river, ten miles down from the country club, made the headlines of the Sunday paper the next day and was all over the nightly news.

On Monday, July 13, Annette Huddle's father went to the Marion County Police Department. He was bleary eyed from fatigue and worry. His daughter hadn't come home from work since the previous Wednesday. He was asked to view the body fished from the river. When he saw it, he cried out, "It's Annette." He told the police that the last place he knew his daughter to be was the country club.

The police department gathered the staff of the country club and brought them all in for questioning. Paul Mack, Cora, and the other employees of the club were asked to describe the last time they saw Annette. Cora, grief-stricken about her friend, told the police about the conversation they had, that

Annette was supposed to see Mack later for an important meeting about her future. She wanted to be a flight attendant, she told them, and he had promised to introduce her to someone influential. Questioned by the police, Mack denied killing Annette. Unfortunately, no one saw Annette leave work on July 8, because she was the last one to leave. There were no witnesses who could attest to seeing Annette with Mack or anyone else that night or the days following her disappearance.

While some officers interrogated the employees of the country club, others were doing background checks on them. It was then discovered that Paul Mack was on probation. When approached and searched, he was found to have marijuana on him. Since possession of marijuana was a violation of his probation, he was sent back to Marion Correctional Institute. However, because there was not enough evidence, Mack was not charged with murder.

Since the body of Annette Huddle had been floating in the shallow Olentangy River for approximately three days, it was difficult for investigators to determine the cause of death. The coroner labeled it "Death by violence of undetermined origin," meaning that this was a homicide by unknown means. Huddle's body was decomposed and partially clothed, her clothes tugged and pulled in disarray but her limbs still intact. According to friends and family, there was no indication in the days prior to her death that she had been depressed or exhibited any suicidal tendencies. Moreover, interviews with Annette's family revealed that Annette had complained to them that Mack had sexually harassed her in the office.

Annette's wooden, macramé-beaded purse was never recovered. Thirty days after his imprisonment, Mack's apartment was searched for evidence, particularly Annette's bag. A search of the Olentangy River also yielded nothing, but when the contents of Mack's fireplace were sifted, detectives found some coins and charred objects which looked like wooden beads. However, these objects were too scorched and indistinguishable to be used as evidence against Mack for murder.

In August, Mack was paroled, although he was still suspected of murder by the police of Marion County. Though he was not supposed to leave Ohio, Mack went to California. By the middle of the next year, Mack began dating single mother Gail Haden. Only two weeks after meeting her, however, Mack was charged by California authorities with burglary and grand theft. He was sentenced to three years in prison. While incarcerated, Mack married Gail, wife number seven, who stayed with him for two years.

In March of 1985, Mack was paroled. Once again, the rules of his parole didn't deter him and that same month he went to Hawaii with a married woman. He returned to California and moved in with another woman, Carol Lee Connors, but didn't marry her. While living with Carol Lee, Mack was seeing yet another woman, Faith Denny, but didn't marry her, either. At this time and all through the next year, Mack forged various papers, owned his own suspender business, and often asked friends and other young women to help him with promotions. By this time, Mack had literally forged himself a new life, obscuring his past and obliterating Annette Huddle's memory.

## CHAPTER FOURTEEN

## *Fatal Seduction*

HE seemed to come from nowhere—a man without a past—but then again, Paul Mack was always able to settle easily into a new community. A professional con man, he was like a chameleon, able to drift in and out of places and personas and blend with the locals via forged documents and various aliases. Some even likened him to a serpent, sneaky and hiding out close to the ground. After his camouflage was shredded in Marion, Ohio, Mack migrated to Sacramento, California. In Sacramento, Paul Mack appeared to be a legitimate, self-employed businessman, selling novelties, clothing, and sports items to a variety of outlets. He provided suspenders and baseball caps for two Sacramento baseball games and regularly sold silk-screened T-shirts and hats at a local flea market.

One restaurant to which he sold his products was the Warehouse. The bubbly hostess and new entertainment director, Karen Winslett, had worked at the restaurant ever since she was sixteen years old. The manager, Jim Walker, was a friend of her family who believed in her talent and ability. Although Karen was busy handling contests, parties, and other weekly entertainment events, she was an enthusiastic employee and Jim allowed her to deal with Mack when he came by to market his promotional gear.

One afternoon, the good-looking, well-dressed Mack had gone there to talk business. "Good afternoon and welcome to the Warehouse Restaurant. My name is Karen. Do you prefer smoking or non-smoking?" Winslett asked.

"Neither," Mack said, putting his briefcase down to free his well-manicured hands. "I spoke to Jim Walker earlier and he told me to ask for Karen. Would that be you?"

Karen, a bit perplexed, shook his hand and hesitantly said, "Yes," and then instantly remembered the talk she had with her boss. "Oh, you must be Mr. Mack. You're here to talk about putting our logo onto T-shirts and hats, right?"

"That is correct, young lady. Is there somewhere private we can talk?" Mack asked, picking up his briefcase.

"Sure, let me just get someone to relieve me up here, and we can have a seat in the back of the restaurant. Did you bring samples with you?"

"Yes, I did," said the confident businessman in his well-pressed gray suit. "They are right here in my briefcase."

Karen excused herself and went through the door of the kitchen to find someone to take her place as hostess. A waitress, Liza Barnes, whom Karen had become friendly with, volunteered to go out front while Karen graciously led Mack to a table away from the other patrons in the restaurant. Mack gave Karen his usual speech about the silk-screening procedure he used to copy the restaurant logo onto T-shirts and hats and how they were quality products that were inexpensive to make. Because listening to sales pitches was new to Karen, she seemed a little overwhelmed, but Mack was personable and told her a few jokes to make her feel at ease. Although Karen was generally cautious and leery about strangers, she seemed comfortable with this gentleman who got her to laugh so easily. When he was finished with his business spiel, Mack ordered a hamburger and carried on casual conversation with Karen. As the sun shone through the windows of the restaurant, it beamed down on Karen's face and highlighted her curly blond hair, making her look like a haloed angel.

"You know, you should be a model. I hope you don't mind me saying so, but you are a beautiful girl and could make a lot of money in that business," said Mack.

Karen, coloring, gave an embarrassed smile. "Thanks, Mr. Mack. It's what I've dreamed about, but I wouldn't even know how to start or who to call or anything like that."

Mack finished his burger and picked at the coleslaw. "Well, I really think you could make it, but if I've made you uncomfortable I apologize. Anyway, if you ever want to seriously get into the modeling business, I know the right contacts among some people who are always looking for models. I have some equipment and am something of a photographer. Anyway, if you want to, we could talk about it some more, and I'll try to help you."

As he got up from the table and picked up his briefcase, Karen, wavering, shook his hand and said, "Well, I have competed in a few local beauty pageants, and there's another one coming up that I've been prepping for. But I only recently earned this position as entertainment director, and I really like it. Anyway, thank you for the offer. I'll think about it. Thank you for cutting us a deal with the T-shirts and hats. I can't wait to see how they all come out. My boss will be really happy."

"Give him my regards. It was nice meeting you, Karen, and do think about my offer. It's genuine," Mack said, wearing a smile as he walked out of the restaurant. He knew she'd be calling him, though it might take some time.

During the next few months, Karen won the title of Miss English Leather. Officially a beauty queen, her aspirations to be a model now became a major focus. She worked out at the health club to keep an athletic figure. When the Warehouse Restaurant closed, Karen found a job at Chadwick's Restaurant as an evening-shift cocktail waitress. Occasionally, Karen found jobs to model swimwear and dresses. Though she lived far away from her parents in Vancouver, Washington, they were still proud of the life their daughter was making for herself. They supported her aspirations and liked her responsible and dependable boyfriend of three years, Greg Harvey.

Early on the morning of Monday, February 16, Greg awoke and left Karen asleep in their bed to shower, get dressed, and go to work. When he got out of the bathroom, Karen surprised him by being wide awake and on the phone, jumping excitedly, and signaling to her toweled boyfriend to look at a napkin to see what she had just written. However, Greg was so focused on getting dressed that he hadn't any time. After Karen hung up the phone, she jumped over the bed, hugged

Greg, and showed him the note. "Guess who that was? An old supplier of ours at the Warehouse Restaurant, Paul Mack. Remember, I told you he had modeling contacts?"

Greg didn't remember but nodded. He was happy for Karen but anxious to get going.

"Well," she said, looking over at her impatient boyfriend, "you will be really glad to hear they're paying me five thousand dollars to model."

At that, Greg was dumbfounded.

"He told me," Karen explained, "that I'm a finalist for modeling for a Budweiser calendar."

Greg gave her a big kiss and promised her a congratulatory dinner that night as he walked out the door. Karen was overjoyed and went to work that evening with an enormous smile on her face; she even practiced poses in front of the ladies room mirror on her breaks. After work and a romantic dinner with Greg, Karen called her friend, Liza Barnes, the waitress with whom she stayed in touch after the Warehouse Restaurant closed, and told her the news.

"Can you believe my luck, Liza?" Karen yelled into the phone.

"I always knew you were meant for bigger and better things, Karen, but I had no idea that you would reach celebrity status so soon! Just think, all these men are going to buy this calendar, look at your picture, and put you up on their walls! I wish I could be a Budweiser girl. Just how did you get involved with this whole thing anyway?"

"Well, do you remember last year when we were at the Warehouse Restaurant and Jim Walker had this good-looking older guy come in to talk to me about buying T-shirts and hats with the restaurant logo on it?"

"Oh yeah," said Liza. "I still have the shirt. I wear it to bed!"

"So do I," replied Karen. "Well, that's the guy. His name is Paul Mack. He offered to help me with my modeling back then, but I was so busy and hadn't won a title yet, so of course I didn't think I was good enough to be a real model. But after Miss English Leather, he contacted me and said that he knew some people who were looking for models for the calendar, so he showed them some pictures of me, and I guess they liked them because they want me to do it, and Mr. Mack wants to take some more pictures of me. He said probably Thursday morning would be best for him."

"Wow, Karen, that sounds great. I'm telling you, after this, things will never be the same for you again, because a whole new world is going to open up for you. You should be proud of yourself!" Liza paused for a moment. Then she said, "The only thing I'm wondering is how this Mack guy got any pictures of you. You never mentioned to me that you had photos taken, so where did he get the pictures he told you he showed to the Budweiser people?"

Suddenly, Karen wondered the same thing, but she wasn't going to dwell on it or jinx her good luck. "Oh, he must have gotten them from Len Rogers, the guy who took pictures of me that time you came along. You remember Len, right? When you went with me to his place, you said he was cute, and I told you he was taken. Well, I'm sure Mr. Mack got the pictures from him."

Liza was disenchanted and said, "I don't know about that, Karen. It sounds kind of strange to me. How would he know Len? Anyway, you should definitely take someone along to the shoot like you usually do. There are a lot of creeps out there. And you need to ask Mr. Mack where he got your pictures. I mean, what if he was stalking you or something, and these are candid shots of you getting out of the shower or something like that?"

Karen began to giggle. "Liza, what is going through that mind of yours? I always shut the blinds whenever I change in the house. Seriously, though, Mr. Mack must be a really nice guy, or he wouldn't have helped me. Also, you know that I would never take my clothes off at a photo shoot, and I always make that clear at the beginning of every session I go to. Anyway, he's practically twice my age, so I'm sure he's either married or has a girlfriend, and I made it clear to him that I have a boyfriend."

Liza sounded unconvinced. "All right, but if you want

someone to go with you, I have this Thursday off so I'm available."

"Thanks. Mr. Mack said that Thursday is probably when he can do the shoot, but he has to call back to make it definite. Anyway, I'm sure Greg can come with me since he has a light schedule at work this week. But you and I should go to lunch that day. We haven't seen each other in ages, especially with me being away in Mexico. And if the shoot is Thursday morning, we can meet at our usual spot afterward to celebrate."

"Great! So I'll meet you around noon this Thursday at the parking lot between The Chowder House and Ruby's Cafe, right?"

"I'll be there, Liza. Don't forget, okay?"

Liza laughed. "Me, forget? Aren't you the one who has to write little notes on napkins and leave them everywhere as reminders! I have to go now, but I'll see you Thursday, okay?"

"I'll see you then, Liza." Karen laughed as she hung up the phone.

To Karen's surprise, she didn't receive a call from Mack that night or the next two days. She assumed with disappointment that Paul Mack was too busy to meet with her Thursday, but she hoped he'd call soon to reschedule.

The morning of Thursday, February 19, was like any other morning that week. Greg got up at 7:00 A.M. to shower, get dressed, and go to the office. Before leaving, he noticed that Karen was stirring.

"Hey, sleepyhead," Greg said, nudging Karen's feet, "Are you going to stay in bed all day? I was thinking of leaving work a little early today. Will you be around to do something?"

Karen was still groggy and her voice was an octave lower than usual. "I'm supposed to meet Liza for lunch at noon. She's off today. Then I'm going to the gym. I'll need to shower and get ready for work after that. I'm sorry, honey, but I don't think there will be much time to do anything before my shift starts."

"That's alright. I'll stop by the restaurant after work, okay? I'll see you later, beautiful." Greg kissed her forehead and left.

Karen wrapped herself in the sheets and tried to doze off, but a short time later, the phone rang. It was Paul Mack.

"Hi, Karen. Sorry I didn't call sooner, but I just cleared my schedule. Can you come for the photo shoot in an hour and a half?"

"An hour and a half?" she asked. How was she going to get ready that quickly? She sat up and saw her reflection in the mirror. *My eyes look puffy. I shouldn't have gone to bed so late*, she worried.

"Yes. Is that okay? Can you make it?" Mack said.

She looked away from the mirror. "Yes, I can make it."

"Great. I'll see you at my house in a little while. Let me give you directions."

Karen took down the directions and hung up the phone. She was a little nervous about going alone, but knew she couldn't miss this opportunity. She jumped out of bed and got into the shower. When she got out, she hurriedly dressed, made herself up, and packed her favorite pink two-piece bathing suit, a leotard, and a lot of makeup. She laid out the cocktail dress and stockings she wore to work on the bed in case the photo shoot ran much longer than she expected. Karen ran out of the house at 9:30 and didn't even think to call Liza to tell her she probably wouldn't make it to lunch or to ask Liza to go with her. However, Karen did remember to leave Greg a note with Mack's address, the directions to his house and a cryptic message:

Dear Greg,
    Went to shoot the Budweiser calendar ad. I'm scared to go by myself, but I have to. Wish you were here. If I'm not home—if my dress isn't gone—get my dress and come and get me.

Thirty minutes after Karen left for Mack's place, Greg returned to the house to pick up some papers he'd forgotten. He didn't notice Karen's car was not outside. "Karen, I'm sorry," he called out as he entered the front door. "I've got to work all day."

Not seeing Karen, he wondered if she was still asleep. Walking into the bedroom, Greg was surprised that Karen wasn't there. He saw her dress laid out, read the note on top of it, and assumed that since Karen was nervous and Liza had the day off, Karen asked Liza to go to the photo session with her. He knew Karen was careful to never go to a photo shoot alone unless she knew the photographer very well.

Con men often feed upon the assumptions of others to get away with their evil deeds. Karen Winslett had no idea of this when she stood before the lair of Paul Mack.

Mack answered the door dressed in a French shirt with his initials embroidered on the pocket and black gabardine pants, looking very extravagant and very professional. The gold chain he always wore hung from his neck. "Good morning, Karen. You look great! Your hair—wow! Come in. Did you have breakfast yet? Do you want something to drink, maybe orange juice?"

Karen stepped into his house. "Well, I don't usually eat before a modeling session. You know, I don't want to look bloated or anything. But some juice would be really good. I didn't have time for breakfast, and without it I don't have a lot of energy."

Looking around, Karen felt nervous with Mack. She set her bags down by the door and walked inside. His place was spare but well furnished and neat. She didn't see any photography equipment in the room, but she thought it probably was in another room that served as a studio.

"Why don't you sit down while I get the juice." Mack indicated the couch. As Karen sat down, she noticed a mirror on the opposite wall. When Mack left, Karen walked over to the mirror and practiced some poses until he returned with two glasses.

"Hey, getting in a little practice, I see." He laughed.

Embarrassed, Karen accepted the glass of orange juice Mack handed her and said, "Thank you."

He held up his glass and toasted, "To your career."

She took a heavy gulp. "It's kind of bitter," she said, grimacing.

"It's fresh, that's why." Paul nodded. "You're probably used to the junky concentrates. This is much better for you. Drink it all down."

Not wanting to be impolite, she obeyed.

She began to feel a bit strange and made her way back to the couch. Mack sat down near her. "Did you know that this Budweiser deal is supposed to be long-term?" he said, patting her leg. She shrank back but he seemed unperturbed. "They not only want you posing for their calendar, you're also going to have to come back here for other promotional sessions with their products and things of that sort. But I know you're up for that. So it looks like you and I will be spending a lot more time with each other. What do you think?"

Karen smiled but then frowned. Mack was sitting even closer to her, and she tried to move away across the couch slowly as she spoke. "Well, actually I didn't know that this was going to be long-term. I'm planning on moving to San Diego for good sometime this year with my boyfriend. I'm sorry, Mr. Mack."

She began unsteadily to get up from the couch, but Mack reached for her hand. "Karen, wait," he pleaded, letting go of her hand as she sat back down. "Maybe we can work a deal out with the Budweiser people so that you can do this session here and do the others in San Diego."

Karen wavered. "Mr. Mack, you've really been awfully good to me, but I have to talk to my parents and my boyfriend."

Mack looked at Karen wryly and said, "It's my pleasure. Let's talk about it after I speak with the Budweiser people. All they told me was that they saw your picture and wanted you for the calendar, but I'll see what's on their minds. But for now, you think about whether you still want to do it."

"Mr. Mack, I'm not really feeling too well. I feel dizzy."

"It's probably low blood sugar. Let me get you another glass of orange juice."

Mack went to the kitchen while Karen slumped on the couch. He took a little longer than before, but she thought that it was because he was frustrated with her. Karen felt badly.

She caught her tipsy-looking reflection in the mirror and tried to steady herself. *What is wrong with me?* she wondered. Just then, Mack returned with more orange juice.

"Here. Drink this," he said, handing the glass to her.

Walking over to a closet, Mack opened it and took out a camera. He bit his lip as he watched her becoming pale. "Okay, then. Well, I guess we'll have to get you warmed up. Let's see some poses. Just go with whatever feels good and be natural."

Karen tried to smile, got up from the couch and despite feeling ill, began to work some poses, putting one hand on her hip, both hands on her hips, one hand to her chin and folding her arms. Mack cheered her on with comments like, "That's perfect," "You're beautiful," and "You'll look great in that calendar."

But after a few minutes, Karen felt nauseous, put her hand to her head and stumbled towards the couch. Mack stood up to catch her, as she looked like she was going to faint, and laid her across the couch. She said, "Oh my God, Mr. Mack, I'm so sorry. I don't know what's wrong with me. I just feel really ill. I think your orange juice was bad. You should throw that stuff out."

"I will, Karen. Don't you worry. I'll go get you something for your head and dump out the juice right now." And with that, Paul Mack got up, and beauty queen Karen Winslett shut her eyes.

Greg Harvey worked until 4:00 P.M., at which time he drove straight to Chadwick's Restaurant, thirty minutes away, hoping to tell Karen about a new assignment his boss had given him. But he didn't see her there. He spoke with a few waitresses and her manager, none of whom knew where she was. They told Greg that she had failed to show up for her shift and she hadn't called as she usually did if she was late.

Greg drove back to the house, ran into the bedroom, and saw Karen's clothes still laid out on the bed. Feeling unnerved, he grabbed the note Karen left and took it with him in his car as he followed the directions to Paul Mack's house.

Ten minutes later, Greg stood at the door, knocking. A young woman with long brown hair and in her mid-twenties, Stacy Carter, answered the door. Greg tried to see inside the house, but he didn't see any photography equipment anywhere.

"I'm looking for my girlfriend, Ms. Karen Winslett. Is she here?"

Before Stacy could answer, Mack came up behind her and said, "We don't know anyone by that name. I'm sorry."

Greg apologized for wasting their time and, frustrated, went back to his and Karen's house. After five minutes of trying to calm himself down by looking through Karen's address books and dresser drawers, and even doing some push-ups, the phone rang. It was Paul Mack.

"Look, I'm sorry. You were just here at my house. I do know your girlfriend, Karen. It just completely slipped my mind."

"Do you know where she is?"

"Well, she was supposed to show up this morning for a job interview, but we discussed it beforehand over the phone and decided to just cancel our appointment when she told me she was going to move to San Diego."

"Thanks. She never showed up at work today, and I'm just a little worried. Thanks again for calling, though." Greg was not as relieved as he thought he would be after speaking to Mack.

When the next few hours passed with no word from Karen, his fear escalated.

At eleven that night, Greg called the police to report his girlfriend missing. They asked him if anything was missing from the house, and he told them that besides her car, there were some articles of clothing missing, a pink two-piece bathing suit, a leotard, a couple of handbags, and a counter's worth of cosmetics. The police told him they could not issue a missing person's report until the next day when she would be gone twenty-four hours. After hanging up, he bit his nails nervously as he tried to fall asleep.

The next morning, Friday, Greg called Karen's friend, Liza,

and asked her if Karen ever showed up for their lunch. Liza said no. "I'm annoyed with Karen because she left me there, waiting in the parking lot. I waited an hour before I left."

"Liza, she never came home," Greg said in an emotional voice. "I don't understand it."

"You mean she's disappeared?" Liza asked, her own fears for her missing friend rising.

"I have to call the police back," Greg told her. "Maybe by this time they'll listen to me. I knew as soon as she didn't come home last night that something had happened to her."

# CHAPTER FIFTEEN

# Bad Dreams

A year before she met Paul Mack, while Margie had been day-dreaming of the muscle-bound hunk on her postcard, a young woman was missing and her worried boyfriend was again headed to Mack's home. Around 5:30 P.M. on Friday, Greg Harvey knocked on Mack's front door. When Paul answered, Greg said, "Please, you're the last person who talked to Karen that day." Once again, Greg asked Mack if he knew anything about Karen's whereabouts, and Greg told him that he had contacted the police.

Mack answered Greg with recalcitrance. "I already told you," Mack adamantly said, "your girlfriend was supposed to come over that morning, but she never did."

Driving away, Greg, his suspicions aroused by now, began going over Mack's story in his mind. First, Mack had said that he canceled his appointment with Karen after finding out she was moving to San Diego. This time, however, Mack told Greg that she was supposed to show up but didn't. These thoughts bogged Greg down as he faced another night without his beauty queen girlfriend.

After Greg Harvey left, Paul Mack nervously paced back and forth in his living room. Then he came up with a plan. He picked up the phone and gave his brother a call.

"Hello?" said the voice over the receiver.

"Todd, it's Paul. I know I haven't talked to you in a while, but I need to meet you tomorrow morning. It's important."

The two arranged to meet and hung up.

On Saturday morning, Greg Harvey went to Mack's neigh-borhood and showed pictures of Karen to the neighbors, asking if they had seen Karen or her car that fateful Thursday. Everyone he asked explained to him that he or she had already left for work and didn't see anyone.

While Greg was canvassing his neighborhood, Paul Mack was meeting with his brother, Todd.

"I'm in some trouble," Paul told his brother. "A local girl here is missing, and she was supposed to come to my house for a job interview about two weeks ago, but I canceled at the last minute. After she was reported gone, her boyfriend came here, saying she left a note that she was at my place. So the police will think that I was the last person to see her. I'm sure they'll be calling to interview me very soon. In all honesty, I was alone that day, but I can't tell them that. They'll never believe me. I want to tell them I spent the day at your place with you."

"What! Paul, you know I don't like lying, especially to the police."

"Todd, please, I know you don't, but this one time, could you please do me this favor? The police are never going to believe that I was by myself that day, so you have to tell them that I came over to your house and that the two of us just sat around and listened to records. Once they talk to me, they're going to have to confirm my story with you. Can I count on you?"

Todd reluctantly agreed.

That afternoon, Paul received a phone call from Detective Frank asking if he could stop by that evening to ask him a few questions. Paul told him that he could and hung up. Then he resumed his nervous pacing from the previous day.

The attractive brunette with whom he lived returned from an afternoon of shopping and interrupted Paul's thoughts. It was Stacy, Paul's girlfriend.

"Are you okay?" she asked, a concerned look crossing her face.

Paul put his arms around Stacy and said, "Sit down. We have to talk."

"What's wrong?" she asked, as she sat down on the couch next to Paul.

Paul began, "About a year ago, I met Karen Winslett at the restaurant where she worked. The manager assigned Karen to assist me in designing a logo for the restaurant's jackets. I talked to her at the restaurant several times and on the phone. Then, after the restaurant closed, we talked once about her going into sales. Now she's missing, and the police will be here later to question me. It's no big deal. They have to question everyone who knows her."

"Oh my God! How awful!" Stacy screamed. "Why you?"

"I guess I was one of the last people who talked to her. The guy that came here the other night was her boyfriend; he said he was looking for her. Maybe it's one of those domestic brawls. He might even have killed her or something. They say most murders are committed by someone the victim knows." Mack looked at his girlfriend and shrugged. "Who knows? Anyway, I'll go fix dinner."

After Paul left the room, Stacy was dazed. How could the police think Paul was implicated in the disappearance of this girl? But she figured Paul didn't seem too upset, so she told herself to put the conversation they had just shared out of her mind.

After dinner, Detective Harnot and Detective Frank arrived at Paul Mack's home. Detective Frank asked Paul to speak with them alone.

"No," Paul responded. "I want Stacy to be here."

Detective Harnot stated, "It might be necessary for me to tape record this interview."

Looking uncomfortable, Paul said, "I don't want to get into any trouble."

Detective Frank said, "I'd advise you of your rights before taking any statement from you if you were under suspicion."

Mack then agreed to the interview, and Detective Harnot asked, "What sort of business are you in?"

"I have a promotional firm that does wholesale silk screening," Mack answered.

"Tell me about Karen Winslett," Detective Frank said.

Mack answered, "Karen had talked to me about opportunities for women in sales. She seemed interested in this type of work. I explained to her that I knew lots of women who were successful. Karen worked with me on some promotional items for the restaurant where she worked. Lately, I've been thinking of going into the beef jerky business. If I do, I'll need someone to help out with sales in the silk screening business. I called her and she seemed interested, so I suggested if she wanted to do it she should fill out an application for me sometime."

"Did you discuss how much money she might make?" the detective asked.

"No, we never talked about money. I just said I'd get back to her," Mack relayed.

Detective Frank asked, "When was the next time you talked with her?"

"Just a few days ago, I called her," Mack answered. "She said she was definitely interested in the job. I told her that she'd work on commission. Karen then told me that she was moving to San Diego near the end of the month. I told her then it wasn't worth my time to interview her or have her fill out an application."

Detective Frank looked at Mack appraisingly, then asked, "Do you do any studio photography?"

Mack said, "I don't have a studio. All I own is a small Vivitar camera."

"When was the last physical contact you had with Karen Winslett?" Detective Harnot asked.

Mack responded, looking thoughtful, "It was months ago, at the restaurant. Any other contact has been over the phone."

"How did you learn of Karen's disappearance?" Detective Harnot asked.

"Her boyfriend came here twice looking for her. The first time he came, Thursday night, I told him that I hadn't seen Karen. He said that Karen told him she was coming over to my house for a photography session for a calendar. I told him I didn't own a studio, as you can see, and suggested he call the calendar people. He didn't seem satisfied with that answer, so he came back the next day—yesterday—and I told him the same thing."

Detective Frank furrowed his brow and asked, "Could you recall to the best of your ability what you did Thursday, February nineteenth, the day Karen Winslett disappeared?"

Mack answered in a thoughtful but casual voice, "Thursday morning I called Karen. I went to my brother's house right after. His name is Todd Mack. We listened to music. After I left my brother's house, I picked up some dry cleaning and came home to get a jacket to be embroidered at work. I was at work until five P.M. I came home again and started dinner. Stacy came home soon after. Stacy was here with me all night. On Friday morning, I went and got my hair cut at nine-thirty A.M. I went to lunch with a friend and just worked the rest of the day."

"If it was necessary, would you be willing to take a polygraph test?" Detective Frank asked.

"Yes, of course," Mack said, nodding.

The detectives thanked Mack for his time. As they left, Stacy seemed shaken while Paul felt nothing but relief.

The next night, the phone rang, and Mack raced to pick it up. "Hello," he said animatedly.

"Paul," his brother, Todd, said, "the cops have been here. I told them you were with me that day, but I got confused. I'm not sure they believed me."

Losing his usual composure, Mack screamed, "I told you to tell them we spent the day together listening to music and hanging out! Is that so hard?"

"It's not that easy! I'm not like you!" Todd screamed back as he slammed the phone down.

Mack sat down on the couch in disbelief.

"What a stupid jerk!" he yelled. His angry voice echoed through the empty house.

Mack ran his fingers through his hair. He tried to think. If they found out he wasn't with Todd, he would just tell them he was nervous, scared to death, because he was alone that day. "So I convinced my brother to be my alibi," he said aloud.

After a sleepless night, Mack arose and quickly dressed.

Not bothering with coffee, he grabbed his jacket in disgust and went to work.

However, when the police didn't contact him over the next few days about Todd's story, Mack thought his brother had been overreacting as usual and he began to relax.

Later that week, Greg Harvey decided to contact Detective Harnot. He telephoned the police station and gave the detective a thorough description of his two conversations with Paul Mack, noting the inconsistencies in Mack's story. The detective thanked him for his help before hanging up. It had been a full week since Karen disappeared and a distraught Greg didn't know what to do with himself. He decided he should try to keep his mind occupied, but as he turned on the television, Greg found there was no escape from his pain: Karen's picture was on nearly every local news broadcast.

Paul Mack, however, was getting on with his life as though nothing had happened. He never talked to Stacy or Todd again of the incident.

On March 3, the body of Karen Winslett was found. Missing nearly two weeks, her body was discovered in the back of her blue Datsun 260 Z hatchback in the parking lot of the Colonial Motel. Bob McLean, a meter reader for the electric company and coincidentally an acquaintance of Karen's, was going about his duties at the motel and thought he recognized his friend's car in the parking lot. Upon closer inspection, he saw the phone number on the "For Sale" sign on the floor of the passenger side and knew for sure that it was Karen's car. Bob knew that his friend had been missing, so he ran to find a phone to call the police and luckily ran into two deputies at the coffee shop next door. The policemen walked over to the car and told Bob to stand back as they opened the trunk. Bob screamed as the pungent smell hit him and he caught sight of the horror inside. A coat lay atop the carpet in the rear of the car, and there was a lifeless hand protruding from underneath the carpeting. When the carpeting was lifted by one of the officers, the three men glimpsed the badly decomposed body of a female with blond hair. The crime unit was summoned, and eventually, a tow truck moved the vehicle with the body to the coroner's office for examination. A forensic team began its investigation.

Because the body was so decomposed when it was discovered, officers doubted whether the cause of death could be determined if she died from soft tissue damage, like strangulation. From dental charts, the body was identified and confirmed to be Karen Winslett, and her parents, who lived out of state, were notified. Greg Harvey was sitting alone in the dark in his living room when Detective Frank came to question him. Greg told him the same things he had said when he first contacted the police about Karen's disappearance: that she was home when he left for work but when he got home later, he found only a note that lead him to Paul Mack. He also repeated what he told Detective Harnot about the inconsistencies in Paul Mack's explanations the two times Greg went to Mack's house.

The autopsy and toxicology tests revealed Karen Winslett had died of a toxic dose of Percodan, a prescription pain killer. The amount was massive.

Detective Frank and Detective Harnot determined Karen Winslett did not have a prescription for Percodan nor did she suffer from any health problems. Karen was not suicidal nor did she have a history of drug abuse.

They were suspicious of Paul Mack and thought he might have lured Karen to his home with the offer of money to pose for a calendar. Then, they speculated, Paul Mack served her a drink heavily laced with Percodan in order to seduce her, take her life, and hide his crime.

Their suspicions were bolstered when a background investigation of Paul Mack turned up the fact that he had been the prime suspect in a similar murder of a nineteen-year-old girl in Ohio. They also learned Paul Mack had an extensive criminal past: he was a many-times convicted forger and burglar and had been freed on parole two years earlier.

The next day, Detective Frank, Detective Harnot, and Officer Warren arrived at Paul Mack's home to serve a search warrant. Mack answered the door, and the officers formally identified themselves. They advised Mack of the search warrant for the residence and demanded entry.

The officers made a thorough search, located and removed vitamins, diet supplements, Traumatex, Geritol, vitamin C, and oyster shell calcium. They took a pen, assorted hairs from a brush, the floor mat and carpet from Mack's car, a Visa card in the name of Stella L. Brown, and a black vest which contained a loose white powder of unknown origin. Officer Warren also collected samples from the bedspread and carpet, which was brown in color, for future comparison with any trace of evidence found on Karen Winslett. The officers left with the evidence they collected.

Mack never said a word to Stacy about the police search when she arrived home. He acted as if nothing had happened.

A few days later, a woman from the motel staff came forward, telling the police that she had seen a man resembling Mack's description: medium build, dark hair and wearing nice pants and a pressed shirt, sitting alone in Karen's car the day she was reported missing. In addition, Mack's friend, Chris Jackson, told the police that early that day he had picked up Mack at a gas station near the motel because Mack called and told him he just had a fight with his girlfriend and had no ride home. Among the items found in the glove box of Karen's car was an invitation to a Halloween party, signed on the back, "Sincerely, Paul S. Mack." Investigators' suspicions peaked when they discovered from Mack's dentist that he had access to Percodan and had filled prescriptions of that drug on at least eight occasions during the past two years.

Twenty-four hours later, Detective Frank and Detective Harnot returned to Paul Mack's home. Mack agreed to surrender to them for questioning on Monday afternoon, which gave him time to get his affairs in order. Mack professed his innocence over and over as the detectives left his home. Although they were wary of his sincerity, Paul Mack seemed so immersed in his job and had strong local ties—specifically, his fiancée and his brother—they did not fear he would flee.

However, when Stacy arrived home that night, Mack's suitcases were packed. He explained to his tearful and frightened girlfriend that he was innocent, but because he'd been in trouble before he didn't have a chance. His only move was to run. Without giving Stacy an opportunity to react, Paul walked out the door and disappeared into the night. Shocked, Stacy sat down and cried in disbelief.

When Mack failed to surrender on Monday, April 13, an all-points bulletin was put out for his arrest. The release stated that Paul Mack was last known to be driving a maroon Jeep Cherokee. "Anyone who has seen Paul Mack or knows of his whereabouts please call the sheriff's department."

The following day another release stated that Paul Mack's Jeep Cherokee had been recovered. Unknown to the police, Mack had rented another car.

In Logan, Utah, he called the sheriff's department to try and make a deal to surrender in exchange for bail. No deal was concluded and Mack had left his Logan address by the time the police arrived. The search for him extended to Colorado Springs, where Mack once worked as a chef, and to Arvada, Colorado, where he purchased oil and a filter on a credit card. The authorities cut off Mack's bank cards. They figured he would run out of money soon. But they did not count on his cunning and his ingenuity.

The FBI joined in the search after Mack crossed state lines. All agents were put on alert. Their bureau chief stated they would go wherever the leads took them.

Meanwhile, meticulously searching, Detective Frank and Detective Harnot flew to Denver to meet authorities in the state to which Paul Mack was last traced.

In May of that year, Paul Mack, no doubt enjoying the fact that the Sacramento police would never think him so close, arrived in Salt Lake City. Approximately two months later, he entered Margie Danielsen's life and her heart. She thought he was the man of her dreams. However, doubts and fears crept in, until the day she went to the police with her suspicions and found out that the truth about Sean Paul Lanier, alias Paul Steven Mack, was even more terrible than her worst nightmares.

# CHAPTER SIXTEEN

## The Chase

"How do I digest all of this?" Margie asked bitterly, listening to the detectives in the police station tell of her husband's alleged crimes and hearing him called Paul Steven Mack. How strange it sounded to Margie. She remembered how long it had taken Sean to respond to the name Sean. Nevertheless, he was Sean to Margie, and it was as if the policeman spoke of someone else.

Margie sat silently in a state of shock as Detective Frank continued. "There's more." He looked at her sadly. "Paul Steven Mack has been married seven times." *So Jed McCall had been right*, Margie thought, wincing. "He has a very lengthy rap sheet, including theft, bad checks totaling more than ten thousand dollars, forgery, burglary, embezzlement, car theft, and various scams as a con man. In California, Mack's criminal history dates back years, including numerous arrests for manipulative crimes, as I call them, that is, bad checks and receiving property under false pretenses. Mack was first arrested at age fourteen. He served a hundred-day jail term for fraud and was paroled. He returned to prison twice for parole violations. He's lived in California, Nevada, Colorado, and Idaho, as well as Ohio and Utah."

"My children and I are lucky to be alive!" she suddenly blurted out.

Frank nodded.

"We've also been checking on unsolved homicides in Salt Lake," Detective Conrad added. "There have been two or three during the time Paul Mack has lived here. One involved a woman."

The words the detectives spoke turned Margie's fears into reality. A reality she wanted to forget but knew she never would.

"We're glad you never gave up your pursuit of the truth," Detective Frank said. "He may never have been caught otherwise. I'm amazed and impressed at your perseverance."

"I've been so frightened," Margie confessed.

"I understand, and it's not completely over yet. With the fingerprint match you've given us, we're almost ready to close in. We want you to be very careful, but when you get home we'd like you to look for any prescriptions in the house, since one of the murdered women was poisoned by a massive dose of Percodan."

Margie took a deep breath and let it out in a rush. "I know he has some Percodan. I found the bottle after one horrendous night when he must have given me some because I passed out." The memories of the the night she thought Sean raped her made her shudder. "I'll look for others," she said.

"Thank you," the detective responded. "You might want to know how Mack changed his appearance. He used steroids to add bulk and muscle to his body."

"Steroids!" Margie said, astonished. "He told me he took vitamin shots! He lied about everything!"

"Mack also did cocaine," Detective Frank stated.

Not surprised anymore, Margie responded, "One day before we were married, he was shaky when he came to my house and then left in a hurry. He told me he was a bit diabetic." She looked down. "He always has an answer for everything."

"Con artists are very good at explanations," Detective Frank reassured her. "Besides his weight gain, Mack shaved off his mustache and lightened and changed his hair style. He wanted to disguise himself. His patterns followed him, however, and that's what did him in. His patterns of changing the stories about his past and trying to con people made you suspicious and led you and the woman who saw him on *America's Most Wanted* to us. We're very glad you acted upon your suspicions."

"What's next?" Margie asked quietly.

"We have to get the prints from the pawn shop and some other last things checked out and if the facts confirm our suspicions, warrants will be drawn up."

"And then?" she said.

The two detectives looked at each other. Frank nodded at Conrad. "If we're right, we'll plant a special SWAT and tactics team down the street from your home, behind the church. Then we'll surround the house and ask Mack to surrender. I think it best that you get the girls and yourself out," Conrad said.

Margie shook her head. "If we do leave, he'll be suspicious. And we may be in worse danger, if not from him, from his friends who'll surely follow us."

"Just be careful," Conrad told her.

"Everyone keeps telling me that. I'll do my best."

The men stood up as Margie prepared to leave. Detective Frank, who had done most of the talking, warned Margie to be prepared afterward for news reporters and television cameras. Another pain hit Margie's heart.

"I'm so embarrassed! And what will the children tell their friends? Why does everyone have to know? What if he finds out?" she blurted out. "Can't you keep my part in all of this secret?"

"We're planning to do that," Detective Frank explained, "but the news reporters always check the police blotter every day looking for a big story. This is a very big story. They'll find out you're married to him and seek you out. You have no reason to be embarrassed. You're very brave. It's not your fault, but we don't want you to be in further danger. You're right about Mack's friends and the threat they pose. He's charming, but he's also vindictive, so we'll keep your discoveries to ourselves."

Before Margie left, Detective Frank said one last thing. "You will feel anger. You will feel hate. You will even feel love. I'm sorry you suffered through this ordeal. But you and your children are alive, and you all still have each other."

"Yes. That's the most important thing."

Tears flowed down her face as she thought of the two young women who were now dead because of Sean. They'd never experience the joy of motherhood. Margie thought of their mothers and the horrible agony they must feel from the loss of their daughters. News reporters seemed insignificant when she thought of Sean's victims. Margie thanked the detectives for their information, compassion, and understanding.

At home, before Sean got there, Margie decided it would be better if the girls didn't know anything. She decided she would send them to their father's after dinner.

Somehow, she got through the next hours. She managed to prepare dinner and make small talk with the girls and Sean throughout the evening, even though her heart was pounding. The girls were picked up by Joel at nine.

Sleep did not come to Margie that night. She desperately wanted to sleep. She wanted to wake up and find out this was just a dream. Margie watched Sean as he slept next to her and thought of how much she had loved him. She thought of the night she was so sick. She knew now that Sean did drug and rape her. The very thought of that night made her physically ill. She went into the bathroom, turned on the shower, and ripped off her nightclothes. She opened the shower door and stood under the hot steamy water, her tears mingling with the running water. Margie scrubbed her body with soap and a brush to rid herself of any trace of Sean. She felt dirty and ashamed that she had fallen in love with a murderer.

Margie felt tired and weak as she called to check on the girls and then crawled back into bed. Still she did not sleep. She was grateful that Sean did not wake up as she lay staring at the ceiling. She waited, just waited, for the unknown events of the next few days.

At five-fifty-three, the bedside phone rang, breaking the early morning silence. Sleepily, Sean answered it. Lying next to him, Margie could hear the agitated voice of one of the strange men who had been watching the house on the other end. "Of course," Sean, keeping his voice low, said into the telephone. "I'll be right there. Just give me a few minutes to get dressed."

Before Margie could say anything, Sean whispered to her, "A business matter. I have to go to the restaurant right away."

Margie murmured a response, pretending to be half asleep. Sean pulled on his clothes at record speed and, as Margie lay listening to his movements, exited through the bedroom window just as police officers began to pound on the front door. Margie flew out of bed and grabbed her robe.

Answering the door, a red-eyed and tearful Margie explained to the police that Sean had escaped.

Detective Conrad tried to convince Margie to go with the police to apprehend Sean. "You might be able to talk him into giving himself up before anyone gets hurt," Conrad said.

For a moment, she stared at Conrad while his words ruminated in her brain. "Before anyone gets hurt? Two women have been murdered. My children and I and countless others have already been hurt."

"I'm sorry. I know how you feel," Conrad said sympathetically.

"Do you?" Margie said stiffly.

"I'm sorry," he said again. "Please, Margie, we have to go after him right now and we need your help."

Margie hesitated, a look of indecision on her face.

Conrad put his hand gently on her shoulder. "I don't mean to pressure you, but time's running out. Will you please come?"

Despite her fear and misgivings, Margie realized that perhaps she could help end the torture here and now. She pulled a coat on over her bathrobe and slipped on shoes, then followed Conrad outside and got into the squad car.

With Margie in the back, the dozen unmarked police cars that had been stationed near the house began to pursue Sean, who had not yet gotten very far. As they raced through the streets, dodging and weaving, she suddenly realized where Sean was leading them.

"He's headed for the canyon and mountains. He always took me there on our dates," she said.

She could hear the skidding of tires and the roar of the sirens as the police followed him in hot pursuit. Sean was a skillful driver. She watched as he kept careful control of the car through the sudden switchback turns which, at any moment, could have plunged his vehicle downward off the narrow road.

"If his brakes fail, or he makes a wrong turn, it'll send that Toyota spiraling off the highway and down those boulder-strewn embankments," Conrad said.

Sean's face was drenched in sweat as he looked through the rearview mirror to see some of the squad cars with their sirens screaming in hot pursuit. He knew the others could not be far behind, but he kept going, even as officers called out on microphones, "Halt or we'll shoot."

Margie knew that, like her, he could hear bullets whizzing by. But Sean didn't stop.

Finally, on a short, smooth patch, Margie called Sean on his car phone from the one in the squad car.

"Honey," he said in a breathless voice, "there must be some mistake. A bunch of police cars and some others are after me."

"I know," she said, though she did not tell him she was in one of the cars. She could not believe that he was still playing the lying game he had played for so long. But nothing surprised her anymore. With Conrad coaching her, she asked, "Sean, why did you run if you've done nothing wrong?"

"Run?" he said quizzically. "I told you I had to get to the restaurant in a hurry. And then suddenly a bunch of these cars started to chase me. Do you know what's happening?"

"No," she said quietly, "but I think you do. Please let the police take you in. You can explain all this later."

He rounded a turn. "I have to go," he said and hung up.

She called him back. "Please, Sean, they have you trapped. Turn yourself in." But Sean drove on. At the next bend in the road, a long S-curve, he stepped on the gas.

"We've got to get ahead of him!" Conrad began to radio directions to the other cars.

They drove on. Light was streaming in the windows as they rose higher and higher into the mountains. The early morning sunlight made her eyes tear. Squinting, Margie saw a blockade of squad cars with their lights flashing way up ahead of them. Sean was trapped, and though she told herself she must be crazy, she was weeping. She prayed that he would stop, that he would not plunge his car into the canyon below rather than be captured.

Suddenly, Sean saw the cars too.

She called him again. "Please, Sean. You have to give yourself up."

For a moment, there was dead silence. Then she heard his car screech to a stop and saw the officers come from all directions with guns drawn, surrounding him. She and Conrad stayed in their car and watched from a distance.

"I don't want him to see you," Conrad said. "You'll be safer that way. He could be vindictive if he thought you helped us get him."

Margie did not want to get closer, but somehow she felt Sean had seen her, but, *Maybe not*, she told herself.

It was over. Two of the officers handcuffed Sean and guided him into the back seat of their squad car.

"I'm glad he gave himself up," she said to Conrad later on the ride back to her home.

Margie breathed a heavy sigh of relief when they got there. She longed for solitude, but as soon as she walked into the house she heard the phone ringing. It was Sean. He was calling from the police station.

"I've been arrested for murder," he said in a casual voice. "Honey," he went on, "you might have to post bail."

"Oh God!" Margie screamed into the phone. "I can't believe this." She paused. "Or you."

She hung up wishing she could disconnect her memories of Sean Paul Lanier as easily as she had broken off the telephone connection.

Another sleepless night had turned into morning. She tore off the bedding she and Sean had slept on and threw it in the garbage can. Her eyes burned from the many tears she shed. *How could you ever imagine events so terrible? Murder. You read about it in the newspaper and see stories on television. Even those don't seem real. It never happens to you.* Margie exhaustedly lay on the bare mattress, still wearing the pajamas and bathrobe she had left the house in, and stared at the ceiling, until the bright beams of sunlight filtering into the room told her she should get up and face the day.

When Margie's children came home a few hours later, Margie sat down and told them what happened. Margie didn't know if they fully realized what she told them, because it was hard for her to believe it too. Julie, June, and Jessi were full of so much love and compassion for their mother that Margie drew strength from them. She knew together they would survive.

Margie's daughters wanted to go to school even though they'd be a little late. Margie thought school was a good idea to keep their minds occupied with something normal.

After the girls left, Margie began going through Sean's things. She found unpaid bill after unpaid bill. Upset, Margie called her lawyer, Ray Wells. When he heard what had happened, he canceled all his appointments and came straight to Margie's house.

Ray arrived with his briefcase and gave Margie a hug. He seemed so big and strong to her. He was over six feet, a bearlike man with light brown hair and mustache. He put his glasses on as he sat down at the kitchen table. Together, they began to sort through all the bills Margie had found among Sean's belongings. Margie discovered that Sean had taken out loans everywhere.

"My house payment is twice as much as it was," she explained to Ray. "I turned over my bank account to him and let Sean take care of the finances, and I don't know about any of these bills."

"Looks like he used the title to the house to secure a large loan," Ray told Margie as he looked through the papers.

"I remember signing papers that I never read because I trusted Sean," Margie explained. "I guess I'm in for a lot of heartache because of my trust. How do I ever believe in anyone again?"

"It looks pretty bad, Margie, but you've shown a lot of courage. You and the girls will get through this."

While Margie and Ray examined the mound of bills, news reporters began to line the quiet street Margie lived on. When her doorbell rang, she looked out the peephole. She knew her lost dream was even more of a nightmare now.

"Oh, Ray!" Margie cried. "I can't face them! I need to get my thoughts together first! I haven't slept in days because of this turmoil!"

"Don't worry," Ray reassured Margie. "I'll talk to them for you."

Ray opened the front door and told the reporters, "We have no comment at this time." Then he quickly shut the door.

Margie watched the media people as they left her home. Instead of getting into their vehicles, they began walking from one neighbor's house to another.

"Oh God. This gets worse and worse," Margie cried.

"Paul Mack has complicated your quiet peaceful life in more ways than one, Margie," Ray commented. "Now you have this financial mess to deal with too. At least he didn't finalize the paperwork to buy the health club."

"What health club?" Margie asked through her tears.

"Salt Lake Fitness, the club that you belonged to."

Margie felt overwhelmed trying to sort out the truth from the lies.

Soon it would be time for Margie's daughters to come home from school. The news reporters were still camped out on her street. Margie called her ex-husband, Joel, and explained the situation to him. Like everyone else, he was in shock. His words sputtered into silence. Joel agreed to pick the girls up from school and take them home with him.

Margie felt drained and tired as she hung up the phone and sat staring into space. When the phone rang, the sudden sound startled her, and she asked Ray to answer the phone in case it was a news reporter. He passed her the telephone. It was Detective Frank. "I want you to come down to the Salt Lake Jail tomorrow," Frank said. "Mack said he'd sign the papers to extradite him to California for trial if he gets to see you first."

Holding her hand over the receiver, she whispered the conversation to Ray, who took the phone.

"We'll both be there," Ray told the detective and hung up. He turned to Margie. "I'll draw up papers to get your house back in your name as well as a power of attorney for you to deal with the financial situation."

Ray left to get the paperwork ready for the next day. She called Joel, who told Margie that he'd be glad to keep their daughters another night. The news reporters finally left, one by one.

Margie called her friend Nila to explain what had happened and to ask if she could spend the night with her. After she arrived, they sat talking.

"It's hard to think about anything but the stranger I married. How do you go on with your life after an experience like this? How do you believe again? How do you trust?" Margie cried.

Nila just sat silently, letting Margie spill out her misery.

Finally Margie pulled herself together. "I know there's no answer anyone else can give me," Margie said. "I have to find the way back for the girls and me by myself."

# CHAPTER SEVENTEEN

## The Stranger

PAUL Mack paced with nervous intensity in his cell in the Salt Lake City Jail. All he talked about was Margie, his new wife. He told his cellmate in a conspiratorial tone, "I do love her. I wanted to live here with my new family for the rest of my life. I am Sean Paul Lanier! I changed my life! How do I convince Margie I haven't done anything wrong? How can I prove to her that I am who she thinks I am? I want to go back to her! I want her to wait for me."

The man lying on the cot across the cell did not answer him.

The tiny cell was quiet except for the sound of Paul Mack pacing, back and forth, back and forth, as he raked his fingers through his hair. He said he was afraid of what lay ahead of him. He said all he wanted was his wife to stand by him and believe in him, to help get him through all of this. "I know that after the trial I'll be a free man. I want to come back to my life in Salt Lake City with my new wife and family."

He stood still now, his face a mask.

"If Margie stands by me through this, I can do it. I can prove my innocence and come back to her," Mack said.

Paul Mack's words were interrupted by a deep voice. "Stand back!"

Keys went into the lock as Paul stepped back toward the wall. With a click, the cell door opened.

"Come on. You can take a shower," the huge bulky guard grunted.

*    *    *

Meanwhile, Margie was preparing herself to face Sean, going over in her mind the questions she wanted to ask, questions she knew might never be answered. Nevertheless, she was determined to help the police, as well as herself, to be sure Paul Mack would never be free again. Feeling dizzy, she went to the bathroom and threw cold water on her face. She forced herself to finish dressing. "I'm going to get through this," she told herself.

Ray Wells drove up. Margie was waiting in the driveway.

"Margie, you look so pale," he commented as he opened the car door for her. "Have you slept or eaten at all?"

"No," Margie said. "I couldn't. I just want to get this over with."

Ray explained the documents he had drawn up for Sean to sign as they drove to the Salt Lake Jail. Margie didn't hear a word Ray said even though she knew she should try to listen. She just stared out the window of the car at all the people going about their normal lives. Margie felt like she was never going to be normal again. But as they rode, her thoughts crystallized. She knew what she had to do.

Once they arrived at their destination, they made their way into the jail and took the elevator upstairs where they met Hank Conrad and Jay Frank.

"Margie," Detective Frank said, "you look tired."

"I am," she said, "but at least we're all safe now, thanks in large part to you."

Hank Conrad said, "You were very brave."

She shook her head. "I don't feel brave. I just did what I had to do."

"Margie," Detective Frank said, "after your attorney gets his papers signed, we'd like him to leave the room. I want you to obtain as much information from Mack as you can. Do you think you can do that?" He spent some time explaining what they needed.

"Yes," Margie said quietly. "The one thing I request is that you be close by and Sean be handcuffed. Knowing he is a murderer scares me to death. I felt fear of the unknown with Sean before. Now, that fear has turned into overwhelming terror. But I'll help you despite my fears. I want to be sure he doesn't inflict this terror on any more innocent women."

"I understand," Detective Frank said soothingly. "I'll be close by, and Mack will be handcuffed."

The interrogation room was small, with a table and four chairs in the middle of the room. Two chairs were on each side of the table facing each other. The atmosphere was cold and unnerving. Margie sat across from Ray in silence. He looked as jittery as Margie felt. Margie's back was to the opened steel door so she didn't have to see Sean walk through it. Her heart pounded with fright as she fought the urge to get up and run away.

When Sean walked into the small room, the door was locked shut behind him. Margie did not turn to look at him. She did not bring her eyes to meet his as he sat down next to her facing Ray across the table.

Ray, who was not a criminal lawyer, looked shaken but determined as he began to explain the papers to Paul Mack. "From Margie's standpoint, there are so many unknowns right now that we need this paper to protect the house in case a sudden judgment pops up. This grants the property to Margie. This other paper makes it possible for her to endorse checks cashed for insurance proceeds and sign financial documents for a period of six months."

Sean signed the papers with handcuffed hands. Margie was instantly relieved. Ray called for the detective, and the door opened. Ray walked out of the room in haste.

Sean asked the detective, "Can I pull my chair closer to her?"

"No!" the detective said. "You can sit right where you are! There better not be a problem! I'll be right outside the door!"

The detective backed out the door, and Margie heard a loud click as he locked it. Sean and Margie were alone.

At last their eyes connected. Margie gazed into the eyes of a stranger. She did not know this man. He was not the man she married.

"I know I'm never going to see you again!" Sean bellowed as his eyes filled with tears. "I just know it!"

Despite everything, Margie almost felt sorry for him.

"I never did what they accuse me of," he cried. "I want to come back to you! I need you! What did they tell you?"

"They asked questions," Margie answered. "They wanted to know where we met, who you were with when we met. They wanted to know about your behavior and if you did drugs."

"What else did they say to you?" Sean asked with anxiety.

"They said they couldn't tell me much, just that you were a suspect in a murder," Margie said, trying not to make Sean more nervous. She knew she had to put him at ease if she was to get the information they all needed. For a moment, she thought of her daughters and her resolve stiffened.

Sean was, as usual, interrogating Margie instead of her acquiring answers from him. But she wasn't going to be put off, not this time. "What *is* the truth about your past criminal record, Sean?"

"It's true I've been on parole," Sean said. "I completed that parole with success. I finished my obligation."

He paused and said, "I just don't know what to do because I didn't do it! How do I prove my innocence?"

"Why didn't you stay in California if you didn't do it?" Margie asked. "Why did you run?"

"Because I didn't have an alibi," Sean explained. "I was by myself at home. And later I was seen near the area where she was found. I've been in trouble before. I told my brother to lie. How much are they going to put me through? That is what happens when you're in trouble once! Who is going to believe me? This is my life! Right now I am scared to death! I told them everything. I had an attorney. He told them everything. They started a war against me, a total war!"

Margie wasn't taken in by his histrionics. "Why did you get in trouble before?" Margie questioned.

"I was accused of embezzlement in Ohio. I went to prison for the charge. I was out on parole when a girl in Ohio was found dead. They didn't have a case against me. They harassed me, so I went back to California."

"Why didn't you tell me all this, Sean?" Margie asked.

"You'd never have given me a chance because of my past. You're good and kind and beautiful, everything I've ever wanted. There's no way I wanted to tell you. I wanted to change and be the kind of man you deserve. Margie, I want to come back to you. I want to prove myself," Sean said.

"How are you going to prove yourself?" Margie asked, trying not to show her disgust.

Sean leaned toward Margie and said, "By proving my innocence, by somehow fighting. You are the one thing I am fighting for. I'm not fighting for myself. I'm fighting because I want you. You are the only good thing that has ever happened to me and I want to spend my life with you. I want to come back to you. I know I hurt you. I left you with bills. I didn't plan on this."

"Prove you're innocent?" Margie said flatly. "How will you do that now?"

"I can and will," Sean replied. "The difference now is that I can take you to my parents, my daughter."

"They're not dead?" Margie asked in amazement.

"No," Sean said. "I wanted to protect you."

"Protect me?" Margie bit her lip, not wanting to let him see how deeply he'd hurt her.

Sean cried out, "I know you hate me! Don't convict me! You're just bitter now. You'll be the one person that will be my jury."

She wasn't about to be put off. "Did you poison that girl, Sean?" Margie asked with boldness.

"That's what they said," he answered. "But you know me. You know I couldn't do it."

She continued to probe. "Did you know the girl?"

Sean replied, "I never took her out, if that's what they told you." Margie was silent. "I knew her boss. Everything is circumstantial. I was on Percodan for a root canal."

She looked at him. "Isn't that the same kind of pill you gave me?"

He nodded, and chills ran up her spine. Luckily, he could not see the emotions churning inside her. He was too intent on explaining himself, excusing himself.

"I ran away to save money to go back and fight," he said. "Then I met you and I didn't want to leave."

The detective knocked on the door. "I'll give you five more minutes. That's it," he said. It was obviously a signal to see how Margie was feeling.

"Thank you," she called out to show him she was all right.

Sean gazed at Margie with sad eyes and said, "I know you want out. If you leave me, I have nothing left to fight for. I have nothing! All I will have is you in my heart. I love you! I will come back. I will get you back! I know I did you wrong, but I didn't mean to. I never meant to hurt you or the girls!"

"You lied to us," Margie said quietly.

"I'm going to get out of here," Sean said, shivering, "and I'm going to come for you and the girls. You'd better believe it."

Margie took a deep breath. "I don't think that's possible."

"I live for you! Don't hate me! Don't judge me!" Sean cried. He looked at Margie one last time and said, "You are my fight. You are my strength. You are everything. I love you, and I'll never let you go!"

Luckily, at that moment the guards came in and led Sean away.

Detective Conrad walked in a few seconds later. Margie stared at him, fear filling her. "What if Sean gets out? Oh, my God," she murmured. She glanced up at Detective Conrad, and his hand gently touched her shoulder. "Did you hear all that?" she asked him.

"You did just fine," he assured Margie as he helped her up from the chair and gave her a hug.

They walked out of the room and Margie saw Ray. "He's unbelievable. He's swearing he'll get out and come back," she said as they walked toward the detective's office.

As soon as Margie sat down, Detective Frank walked in. "Margie, you've really been a great help," he said. "Let me tell you about our case now. Paul lived with his girlfriend, Stacy, at the time of this murder. We believe the girl was poisoned in their home. Paul fled to Utah after he was questioned by the Sacramento police."

Margie's eyes widened. "He told me Stacy was killed in a car accident in Ohio. He was full of lies!"

The detective handed Margie two pieces of paper. One was a copy of the phone bill from Sean's apartment. There were calls to California, Ohio, Colorado, New Zealand, and France listed on it. Margie remembered Sean's receiving brochures from a chef school in Paris. "He went to a lot of trouble to make his stories believable," she said. "But he's a monster. I have to make sure he never gets out, because whatever he says about loving and protecting the girls and me, it's all more lies. He'll figure out who led you to him. He knows, and he'll get even if he's ever freed. He killed those girls because they rejected him, and mine is the ultimate rejection."

The second paper was an application for a social security card. It stated Sean was fourteen years old.

"He tried to cover everything, didn't he," Margie said to the detective.

Detective Frank just nodded and continued, "Margie, *America's Most Wanted* is here in Salt Lake to cover the end of the story and wants to talk to you. Before you say anything, I want to explain. It is in your best interest to let them interview you and do an interview with the local news stations. The reason I say this is you need to impress upon people that you were not in on this. You were the victim. I think your story needs to be told to clear the air."

Margie was hurt that some people might think she was involved in such sordidness. "I guess they don't know me though," she reflected.

Margie realized that getting the truth out was important, especially for her daughters. Margie said, "Yes, I will do it."

The Sacramento detective made a phone call, then turned to her. "A camera crew will be at your house this afternoon," Detective Frank informed Margie.

He went on, "I don't know if you're aware that the show's host, John Walsh, has suffered a tragedy in the past. His son, Adam, was kidnapped as a small child and murdered several years ago. So he understands others' pain and is committed to seeking out criminals who prey on others.

"I've learned from this case that television can be a forceful medium," Detective Frank continued. "A lot of people who have committed violent crimes are behind bars because ordinary citizens called in and the show cooperated with the police to track down criminals."

Detective Conrad walked Ray and Margie to the elevator. They rode down to the first floor in silence.

"I'm glad that's over," Ray said to Margie on the way home.

"It won't be over till he's convicted and sent away for good," she said. "And I have to be sure that it's going to be done if my daughters and I are ever really going to be safe."

Ray left Margie at home after she reassured him that she was okay.

At home, Margie kicked her shoes off and lay down on the couch. She knew there was no chance she'd be able to sleep. Margie tried to rest, but her mind was engulfed with thoughts of Sean, her suspicions, and how she never dreamed of the nightmare her life and the girls' turned into.

Suddenly, the phone rang.

Margie recognized Detective Frank's voice. "The camera crew will be at your house within the hour," he informed Margie. "Remember, Margie, how lucky you and the girls are to be alive."

"I'll remember that and the fact that I don't want anyone else to endure this," she said.

A chill went through Margie as she thought of the many times she and the girls were in danger.

An hour later, there was an army of people around her telling her where to sit and what to do.

"The light's better over here," one man said.

"No, the light is better there," another one declared.

"Here, Margie, sit on the couch," a lady suggested.

"No, have her sit in this rocking chair," someone else said.

Lights flashed in Margie's face. Everyone seemed so rushed. Then, the room grew quiet as the questions began. One question Margie found particularly difficult was why she married Sean.

She answered, "Because I loved him."

She paused and went on, "He talked me into marriage just like he conned me into everything else. In truth, I never knew the man he really was. That man was a stranger."

Had Margie loved Sean? "I had always thought so, but maybe I loved the 'fantasy' he projected for me. Sean treated me the way I always wanted to be treated and loved. I fell into his trap of charm and romance."

The television people thanked Margie. They grabbed their equipment and were out the door as fast as they came in. They had a story to tell. Margie was left alone once more.

She sat down on the couch, thinking about Sean's last words to her, of his promise to get free and return. "I've got to be sure that never happens," she murmured. It was then she thought about his revelation that his parents and daughter were really alive. "I have to find them and talk to them," she said out loud.

# CHAPTER EIGHTEEN

## First You Cry

THAT night as she tried to sleep, images of Sean, of the past, assaulted her. No wonder she had felt fear! The charming, romantic, good-looking, and kind man she had married was a murderer!

Her mind raced. She had thought so many times her fear was just imagined. She had never felt such a feeling before in her life. Feelings came and went. Reassurances came and went. She made excuses. He made up lies.

The past flooded back. She had felt this fear mostly when they were dating. She thought of the first time she was overwhelmed with terror, on the ride up the canyon, the two of them alone on a deserted road deep in the mountains. She had thought she was losing her mind. But she wasn't losing her mind. Her instincts, angels, God, something had warned her.

Margie opened her eyes as tears ran down her face.

"What a mess!" she cried. "What a nightmare!"

She got up and splashed cold water on her face. Back in bed, she closed her eyes once more and again, the memories raced through her mind.

The work-out clothes left in her home by a charming man who broke in, destroying the security she once felt. A chill ran up her spine. And the feeling of invasion—of fear.

Taking her daughters without her permission. The ultimate fear—losing your children!

The escape in the rain after facing a monster she didn't know. Him demanding her to come into his apartment. Her running away.

The rape.

"He might have killed me then," she said to the empty room, her eyes now open and staring. "I can't think of that! It's too horrible!"

Margie went back over Sean's strange behavior while they were dating.

*Why did I let these things go and marry him?* she questioned. But she knew the answer. *He changed his behavior so dramatically that the fear vanished, and I fell in love with him. I believed him. The fear was gone.*

"Conartists!" she exclaimed aloud. "Very good at what they do!"

Suddenly she remembered something she had forgotten, an incident that now was clear in her mind.

One evening after they were married, Sean had called her into the bedroom. Her daughters were gone that night. There he was, sitting on the toilet in the bathroom with the door open. She was surprised and turned away.

With a raised voice he said, "Don't turn your back on me!"

She turned around facing him, backing up until she felt the bed behind her so she could sit down. They had some kind of argument, the details of which she couldn't remember. Yet she remembered how it ended.

"I'm going to the store!" she said, defying him.

"No, you are not!" he yelled, his piercing blue eyes turning a steel gray, those eyes stabbing her, grazing her heart.

She trembled and sat back down. She was afraid to move, afraid to think. Should she say something or would he strike out in anger? She sat frozen in silence.

Soon he was okay and back to his normal self. Her fear ended as quickly as it had begun. She dismissed those few minutes of fear until now.

She got up and decided to take a long, soothing bath to relax her.

She thought about the fear she felt whenever Sean raised his voice or his eyes hardened as he looked at her.

Images went through her mind of the night he had raped her. What had happened that night only this man, this demon, knows. Rape, murder, the long rap sheet from a man who looked so normal on the outside—like Ted Bundy.

"Good heavens!" She began to cry. "You can never trust anyone! The fear. Listen to the fear."

Now she saw there was a reason for her fear, an explanation for his strange behavior. It was the not knowing part that had almost driven her crazy. But it all made sense now. This man had never been what he appeared to be. He was a murderer, a con man!

Margie felt weary as she stepped out of the tub and reached for a towel to dry herself.

"Maybe I can sleep now," she murmured.

She crawled back under the cool sheets and closed her eyes. Trying to analyze everything helped and didn't help. The only conclusion she had was that it was not physical violence but the mental and emotional violence that had most tormented her and the girls. She knew now that she and the girls had narrowly escaped being killed.

In the morning, Margie's children went to school. The girls hugged Margie in earnest as they lingered at the front door. They didn't want to leave their mother alone. Margie assured her daughters that she was fine even though she looked exhausted.

Margie spent the day trying to decide her next move. All manner of collection agencies had begun to badger her. Everything Sean had bought for the house—appliances, furniture—had been bought on installment plans. The payments were never made.

*Where do I go to begin to reclaim my life and my children's lives?*

Margie's neighbors and friends saw Margie on the news. To her surprise, they called with words of encouragement and praise. Beautiful cards were left in Margie's mailbox and on her front porch.

Margie was overwhelmed by the response. They told her things like, "Hang in there. We love you. You are a wonderful lady. We care. You have our love and support. Your strength will see you through. You are a good mother. You have always conducted yourself with a touch of class and even through this you have not faltered."

The love and support from strangers and friends and most of all from her daughters gave Margie strength. She began to feel ready to face whatever lay ahead of her. She thought again of contacting Sean's family. She wanted to be sure his jail term was only the beginning and that his lies would never torment her again. But first she needed to find out about his life so she could sort out her own. But first things first. Margie called her lawyer. She had to start with the financial mess Sean had put her family in.

"I have a lot to deal with. I know I can do it," she told herself over and over.

After his office hours, Ray Wells came over. He suggested she declare bankruptcy because of the financial burdens left by Sean.

"I hate the idea of declaring bankruptcy, but I don't think I have any other choice," Margie said.

"I can't find twenty-five thousand dollars from when you refinanced the house with Sean," Ray stated. "Do you know where the money is? You also need to deal with the loan for eight thousand against your car," Ray continued. "Otherwise, you'll lose the car."

"No!" Margie bellowed. "I bet the money's in a bank in Switzerland, or better yet, New Zealand." The tears flowed once again as Margie realized the mess she was in. She signed the papers Ray brought for the annulment of the marriage, and then he left.

A creditor called and demanded to pick up his merchandise immediately.

"This afternoon is okay," Margie told him stoically.

"There go the refrigerator, stove, and stereo," she said to herself with a sigh.

She called her ex-husband, who offered to come over. "I'll stay until the men are finished removing the appliances."

Margie was thankful for Joel's willingness to stay. She didn't want to be alone when the men came.

Joel sat down at the kitchen table. Margie made coffee.

"I'll go today and get you and the kids a new refrigerator and stove," Joel said with a look of pity. "Do you want to keep the stereo?"

"No. I don't want the stupid thing or anything else Sean, I mean Paul, gave us," Margie said. "Thank you for the new appliances, though."

A short while later the doorbell rang.

"They don't waste any time, do they?" she said.

Joel jumped up from his chair. "You can wait in your bedroom if you want. You've been through enough today."

"No, it's my mess. I'll clean it up," she said firmly. "I'll just feel better if you're with me."


Detective Conrad called soon after Joel left.

"Paul Mack is on his way back to California," the detective informed Margie. "He signed the extradition paper."

"Would you read to me what it says?" Margie asked.

"Sure. The paper states 'a demand to surrender to the State of California on a charge of homicide.' It also says he has 'a right to demand and procure legal counsel, that his counsel may test the legality of the arrest by having the said Honorable Court fix a reasonable time to apply for a writ of Habeas Corpus. Paul Mack freely and voluntarily and without promise of reward or leniency is the identical person whom the aforesaid criminal proceedings have been instituted in the aforesaid State. With the full knowledge of aforementioned rights and privileges, Paul Mack hereby waives all of the aforesaid rights to return to said State. The consent and waiver to extradition is made without reference to guilt or innocence and in any way prejudicial to the case and is not an admission of guilt.' "

Margie was relieved to hear Sean was on his way to California. But she knew it was only the first step to getting him out of her life permanently.

A friend in California sent Margie some of the newspaper articles about Paul's case. The story was big in California. Margie read the articles over and over. She soaked in any information she found. She wanted answers, yet the answers never seemed to come.

The dramatic articles were headlined: "Killer Still on the Loose," "FBI Agents Join Search of Poisoning Suspect," "TV Show Leads to Killing Suspect," "Businessman Sought in Slaying of Hostess," "Alleged Killer Identified," "Suspect Charged in Killing," and "Murder Trial Ordered."

A few articles from Salt Lake City newspapers said, "TV Show Triggers Arrest of Salt Lake Chef Suspected in Two Murders," "Slay Suspect, 39, Is Heading for California," "Slay Suspect Taken to California," "Extradited Utahan Has 19-Year History of Fraud Charges."

Margie was not surprised that thirty-nine-year-old Sean lied about his age. "He lied about his whole life." Margie, who had become part of it, was surrounded by lies, murder, and heartache.

The last newspaper article Margie received from California took her by surprise. She hadn't realized that news which concerned her private life would spread so far. The article revealed her own lawsuit:

Mack's Eighth Wife Seeks Annulment

The eighth wife of suspected murderer Paul Mack filed for annulment of their one-month-old Salt Lake City marriage, court records show.

Mack, thirty-nine, faces charges in the murder of restaurant hostess Karen Winslett. Mack, who was going by the name of Sean Paul Lanier and had lived in Salt Lake City at the time of his arrest for the Winslett murder, married Margie Danielsen on February 14.

According to the suit, Danielsen said she is seeking the annulment because Mack never told her about his past wives, arrests, convictions, or prison terms. Danielsen, who took the last name of Lanier, is also seeking to regain her former last name.

# CHAPTER NINETEEN

## A Dead Daughter Comes Alive

ALTHOUGH Margie changed her telephone number, Sean of course found it out. He called many times. In fact, it amazed Margie how many times he was able to use the phone from jail. She wondered if he conned other inmates into giving up their time to him, or if he used the excuse that he needed to talk to his attorney about his case.

Since Margie wanted to make sure he didn't worm his way out of jail without her knowing, she took the calls.

*Sean can't hurt me over the phone*, she reasoned.

"Margie," he said over and over. "Never leave me. I don't care what any papers say. This is between us. I'm getting out. I promise you that, and I'm going to come for you and the girls."

Every time he said it, chills ran up her spine.

In actuality, Sean caused problems no matter where he was. He drove her so crazy with his constant phone calls that one night she took the phone off the hook. Later that night the doorbell rang. When Margie opened her front door, a police officer stood on her porch.

Margie's heart sank as she thought, *Now what?*

The police officer asked, "Do you know a Sean Lanier?"

"Yes," Margie answered concerned.

The officer said, "He called the police station because your phone has been off the hook all night. He was worried. Are you all right?"

In shock, Margie uttered, "Yes."

She was too embarrassed to tell the police officer the truth, that Sean Paul Lanier was in reality a murderer in jail in California and she had been foolish enough to marry him.

Margie closed the door and put the phone back on the hook. She turned down the bell so she could not hear it if it rang. Even in jail, Sean tried to run her life.

Once again, Margie had gotten in touch with Jed McCall, the private investigator, asking him to locate Sean's daughter, Nickie, and his parents, whom she thought might be living in New Zealand. Jed found them in the United States. A few days later, Jed called with both their numbers and told Margie the news that he'd looked into Sean's family background and found that his parents were not from New Zealand but were born in the United States. After all the lies, Margie wasn't the least bit surprised.

Margie called Nickie, who offered to come to Salt Lake to meet Margie to find out more about her father. Margie knew the girl needed to know and told her to come.

The moment Margie laid eyes on Nickie, she saw the resemblance to Sean. Nickie's hair was long and brown. Her eyes were the same Dresden blue as Sean's but with a look of gentleness and innocence to them.

Margie was taken by her sweetness and offered to let her stay with her and her three daughters for a while.

Nickie accepted and moved in the next day.

The strange thing was, Nickie seemed to fit right into Margie's little family and got along great with her daughters. She told Margie, "I grew up with my mother in Montana and never knew my father until I found him in California. My brother doesn't want anything to do with him, but I wanted to get to meet and love the father I never knew." She had just found her father when he fled from his crimes.

Nickie stayed with Margie's family for several weeks. She was, Margie thought, a wonderful young woman, the one part of Sean's life that was good; yet, he had caused even her pain.

One night soon after Nickie left, Margie decided to call Sean's parents and see what answers they might offer. Margie's heart pounded as the phone rang. An older-sounding gentleman answered the phone. He didn't speak with an accent and was obviously from the United States and not New Zealand. Margie introduced herself and explained the reason for her call.

Sean's father was very apologetic. "We didn't do anything wrong. We were normal parents. We don't understand why he gets into trouble."

Margie's heart went out to him as she tried to reassure him that she understood.

Then Margie spoke with Sean's mother. She was very upset as she told Margie, "Paul did not do this! I know he couldn't do it!"

Margie hung up the phone after she promised to send them a videotape of her wedding. They sounded so much like a normal family Margie almost forgot their son was in jail for murder. They expressed parental love for their troubled son. There seemed to be no explanation as to why Sean committed these heinous crimes. What makes one person become a law-abiding citizen and another a murderer? Margie didn't find the answers in the conversation with Sean's parents.

With Jed's help, she interviewed other people who had known him.

Margie also went to the library to research the mind of a murderer. She wanted answers. She learned violence gives to some the feeling of superiority and retaliation. A violent crime gives the perpetrator control. Some want to get even with a world they believe has let them down. Does a violent person start out as a child who lies and thinks perversely? Does killing another human come from anger and a desire to control? Criminals seem to start with petty crimes and then move to worse crimes. Their lives are based on lies. Margie read speculations about low self-image, compulsion, distorted thinking, stress, arrogance, abuse of animals, and setting fires. She read about characteristics of extreme dominance, aggression, manipulation, impulsiveness, revenge, insecurity, charm, and guiltlessness.

One book mentioned a strangling as a spur-of-the-moment killing. Margie thought of the girl in Ohio who some believed was strangled.

Margie wondered, Did Sean have problems with women

Margie and Sean Paul Lanier (Paul Steven Mack) on their wedding day.

Sean kisses Margie after their wedding.

Margie, Sean, and their friends head off to Nevada after the wedding.

Sean Lanier's true nature is exposed as he wrestles with Margie's daughter.

Sean Lanier, avoiding the camera, appears on a local television show displaying his culinary skills. REPRINTED BY PERMISSION, *AMERICA'S MOST WANTED*

John Walsh on *America's Most Wanted* shows the home audience photos of the fugitive, Paul Steven Mack, wanted for murder. REPRINTED BY PERMISSION, *AMERICA'S MOST WANTED*

Paul Mack's photo and description as it appeared on *America's Most Wanted*. REPRINTED BY PERMISSION, *AMERICA'S MOST WANTED*

Annette Huddle was only nineteen years old when she was found murdered. REPRINTED BY PERMISSION, *AMERICA'S MOST WANTED*

The home of Annette Huddle, located fifteen minutes away from the Marion County Country Club, where she worked as Paul Mack's secretary. REPRINTED BY PERMISSION, *AMERICA'S MOST WANTED*

The gravesite of nineteen-year-old murder victim Annette Huddle. REPRINTED BY PERMISSION, *AMERICA'S MOST WANTED*

Paul Steven Mack's mug shot taken after his arrest for parole violation by the Marion County Sheriff's Department. Although he was a suspect in the Annette Huddle murder investigation, there was never enough evidence to charge him with the crime. REPRINTED BY PERMISSION, *AMERICA'S MOST WANTED*

Model and beauty queen Karen Winslett, shortly before she was brutally murdered by Paul Mack. REPRINTED BY PERMISSION, *AMERICA'S MOST WANTED*

The home of Paul Mack in Sacramento, California, where he lured, raped and murdered Karen Winslett. REPRINTED BY PERMISSION, *AMERICA'S MOST WANTED*

Convicted murderer Paul Mack, as he appeared a few months before the disappearance of Karen Winslett. Mack liked to keep himself well-groomed, with hair-cuts and manicures on a weekly basis. REPRINTED BY PERMISSION, *AMERICA'S MOST WANTED*

Karen Winslett's Datsun 260 Z, as it was found with her body inside by the Sacramento Police behind the Colonial Motel. REPRINTED BY PERMISSION, *AMERICA'S MOST WANTED*

A handcuffed Paul Steven Mack, after his arrest in Salt Lake City, Utah for the murder of Karen Winslett, is announced "Captured" on *America's Most Wanted*. REPRINTED BY PERMISSION, *AMERICA'S MOST WANTED*

After his extradition from Utah, Paul Steven Mack is escorted to the county jail by Sacramento County Sheriff's detectives to stand trial in California for the murder of Karen Winslett. REPRINTED BY PERMISSION, *SACRAMENTO BEE*

Margie Danielsen's courageous investigation helped lead to Paul Mack's arrest.

because the women he wanted rejected him and he refused to accept it? Was Sean's life full of frustration because of financial difficulties? Did he charge items he couldn't afford because of the material status he wanted to achieve? Was he seeking to feel important? Did he kill because his life was out of control? Sean's lies seemed to come more easily with each crime he committed. His stories were believable; he was believable. He may have even begun to believe his own lies. Since Sean got away with one murder he must have thought he could get away with the next as well. Was it a rush to commit a crime and get away with it? *I don't believe he'd stop if he weren't caught.*

From what she learned, Margie began to glimpse what she searched for, a profile of Paul Mack created in her own mind. She saw a young boy who lied, stole, and cheated. He wanted to have the best of everything. Sean was willing to do anything to get what he wanted. He thought he was invincible. Nothing stopped him. One crime led to another as he grew older, until he committed the ultimate crime of murdering two young women because they did not want him. Was Margie the next victim because she'd rejected him? Yes! At first, she had believed his fantasy of love and romance. That saved her life. But later, her suspicions, the ones which ultimately brought him down, also put her life and those of her children at risk.

Did Sean have two personalities? Was he schizophrenic? He portrayed himself as a charming, kind, and wonderful man to achieve what he wanted. What he wanted was evil. No, she decided, *Sean did not have two different personalities. Sean was a wolf in sheep's clothing.*

Some of Margie's preliminary questions were answered by the many theories she had researched. But she knew the real answers lay in the mind of Paul Mack, alias Sean Paul Lanier, and there they would remain.

Her nightmares began in the middle of the night, in the darkness, and would continue through the next three years. Always, the same dreams of terror awoke Margie. She leaped out of bed and ran to turn the light on. The dreams of fear were so real that she never wanted to sleep again.

The first dream consisted of Margie fleeing in the dead of night from Sean. She hid under bushes and fences, dodging bullets fired at her from Sean's gun. The night was silent except for the sound of ricocheting bullets that flew through the air. Margie awoke in sheer terror and raced toward the light switch. She was afraid to return to sleep.

The second dream took place in the mountains. Margie walked down a dirt road in the middle of the day. She passed cabins nestled among pine trees. Shots rang out, and she began to run. She stopped at each cabin door and screamed for help. No one answered the door. Margie turned and saw Sean holding a rope which he pantomimed tightening around her neck. At last, an elderly couple opened their door. Margie ran in as she yelled for help. The older couple hid Margie in a shower with the water running and called the police. Margie later connected this part of the dream to the time she took a shower to erase her memories of Sean. The dream ended with Margie looking out the window and watching Sean run around in a rampage trying to find her.

In the third dream, Sean escaped from prison and kidnapped Margie at knife point. They drove from city to city, state to state. She was afraid to eat the food he gave her, for fear that the food was poisoned. The police caught up to them and there was a shoot-out. Margie would awaken abruptly, not knowing what happened next.

Margie continued to be haunted by the man who was now a stranger to her. She felt she'd never be rid of him. It was especially difficult for her while she was looking for a job. During interviews, she would try her best to look outwardly professional, calm and secure. Inwardly, however, she could barely hold herself together with all the stress she was under. She knew she had to do all she could to make sure he'd never be free again.

Margie's tears finally turned into anger. She made several phone calls and reached the judge on Sean's case. Exasperated, Margie told the judge her problem with Sean constantly telephoning her and the hardship it created for her.

The judge said with compassion, "I will talk to Mack on your behalf at his next hearing. I will inform him that he cannot, under any circumstances, have any contact with you whatsoever."

Margie felt relieved after she spoke with the kind-hearted judge. It bothered Margie how Sean could still torture her from behind bars.

After that, she was offered a job with an insurance company. She gratefully accepted and thought that maybe things were beginning to turn around for her. She was crushed when the company told her that she wouldn't be able to start until after New Year's because the woman she was replacing would not be leaving until late January. That would be more than two months away! Money was tight and she knew it would be nearly impossible to stretch it for that long.

Then, turmoil came at Margie from all directions. Her loveable dog, Socker, that Sean gave her for the first Christmas they shared, died from routine surgery. Margie and all three of her daughters cried for days. Seeing them so heartbroken, Margie knew it was more than the death of their beloved dog—it was symbolic of their lives being broken apart and she was consumed by worry about the effect the big and small traumas were having on her daughters. A week later, the family cat developed a tumor and had to be put to sleep. Margie began to wonder just how much more she and the girls could take.

It had been many months since Sean had been taken to California and Christmas was almost upon them. Margie sold the video camera, her ceramic kiln, and whatever else she could find to buy Christmas presents for her daughters. The veterinarian called Margie a few days before Christmas.

"Is it okay if I give you and the girls a puppy as a gift?" he asked. "I feel badly about all the misfortune you've been through."

Margie was overwhelmed at his compassionate gesture and gratefully accepted his offer. Rex joined Margie's family that Christmas. He brought happiness and fun into Margie's and her daughters' lives. Rex was just what they needed!

Sometimes it's the small things that mean the most, Margie learned. She vowed never to take those things for granted anymore.

# CHAPTER TWENTY

## *Messages from Hell*

FOR an entire year, despite the judge to whom Margie had talked, Sean managed to acquire Margie's new unlisted phone number no matter how many times she changed it.

Finally, Margie and the phone company devised a plan so Sean wouldn't get her home phone number again. The plan seemed to work. Margie and the children's lives were quiet at last. After a few weeks, Margie no longer got squeamish every time the phone rang. The fear and panic subsided. She saw a small glimpse of a normal life once again. The cloud she carried with her started to dissipate. The pleasant spell in Margie's life didn't last for long though.

One day, the phone rang in Margie's private office just as it had many times before. Margie answered as usual, "Margie Danielsen. How may I help you?"

The voice on the other end was pleasant and confident. "How do you like your new job? You work in an elegant new building with a statue and waterfall out front. You look so beautiful in that red dress."

Sean's voice echoed through Margie's ears, down to her heart, and the fear returned, taking over her body. Margie's hand froze to the phone as she tried to release the receiver. It was hard for her to breathe. She took her free hand and forced the phone down until it was secured in its place. She turned off the phone and sat in silence in the busy office.

*How does Sean know where I work, what the building looks like, and what I'm wearing?* she wondered in a panic. *Is he guessing?*

Margie managed to stand on trembling legs and stepped

towards the doorway. She looked around the office, glancing at all the desks. She examined each person to see if one of them might be a traitor. Or worse—Sean. Margie watched her colleagues with distrust. She viewed them all as if in a slow-motion movie. With care, Margie studied each face and each movement they made. She searched for something suspicious. Everyone and everything seemed to be normal.

Margie walked shakily back past her desk and stood at the window. She peered out at the statue and waterfall below. She examined every corner of the ground beneath her. She searched for Sean lurking in the shadows. There was nothing, except the sound of her own pounding heart.

*How could he know all that information?* she asked herself. Suddenly, she thought of a possible answer. *Sean has someone on the outside following me. It could be the two men who watched me and the children in the past. Maybe he asked them to follow me once again. But would they really do something like this for a man in jail? Yet Sean cons people so well without them even being aware of his actions. I bet that's what happened!*

Margie wandered back to her desk and fell into the chair. She stared at the phone. Margie forced her finger toward the button to turn the phone back on. As soon as she made contact with the button, she snapped back her hand as though she were bitten by a poisonous snake. When the phone rang, Margie jumped with fright. She answered the now demon phone with her business greeting and waited in fear for the person on the other end to speak. A woman's voice answered back and Margie breathed a sigh of relief.

Margie was terrorized with each ring of the phone as the day wore on. At last it was time to leave work. She turned off her phone and ran to her car. Again, Margie studied each person who passed her on the way.

*Sean must have convinced his shadowy friends to follow me,* she speculated. *Sean is very persuasive when he wants to be. They must be surveying me at this very moment for him!*

There were so many bizarre scenarios swimming around in

Margie's head. And Sean was very capable of carrying out every one of them.

Once Margie was inside her car, she quickly locked the door. She drove home shaking, still upset from the unwelcome intrusion in her day.

A week went by before Margie received another phone call from him. Again, Sean knew what she was wearing.

*I'm being stalked by a man in jail!* she thought. *Unbelievable!*

Margie took different routes as she drove to work and home. She left work at different times. She became apprehensive and uncertain of everything and everyone around her. She was guarded and alert at all times.

After work she hibernated at home from the world and withdrew from everyone she knew, except her children. Margie was too afraid to venture out, too afraid to face the reality of her life.

"These phone calls are making my life a wreck again!" she cried.

Margie was too embarrassed to ask for help. She hid within herself, seeking shelter from this nightmare. Aside from working and caring for the girls, the days blended into one another. Sometimes Margie didn't even know what day it was. She just wanted to forget and to be left alone.

"I wonder if Sean will ever allow me to be free again," she wondered out loud.

Margie waited for more terrorizing phone calls from Sean. She anticipated the calls every day. She still felt sick every time her phone rang at work.

"I have to answer the phone," Margie told herself. "I can't let him terrorize me on the job."

Margie prayed with each ring of the phone that it wasn't Sean. She tried to be strong. She tried to be positive. She tried to fight her fear.

And every few days, letters and poems arrived from him. She felt like the nightmare was beginning again.

One day, Margie was at the supermarket searching for a birthday card for a friend. She glanced at the cards in the next section labeled "Romance." She reached for a card and read the words of love and devotion. Margie thought of the poems and cards Sean was sending.

Margie took another card and read the words. The verse sounded very familiar to her. She wondered if Sean had given her this very same card. She picked out another card. Again, she knew the words from somewhere else. Margie read one card after another until she realized why all the cards were so familiar to her. The poems Sean sent her from jail were from these cards. Sean handwrote and signed each poem as though he wrote the words himself. He must have used the words from cards received by other inmates from their wives or girl-friends.

Margie grimaced and shook her head. *He never gives up. He just lies and lies and lies.*

Margie bought a birthday card and drove home. She went to the desk where she kept the poems Sean sent her. One by one, she ripped each one into tiny little pieces and threw them away. Then she changed her phone number at work and the one at home again.

Finally, on a Friday after the girls left for school, she decided she'd had enough. She called Detective Frank in California. "I want to testify for the prosecution," she said.

"Margie, I was just about to call and ask if you would," he said.

# CHAPTER TWENTY-ONE

# Suffer the Children

IT was not only Margie that Sean inundated with letters and calls. He deluged her daughters as well, calling when Margie was at work and sending so many letters Margie couldn't intercept them all.

And it was the girls who looked on wide-eyed as people came to the house to remove the things Sean bought on installment payments unbeknownst to Margie, things Margie could no longer afford.

Margie knew it was just the movers' job. Still, they looked like vultures circling their prey, and Margie worried night and day about the effect such experiences were having on her daughters. They already had suffered greatly during their parents' divorce despite the care Margie and Joel had taken to shield them, and now they had to endure this.

One night, Jessi, now eight years old, awoke screaming. Margie rushed into her room.

"What's the matter, dearest?" Margie asked.

"Mommy, I had this terrible dream."

"Tell me about it," Margie said, sitting on the edge of Jessi's bed and stroking her daughter's long hair soothingly.

"Daddy and I were driving in his car. We pulled up at this gas station, and Sean was there threatening us. Daddy told the man giving us the gas, 'That's my ex-wife's husband, and he's dangerous.' Then Sean ran over and said to me, 'Come with me,' and when I wouldn't, he tried to grab me. Then Daddy pushed this square cart right into Sean's stomach, causing a terrible hole. I screamed, and Sean ran to his truck holding his stomach. And those two men who wouldn't let us come home from the amusement park opened the door and waved at me, calling me to come with them."

"Oh, Jessi," Margie said, "what a terrible dream. It must have frightened you a lot."

Jessi nodded her head. "And the thing is, Mommy, I felt sorry for Sean with that awful hole."

"Jessi," Margie said quietly, "the first thing to remember is that dreams aren't real. You are safe here. Sean is in jail, and don't be sorry for him. He is there because he's done some bad things. Jessi, Daddy and I would never let him or anyone else grab you."

Into Margie's mind flashed the scene of the night the children hadn't come home and the two men who had finally brought her daughters back. She bit her lip and fought back tears.

"Those two men will never scare you again," Margie promised. "If you ever see them, you just tell Daddy or me."

"I will," Jessi said.

"Would you like me to stay here till you fall asleep?"

"Please, Mommy, will you?" Jessi asked.

Margie nodded, got into the bed, and reached out to hold her trembling child. "Now go to sleep, darling," she said. "Mommy's watching over you, and, Jessi, whenever you have a bad dream or feel frightened, let's talk about it."

Jessi eventually fell asleep that night, but in the days that followed, she sometimes became scared, thinking Sean would come after them or show up at her elementary school to take her away.

Margie tried to calmly reassure Jessi whenever these fears returned, but she often felt anger churning inside her at the trauma Sean was putting them all through.

June, her middle daughter, reacted very differently than her younger sister, becoming more withdrawn and silent. "It was a catastrophe with a significance I didn't understand until the horror of it sunk in," June wrote to a friend whose mother called Margie. Although Margie tried to handle June sensitively, she could see that a kind of distrust now pervaded June's relationships. She didn't allow many people to get too

close. And Margie mourned the loss of her daughter's innocence.

"It's too soon for June to find out people can be rotten,"
Margie told Nila. "He took away her last few years of childhood."

Julie, Margie's oldest daughter, was the most bitter. It was
Julie's initial distrust of Sean, occasioned by her feelings that
he was a further threat to her already broken-up family, which
had in the beginning caused Margie the most concern. For
Margie had wanted desperately to give the girls a family life
to replace the one she and Joel had taken away.

One day, Julie was taking her usual long bath when Margie
heard a scream from the bathroom that brought her running.
Though at this stage Julie was shy about being naked in front
of her mother, Margie was not concerned with that now. Her
daughter could be in trouble. Using the tip of a letter opener
she got from the bedroom, Margie pried open the locked bathroom door.

"Julie, what's wrong?" her mother yelled.

"Mom," her eldest daughter said, tears streaming down her
cheeks. "I was just lying here thinking and suddenly I felt
terrified that someone could be out there. I couldn't move and
that's when I screamed."

"Oh, Julie," her heartbroken mother said, "you keep too
much inside. We're safe now. You don't have to be afraid."

In the letters Julie got from Sean from prison, he never
spoke of what had happened but only promised to return by
Christmas. For Margie, the implicit threat was alarming, but
she said nothing to Julie, not wanting her daughter to feel even
more frightened. Julie said she wanted to keep the letters, and
Margie, respecting her oldest daughter's wishes, allowed her
to do that. In the next weeks, she watched Julie release her
anger by crumpling them up and throwing them away and
thought that a healthy reaction. Like her, Julie had begun to
heal, but, as in Margie's case, it was a forward and back movement.

A few weeks later, on a day when Margie was feeling especially low, Julie went out and bought her mother a red rose.

As she handed it to her, she and Margie began to cry. "It's all right, Julie," Margie said. "It's all right to cry over this tragedy and what it's done to our lives." Margie embraced her oldest girl, who at this point in her life usually shied away from hugs but now submitted. "I love you, Julie, and I will always be here for you."

"Sometimes I'm so scared for you, Mom," Julie said brokenly. "And for me and my sisters, because I don't know where we're heading."

"Julie," her mother said, smiling through her tears. "I don't know exactly where we're heading either, but I can tell you one thing. The worst is behind us," she said firmly.

Julie nodded. "You sound like you mean that."

"I do. I surely do."

After that, though more objects like Sean's Toyota truck were repossessed and though more letters with their explicit expressions of love and their implicit threats arrived, things slowly returned to a more even keel in Margie's and the girls' inner and outer lives. Through it all, they learned to pull together, and day by day, Margie and the girls grew stronger.

Margie spent all of her spare time after work with her daughters, but they kept encouraging her to get together with her friends and finally she agreed. "Sean caught us all in the web he spun," Margie said to Nila one night when the girls had gone to stay with their father.

Her friend nodded. "I remember when I mentioned to Sean how silly I felt for giving you that newspaper article that made you check out his knuckles for a tattoo. I didn't like the look he gave me. I remember how I hurried to change the subject."

"It all falls into place now, doesn't it?" Margie said.

When Margie discussed her and the girls' feelings about Sean with her friends, they all agreed they had also been confused, because Sean was good to them too, and so they were doubly angry about his deception now.

"I've discovered anger can be cleansing as well as damaging," Margie declared. "My anger has brought me to the conclusion that it's time Sean's control over all our lives, especially my girls' lives, is stopped once and for all."

## CHAPTER TWENTY-TWO

# Witness for the Prosecution

THE day came when Detective Frank called and told Margie the trial was about to begin. A man in a dark suit waited in the conference room at Margie's office. Margie surveyed this older man with balding gray hair and glasses. He appeared serious and matter-of-fact as he held a chair out for her to sit down. "I'm Duncan Kelly," he said.

He handed Margie a summons and airline tickets. In his clear, quiet voice he said, "You will appear in court to testify in the case of the State of California versus Paul Mack. You will fly in the day before."

Margie stopped him. "I'm going out for the opening," she said. "I want to be there."

"You're going to be a witness so you won't be allowed to attend the trial," he said flatly.

"I want to be there anyway," she said firmly.

"Fine. Here is a check to cover expenses for food and a cab from the airport to the hotel and back again when you are finished there. The hotel is located within walking distance of the courthouse. You will be contacted by the prosecutor once you arrive at the hotel."

Kelly shook Margie's hand and walked out the door. Never had Margie felt so alone. She tried to remember everything that the man just relayed to her. Because he'd done this so many times before, he seemed cold and unmoved.

Lee, Margie's boss, came into the conference room with a look of concern on her face. Margie explained the entire horrible story to Lee. "I want to go out there for the opening,"

Margie told her. Lee gave Margie a long hug and patted her back as Margie started to cry.

"I've been waiting for this," Margie said, "but now that it's here, although I know the trial will bring closure, I feel terrified. Yet it's something I want and have to do," Margie said.

The two women spent some time together. They talked, laughed, and cried. Margie found a friend in the office that day.

That night, Margie explained to the children that while she was gone she would be testifying at Sean's trial.

"Mommy, I'm afraid," Jessi said. "Maybe he'll try to grab you and hurt you."

"No, he won't, Jessi. I promise you he won't."

A few days later, Margie received a phone call from Gerry Sue, Sean's old roommate. She was in Texas working as a teacher there.

"I've been summoned to testify at Sean's trial," she informed Margie. "I'm not looking forward to testifying."

"Though it's the hardest thing I've ever had to do, I want to and I'm going out for the beginning," Margie answered. "I want to be sure Sean never has the opportunity to hurt another person."

"Did you know that Sean never owned the White Horse Restaurant?" Gerry Sue asked Margie.

"Yes, I found that out too," Margie replied.

"Well, he talked me into investing in the restaurant and I lost thousands and thousands of dollars," Gerry Sue stated.

"I'm so sorry! I guess he took us all," Margie said.

Gerry Sue said, "Yes, but I guess money can't replace lives."

"That's true, and it's the thing all we survivors have to keep uppermost in our minds. I lost a lot of money too," Margie informed Gerry Sue. "But the girls and I are pulling through all this."

Gerry Sue said, "You know, I was in love with him. I love him still."

Surprised, Margie sputtered, "Oh, I didn't know that, but, Gerry Sue, you and I are very lucky. What happened to those two girls could have happened to us. The person you and I thought we loved never existed." Margie paused and then added, "Take care of yourself." She said goodbye.

For a moment after they hung up, Margie wondered if Gerry Sue got her operation to be a woman and wished she had asked. "I'm not sure I want to know anything more," she decided. "I'm glad I didn't ask."

The next day, Margie received a phone call from Hal, the man Sean had said was co-owner of the restaurant he'd bought into. She had learned from Jed McCall that Hal was the restaurant's manager and Sean's boss, not a co-owner as Sean had led her to believe. Hal asked Margie how she and the girls were doing.

"Fine. We're taking it one day at a time," she said. "I have to go to California next week for the trial's beginning and then I'm going to testify."

"I've been summoned at the end of the month," Hal stated. Then he asked, "How's Sean's little boy? What happened to him?"

"What little boy?" Margie asked.

"Sean told me that he was raising a small son. He doesn't live with you?" he asked.

"No! And Sean does not have a small son! You and your wife have been here for dinner. You never saw a little boy here, did you?" Margie asked.

"Sean lied? I just assumed the little boy was asleep or something. What would have happened if I inquired about Sean's son at dinner and you didn't know anything about him?" Hal asked.

"Sean was good at making up stories, and we would have believed him," Margie said.

"Wow! He was creative about his lies, wasn't he?" Hal said.

"Too good if you ask me!" Margie replied. "But his day of reckoning is coming."

For some reason Margie remembered the yard sale where Sean sold the things out of the restaurant's storage shed.

"Hal, do you remember when Sean sold the things out of

the restaurant's storage shed for you?" Margie asked inquisitively.

"What?" Hal asked, surprised by the question.

Margie explained the yard sale. "Sean said you asked him to sell the restaurant supplies. He told me that he received a percentage from the profits."

"Hell, no!" Hal exclaimed. "I wondered what happened to everything in that shed! I just assumed the shed was broken into. I guess Sean received a hundred percent on that deal!"

"He told me he didn't take any of the proceeds," Margie said, "because you and your wife needed the money for medical expenses."

Hal laughed bitterly. "We sure were snookered," he said.

Hal wished Margie luck at the trial, and they said goodbye.

*Sean lucked out on all those lies,* Margie thought. *What if Hal had said something about a small son at dinner, or the restaurant's storage shed being robbed? What stories would Sean have come up with?*

The day before her departure for California, Margie packed her suitcase. Although she was strong in her resolution to testify, she wished she did not have to go alone. Facing Sean again would not be easy despite her resolve, she realized.

"This is really hard," she said aloud. "And if I have to do it alone, that's the hardest part."

Then Margie remembered that Nickie, Sean's daughter, lived in California. Nickie, who was in denial about the revelations about her father, was happy to hear from Margie.

"I'll pick you up at the airport so you don't have to take a cab to the hotel," Nickie offered. "I'll take a few days off from work and stay with you through this."

"I really appreciate your support," Margie said. "I'll be happy to have you by my side. I won't be alone after all! You are so thoughtful!"

"I want my father to be vindicated," Nickie stated. "I believe in him so much. I'll stand by you to help the both of you."

Margie was shocked. Nickie didn't really know her dad and

as a child had only fantasized about a father. She had only begun to have a relationship with him when he had run away from California. However, Margie had thought in the interim that Nickie had become acclimated to Sean's real character. Now she knew this was not the case.

"Nickie, I think we should talk about all this face to face," Margie said. "I know it must be very hard for you as it is for me, but we both need to face reality. Maybe we can help each other."

After they hung up, Margie closed the suitcase and threw it on the floor with resentment. Her feelings turned to anger once again. She was angry at what Sean had done to those who cared about him, angry at what lay ahead of her, angry at herself for getting involved with him in the first place.

"First I cry and then I'm mad," she said bitterly. "What an emotional roller-coaster ride."

Margie heard the front door open and the voices of her three daughters.

*Have I been there for them these past two years?* she pondered. *Or was I too caught up in this whole mess? It's time to love and hold my darling girls again!*

Margie ran toward the girls' voices and hugged each one of her beautiful daughters. She cried and told them she loved them. They weren't surprised by their mother's outburst. They knew how much all the turmoil had cost, especially for their mother.

After dinner, Margie helped her girls pack to go to their father's house. "If I've ever not been there for you these last two years, I'm sorry."

"You've always been there, Mom," Julie said. The others echoed their sister.

Margie felt better to hear her daughters tell her that she was still a good mother.

Nevertheless, she did not sleep that night. A letter had arrived from Sean filled with an overtly loving message but disclosing he knew who had alerted the police. Her stomach churned with anxiety as she thought of the trial. *I must be sure he never hurts us or anyone else ever again*, she told herself over and over, but there was a hard knot in her stomach.

Margie hugged and kissed her daughters goodbye in the morning and they wished her luck. Margie's friend Nila arrived to drive her to the airport. Nila kept her busy with nervous small talk the entire way, so Margie didn't think about where she was headed and what she'd be doing.

It was time to get on the plane. Margie gave Nila a hug goodbye. "I wish you were going with me," Margie said nervously.

"You'll be fine. You are strong," Nila reassured her.

"Am I?" Margie questioned.

"Yes! You are!" Nila replied with an earnest smile.

"Okay, if I have to be," Margie said as she smiled.

Nila just winked. Margie took a deep breath, turned around and marched onto the plane. She sat in her assigned seat and gazed out the window.

*I feel like I'm engaged in a dangerous mission and I'll never return to my home and children*, she thought as she looked at the majestic Utah mountains and tried to draw strength.

The plane bolted into the sky, and in that moment she felt she was the only person in the world. It was the first time she had ever been on an airplane and only the second time she had left her home state. She was alone and terrified but never had she been so determined. This was a journey she had to take.

When Margie got off the plane and walked through the gate, Nickie and Margie's eyes met. Margie ran to Nickie and hugged her.

"I'm glad you and I will be together," Margie told Nickie. "There's a lot we have to talk about."

Nickie drove down the freeway as Margie took in the sights. Nickie and Margie arrived at the hotel and checked in. They both carried their suitcases into the room and unpacked. Margie could tell from Nickie's comments that she badly wanted to believe in her father. Margie decided Nickie needed time. She would watch for an opportunity to begin to unveil the truth. First, Nickie needed to trust Margie. They watched television and talked of movie stars and clothes like a couple of school girls. The difference was that Nickie was the daughter of an accused killer and Margie, the ex-wife.

Nickie went into the other room to take a shower. Margie was left alone with her thoughts. The phone rang. A controlled, stern voice replied to Margie's hello. "This is Gene Statlin. I'm the prosecutor on the Paul Mack case. Is this Margie Danielsen?"

"Yes," Margie said. She noticed her voice trembled and sought to calm it.

"Can you come to my office in an hour so we can meet and discuss tomorrow's court day?" Statlin asked.

"Yes, I can," Margie replied soberly.

"My office is right next to the courthouse, just up the street from your hotel," he stated.

"I'll be there. I've been waiting for this day. I'm ready, no matter how difficult this is for me."

Nickie came out of the other room, her wet hair wrapped in a towel.

"I have to go to the prosecutor's office in an hour," Margie said. She looked searchingly at Nickie. She knew Nickie had to be apprised of the truth before the trial began. Otherwise, the shock would be devastating. She had hoped to do it more slowly, but now she knew she could wait no longer.

"I'll take you there," Nickie offered.

"Thank you. I think that would be a good idea," Margie said sadly.

An hour later, Nickie and Margie walked into the prosecutor's office. Margie was there to do battle for herself and her daughters, Nickie to fight for the father she loved but never really knew.

They met Gene Statlin, the prosecutor, who chain-smoked amidst a mess of clutter and notes that surrounded his desk. His thin, sensitive face seemed nervous and tense as he stood up to greet them. Fine lines of wrinkles on his brow showed the pressure he was under because of this well-publicized murder trial. His hair was dark with streaks of gray running through.

Margie introduced Nickie, and Statlin asked to meet with Margie alone first. His brown eyes were tired as he looked quizzically at the two women before him. He seemed uncertain of Margie's feelings toward the man he was about to prosecute for murder, and this uncertainty was obviously increased because she showed up with the accused murderer's daughter. After Nickie stepped outside, he looked at Margie, obviously puzzled.

"I'm on your side," Margie said. "I don't think you know that, but you may be sure I'm here to tell the truth."

"That's good." Statlin gave a weary smile. "We've been left with mostly circumstantial evidence, and it's going to be a hard case to try, since the court has elected not to admit the DNA which links Mack to the dead girl." He handed Margie the newspaper and pointed to an article with the headline, "Judge Throws Out DNA Evidence". Margie gripped the paper in her hand and began to read.

A jury will not be permitted to hear DNA evidence potentially linking Paul Steven Mack to the 1987 rape and murder of a restaurant hostess, Sacramento Superior Court Judge Floyd Robertson ruled Wednesday.

"This technology's time will come, but it's not here yet," Robertson said after hearing three weeks of testimony from some of the world's leading experts in the field of DNA typing.

Robertson found that the technique used to test a sperm sample taken from the undergarments of Sacramento homicide victim Karen Winslett is not yet "generally accepted in the relevant scientific community."

That is the legal threshold that must be crossed before scientific evidence based on new technology can be introduced in a criminal case.

Prosecutor Gene Statlin wouldn't comment on the impact of the ruling, but in his written motion to the court, he said: "It is clear that the people's case depends in large part upon the admission of the DNA evidence."

Mack's attorney, James Clifton, said he was pleased

that the court agreed with his assessment that the technology employed in the Mack case is still in its early stages of development and should be viewed with skepticism.

The typing of DNA, which carries genetic information unique to each individual, is not new, Robertson noted in his ruling. It began in the middle to late 1970s and has gained considerable acceptance in the medical and biological fields where it has been put to use.

But the technique known as DNA amplification, or PCR (polymerase chain reaction), was not discovered until 1985, and while it has produced "impressive and undisputed" results in "a number of important areas, its transfer to forensic labs and the courts has just begun," Robertson said.

Robertson said further testing is needed, as well as established standards and controls, before PCR technology can be reliably used in a courtroom where a man's life is at stake.

Mack, if convicted, could be sentenced to death for the murder of Winslett.

Robertson said that in making his ruling he based some significance on the disclaimer found in a warranty notice that accompanies the PCR test kit. It reads: "The performance characteristics of these procedures have not been fully established."

PCR is just one of the three tests used to type DNA, an unusually complex procedure drawn from molecular biology that identifies distinctive patterns in genetic material.

While the other two types rely on a set of procedures known as RFLP (restriction fragment length polymorphism) analysis, commonly referred to as DNA "fingerprinting," PCR requires much less biological material to be successful.

In the Mack case, "conventional electrophoretic analysis" of the semen evidence was "impaired due to the degraded quality and small amount of the specimen materials," Statlin wrote in his motion for admissibility of the DNA evidence.

Because of that deficit, Statlin said, the specimens were forwarded to Dr. Jeffrey Anders Randolph, a forensic serologist, who applied PCR technology and found Mack's gene type in the sample.

"The frequency of that gene type, according to genetic population data, is slightly less than 2% in the Caucasian population," Statlin wrote.

Jury selection for the trial will begin Friday morning.

Margie felt anger well up inside of her. "I can't believe this, just when I thought Sean couldn't get away," Margie said. "I want Sean to be locked away forever so he can't harm anyone else."

"Well, it's going to be a fight, but you may be sure we'll do our best. We know he did it."

"Look, I'm here to tell what I know about Paul Mack, alias Sean Paul Lanier," she said. "I think we can both appreciate how hard it is for his daughter though. She never had a father, then she finally met him, and now this. She needs to find out the truth, but slowly."

Statlin nodded. "You're really nice to be helping her," he said and went outside to ask Nickie to come back in.

With reluctance, Margie left the prosecutor's office. She wanted to know so much more. No one had the time to answer her million and one questions. They needed to prepare for the next day. But she was impressed by their earnestness. Margie felt their determination to see justice done. She left the attorneys to their work. She would do her part.

When she talked to Nickie about the circumstantial nature of the evidence, the girl fastened on this. "See, Margie, they don't have anything on my dad," Nickie said with delight.

"Nickie, I believe they have the truth," Margie replied soberly.

Nickie continued to discuss her father's innocence as Margie wondered how to prepare Sean's daughter for what she was about to learn.

She decided to go with her instincts.

"Nickie, have you seen your father's arrest record? Have you thought about his lies?" Margie said softly. Nickie didn't answer. In the back of Margie's mind, fear was growing again. *What if Sean's lies convinced a jury as they had so many others? What if he's found innocent? He knows who led the police to him. He'll never leave the girls and I alone.*

Nickie and Margie arrived back at the hotel room and turned on the television set once again. They watched as a newscaster announced that the trial of Paul Mack was to begin the next day. All that was left to do now was wait. Margie called her daughters to let them know she was okay.

"It's going to be a long night," Margie said. Nickie nodded.

The clock ticked monotonously. Everything was in slow motion as the two women waited. They waited into the night, sometimes in silence, sometimes with a bit of conversation. The night lingered on as Nickie and Margie slept on and off, waiting for the next day and what was to come.

# CHAPTER TWENTY-THREE

## Day of Reckoning

MORNING arrived at last. Unlike the restless night before when the two women languished, Nickie and Margie rushed about, getting ready to leave.

They made it to court with time to spare. Standing before them, the courthouse, a tall, gray cement building, looked foreboding. They climbed numerous steps before reaching the front door.

As they made their way through the maze of corridors, Margie's heart palpitated with rapid force. She took deep breaths to try and remain calm. Then, they were there. They stood in front of the door that led Margie to her next and hopefully last step of involvement in the life of Paul Mack, alias Sean Paul Lanier.

Once again they waited, sitting outside the door on a bench. Attorneys soon surrounded them with their briefcases, pens, and papers. Margie wore the blue silk dress she had worn for her first date with Sean Paul Lanier. She felt like she was wearing a red dress in a black and white picture, sticking out like a sore thumb because of all the looks they received.

Finally, Margie said, "Maybe I'd better tell someone we're here." She walked up to the officer at the courtroom door and told him who they were. "You'll have to wait outside until you're called to testify," he informed her. Margie didn't argue with the man, although she wanted to see what was going on behind that door.

Nickie looked at Margie with questioning eyes and Margie said, "It's okay. You need to go in. I'll see you soon." Nickie gave Margie a hug and opened the huge mahogany doors.

Several people followed Nickie in, so the door remained open long enough for Margie to hear the bailiff announce, "The matter of the People of the State of California versus Paul Steven Mack, Number 86116, came on before the Honorable Floyd Robertson, Judge of the Superior Court, at nine-thirty o'clock, A.M.

"The People are represented by Gene Statlin, Supervising Deputy District Attorney for the County of Sacramento, State of California.

"The Defendant, Paul Steven Mack, is personally present and represented by James Clifton as his counsel."

As the doors slowly closed, Margie sat back down on the bench in the hallway. All was quiet. The only sound was her pounding heart.

After his preliminary statements and the excusing of one juror who had a heart problem, Judge Robertson announced, "The information is entitled 'The People of the State of California versus Paul Steven Mack.' M-a-c-k.

"Count one. Paul Steven Mack is accused by the District Attorney of Sacramento County of the crime of violation of Section 187 of the Penal Code, a felony, that on or about February nineteen, nineteen eighty-seven, in Sacramento County, the defendant did willfully, unlawfully and feloniously, and with malicious aforethought, murder Karen Winslett, W-i-n-s-l-e-t-t, a human being.

"There are three special circumstance allegations in Count One:

"One, it is alleged that the murder of Karen Winslett was committed by the defendant and that the defendant intentionally killed the victim while lying in wait.

"Two, it is alleged that the murder of Karen Winslett was committed by the defendant and that the defendant intentionally killed the victim by the administration of poison.

"Three, it is alleged that the murder of Karen Winslett was committed by the defendant while the defendant was engaged in the commission of the crime of rape.

"Count Two: The defendant is accused of the crime of violation of Section 261 of the Penal Code, a felony. That on or about February nineteen, nineteen eighty-seven, in Sacramento County, the defendant did willfully and unlawfully have and accomplish an act of sexual intercourse with a person, Karen Winslett, who was not his spouse, where she was prevented from resisting by an intoxicating narcotic and anesthetic substance and controlled substance administered by the defendant."

The judge looked in the direction of the defendant, who sat staring straight ahead.

"I remind you that Mr. Mack has pleaded not guilty to each of the crimes charged against him. Therefore, in law, he is presumed to be innocent. He may not be found guilty on either count—he may not be found guilty of either crime unless his guilt is proven beyond a reasonable doubt.

"Mr. Mack has denied the three special circumstance allegations in Count One, and, therefore, in law, each one of them is presumed to be not true. And none of them may be found to be true unless it is proven true beyond a reasonable doubt.

"Mr. Statlin, do you wish to make an opening statement?"

Statlin nodded. "Yes, I do, Your Honor. Thank you."

Robertson waved his hand. "You may."

A spectator leaving the courtroom slowly pulled open the mahogany door and Margie saw Gene Statlin, dressed in a navy blue suit, walk slowly to the front. His face was sober, as if the burden of this prosecution, now made even more difficult not only by the passage of time but the inadmissibility of the DNA evidence, weighed heavily upon him. Margie forced herself from her own thoughts to those in the courtroom before her. She wanted to be a mirror which reflected their feelings and perceptions so that later she could evaluate what she saw, heard, and read about the man she had loved so much, the man who had proven to be so very different from all her illusions.

"Good morning," Statlin began. "This is a time when both sides, if they want to, have an opportunity to talk to you a little bit about the evidence in the case. Lawyers call it an opening statement, but literally, it is kind of like a table of contents to a book that one or both of us are requesting to do here.

"You know how you have a real large book you are going to read and you look at it at the outset and you know it is pretty big, and to kind of have a road map to work your way through it you can look at the table of contents to give you an idea of what the chapters are about, to give you signposts of what you will see in the book. That's all I will do here this morning is give you some of those signposts. Probably the easiest part of the table of contents, or to give you the structure of that table of contents, is to start with the charges.

"Now, the Court just read you the charges. That is the charging document, the information. And in this case, it is very, very, simple. Two counts. Count One, murder of Karen Winslett some three-and-a-half years ago. Three special circumstances alleged in connection with that murder: Murder by lying in wait, murder by poison, murder in the commission of a rape.

"And the second charge, the other substantive charge is that of rape. That is how simple this table of contents is. Now, that's the framework within which we work, because all the evidence has to prove the charges before you can find this person guilty.

"Let's talk about some of the evidence now. Let's explore for a little bit the evidence that is going to prove this case beyond a reasonable doubt.

"Those charges start back about three-and-a-half years ago, shortly before February nineteen, nineteen eighty-seven. And you see, before February nineteen, nineteen eighty-seven, Karen Winslett was about twenty-one years old. She was young. She was very, very, beautiful. She was living with her boyfriend at the time, Greg Harvey.

"He's a former high school, college football player with an advertising position and works on assignment.

"And Karen Winslett worked at Chadwick's on Arden Way. She worked the P.M.'s there. The P.M. shift starts about four o'clock in the afternoon.

"And from all the evidence you will understand that Karen

Winslett, before the February in question, was a relatively happy, very healthy, outgoing young lady who wanted to be a model and was working at Chadwick's as a hostess."

People wound in and out of the courtroom. Each time the door opened Margie caught glimpses of what was going on inside and heard bits of Statlin's opening statement. *I want to go in there*, Margie thought. *I want to hear what's going on. I want to know everything. After all the children and I have been through, I should have that right.* But since it had been denied her, she vowed to use every perception and image available to her to learn all she could.

Statlin continued with his opening statement.

"When I say 'wanted to be a model,' she had aspirations because of her physical beauty of posing as a model, either for photography purposes or ads and things of that nature. That was what she wanted to do in the future, and that is what ultimately led to her death.

"Probably the next most logical place to turn to is the day Karen Winslett died, the day she disappeared.

"On a typical Thursday in her life and Mr. Harvey's life, little did they know what would really happen.

"That morning, Greg Harvey, her live-in boyfriend, got up to go to work. His routine when he has an assignment: gets up, takes a shower, and begins to dress. And Karen is still in bed at this point in time. Ostensibly, her plans for the day, meet a friend over the lunch hour, go to work that afternoon about four. Because, as I said, she worked the P.M. shift.

"Greg went to work, but he forgot something.

"When he came home that morning, he arrived home back where they were living together. It was about ten or ten-thirty in the morning.

"Karen Winslett was no longer there. Her car was gone, a pretty distinctive car, a blue-colored 260 Z. She wasn't there. When Greg left earlier would be the last time he ever saw her alive.

"Well, that is how Karen Winslett came to be missing, because, you see, she never, ever came back to the house that

Thursday. She never, ever went to work. She didn't keep that luncheon appointment with her friend.

"Karen remained missing for about three-and-a-half weeks, roughly, from that Thursday, February nineteen, until March third.

"On that date, there was a meter reader, a guy that works at one of the utility companies, a guy by the name of Bob McLean, and part of the route he rides includes the Colonial Motel off Hillsdale.

"He knew of Karen Winslett. In fact, he had seen her in some beauty contest before. He was a customer at Chadwick's. He was an acquaintance of hers and he had known what kind of car she drove. When he happened to be riding his route on March third and he came upon Karen's car, the car was parked in the back parking lot of the Colonial Motel, literally backed into the space. And he really couldn't see what was inside of it because the—you know, the floorboard carpet in the hatch-back that was kind of pulled up over some object in the back of the car.

"As soon as he saw the car, he recognized it; he knew that she had been missing, it had been in the media—he called the cops.

"Officers came out, and, unfortunately, everybody's worst fears came to be true. In the back of the car was Karen Winslett. She was dead. She had been dead. She was badly decomposed.

"Well, that is how we know what happened to her, to a certain extent. But that's not the end of this."

Statlin described how Karen Winslett's body was discovered to be stashed under a rug in the backseat of the car, and that Karen was fully clothed except that her blouse was pulled up exposing her breasts. There was no external signs of trauma except a slight discoloration of the neck. It was this bruise and how and when it was inflicted that would later become an important piece of evidence. For now, Statlin just mentioned it, pausing on the reference for a moment and then going on. He spoke next of the autopsy.

"Aside from having very little, if any, external trauma that the pathologist or autopsy people noted about her, they went further, obviously. They examined her as any good autopsy staff and trained medical doctors would and what they literally found was that she had been a very, very healthy, young woman. In terms of her internal examination there was simply no reason, no reason that she would have died by any natural process, disease process, or anything of that nature. And, obviously, when you have a case like this, they take tissue specimens and blood specimens at autopsy, and, of course, they did an analysis of those. And this fact becomes important.

"What they found upon analysis was that she was full of Percodan. That is a trade name for a drug that is a narcotic-type agent known as Oxycodone. And the interesting thing about this, the tragedy—Karen was kind of a health nut. Really, other than as principles—she drank a bit of wine on occasion, but she was very conscious of not taking pills. The pills that the evidence will establish she took were in the nature of birth control pills, vitamins, pain pills. Those were the type of pills the evidence will show Karen took.

"When I talk about Percodan in her system, she had large undigested amounts of Percodan in her stomach. She has it in the bloodstream. It is in her organs. And Percodan, as I indicated to you, is a narcotic drug, one that will make you sleepy, generally. In a normal person that doesn't have a big tolerance, you get about four, five, you are talking unconscious. Literally in her stomach, undigested in free-base form, she had about four pills. That is not counting what got into her system, what was in her bloodstream, what she had vomited up. Because there was some evidence that she had regurgitated at some point in the time prior to the death.

"So she is full of Percodan." Statlin said the last words slowly, his eyes not on the jury but on Paul Mack, whose return gaze was cocky, sure of himself.

Statlin turned back to the jury. The courtroom was still.

"But that's not all the evidence.

"The car itself was processed. Inside the car was the typical stuff that we collect in our cars, accumulated notes, pieces of paper, gum wrappers, an old for-sale sign when she had had plans to sell the car. Nothing really significant in the car other than a bag, a large red purse—and you will get to see the purse, which contained another string-like bag with her pink bikini in which she modeled occasionally was kind of stashed on top of her as she lay all covered up by a jacket and the car rug.

"Then they found a lot of fingerprint impressions, although the car—as you would expect, the car was all dirt sitting out there, and God only knows how many people in history had touched it. A few of them came back to Karen. All of them couldn't be identified as belonging to particular people, none of which come back to this defendant, Paul Mack. There were just a lot of fingerprints all over this car."

He was painting a meticulous picture of the crime scene, taking the jurors step-by-step through the discoveries the police, coroner, and other experts had made about the murdered girl. "Besides processing the car, the police, the coroner, and others also examined Karen's clothes and Karen in more detail than what I just spoke to you about here.

"Karen, as I told you, had a blouse on. She had socks on. Her feet were inside the boots. She had had a pants outfit on, kind of like overalls that have the straps that come over the top of the blouse, and she had on underwear and a bra. The coat that looks like it would go along with that outfit, and given this was February, was also over the top of her as she was covered up by that carpet, when she was found on March third.

"The panties that she was wearing, the crotch of the panties showed stains. The stains were looked at by a criminalist, by the people who help in the autopsies. There was a large amount of semen present.

"Now you see, Karen's boyfriend, Greg Harvey, when he talked to the police, had told the police that she had had intercourse the night before, but that normally before she ever went anywhere she always took a shower and she usually cleaned herself after they had intercourse. But in these panties, when she was found on March third, the crotch was just full of semen and sperm.

"Unfortunately, because of the decomposition of Karen, how badly decomposed she was, how long she had been in the car, conventional serological testing couldn't be done on the semen and sperm that was found in the panties, or inferentially secreted or purged from her on to the panties. It was too decomposed. In fact Karen's blood was so decomposed she couldn't even be typed under the ABO system. That is how bad it was.

"Nevertheless, you have the presence of that type of sex evidence.

"The only other thing of significance that the crime scene investigation established, and this was a little unusual, was that she had some carpet-like fibers stuck to her clothing. And when I say carpet-like fibers, what I really mean to say is fibers that were upon the outside of her socks, which were inside the boots, on her clothing, including the panties that were underneath her regular pants. There were these fibers. And, as I said, that was somewhat of an unusual finding. And this was done by a criminalist. They take great pains to see if there is any trace debris or trace evidence inherent to victims. Commonly done.

"That is how Karen Winslett came to disappear, what caused her death, and how she was found. That's not all the evidence. Clearly it can't be."

Statlin was ready now to take the jurors minute-by-minute through how and why Paul Mack was implicated in Karen Winslett's murder.

"So let's talk about the evidence that proves who did this to her, who murdered her. Let's talk about this defendant, Paul Mack." He paused to let his words sink in.

"Where do we start? Perhaps the easiest place to start is the day she disappeared, that fateful day, February nineteen, that morning which was the last time Greg Harvey ever saw Karen Winslett alive. You see, that morning—that Thursday morning, I told you Greg Harvey came home because he forgot something. Well, you see, he came home not only to find Karen's car not there, Karen not there, but what he did find was significant.

"Her hostess dress, the one she wore to Chadwick's, was laid out on the bed, along with her nylons, if you will. And on top of her dress, which was laid out on the bed, was a note. And the note essentially went like this: Greg, went to shoot a Budweiser calendar ad. Wish you were here. If I am not—if my dress isn't gone by three-thirty, get my dress and come and get me. She literally gave the directions to where she was going to go pose for this modeling session to be photographed for this Budweiser calendar. She wrote down a couple of streets and then an address. Well, lo, and behold, guess who lives at that address?"

Mack's attorney, Jim Clifton, stood up. "Your Honor, I will object to the way Mr. Statlin is making the opening statement. It verges on a judgment, rather than staying with the evidence."

The judge inclined his head. "I couldn't hear the very last thing you said?"

Clifton spoke louder. "It verges on argument rather than just a statement of what the evidence says."

"The objection is overruled," Robertson said firmly.

Gene Statlin continued. "Well, Paul Mack, this defendant, lived at that address.

"Of course when Greg Harvey came home that morning, other than the fact that Karen had gone over to do a photo session alone, which was a little unusual unless she knew this person, he wasn't that concerned about her absence. He was picking up something and going back down to his job. So Greg Harvey didn't think a whole lot about it. He gets off work and it is after four o'clock by the time he gets back into Sacramento, and he goes by Chadwick's where Karen was supposed to be at work at four o'clock to stop in and say hi.

"She wasn't there. A little unusual. She was, according to the manager of Chadwick's, the type of employee who not only met her shift when she was scheduled, but literally worked extra hours, very punctual. It was somewhat unusual that she failed to report for her shift.

"Greg immediately went home. And the note was still there,

her clothes were still there, the dress—her work dress—and the nylons.

"The next thing he does, he figures out, hey, she is supposed to be at Paul Mack's, and Greg drives over there. You will see a picture of the house the defendant lived in. It is about four miles from where Karen and Greg lived together. Greg beats on the door. A female answers it, not Karen. Paul Mack comes to the door. First thing Greg asks is have you seen Karen? She came over here to do a Budweiser ad. I have the address, this is where she came. This is Paul Mack's first lie: He says, I don't know Karen. Don't know anything about Karen.

"Greg says well, I have got a note, a map. She came over here to do this. Haven't you seen her? She is supposed to be here."

Just at that moment, one of the reporters walked out of the courtroom. Margie peered in and heard Statlin speaking:

"Mack replies, I don't know anything about a Karen. About a minute and a half conversation. That's his first lie." Statlin's voice had a razor edge. Margie could see the jurors were with him now, their eyes focused on his face.

"Greg Harvey leaves and goes back to the house. He is calling people. He is calling even the friend that she failed to meet for lunch. He is calling, trying to find her, find out where Karen is.

"Later on that night, Greg reported her missing to the police. They came out and he gave them the note that took him to Paul Mack's house, the note Karen left.

"Other than the initial lie and the note connecting this defendant to her on that critical day, is that all the evidence? Obviously not.

"We go to the next day, Friday. Karen hasn't been found. The body hasn't been discovered. Paul Mack made a second major mistake. You see, Friday night he calls his brother up on the telephone. He gets him on the phone and he says, hey, I have got to talk to you. And this is really important. It is urgent that I talk to you.

"And, actually, they are not that close. And Todd says,

okay, if it is real urgent, when do you want to see me? Well, Paul Mack doesn't want to talk to him on the phone. He says, I will be at an auction tomorrow, out in Roseville. You meet me there. It is important. I have to talk to you. His brother does that Saturday morning. He meets this defendant, his brother, out at the auction."

Statlin's manner was easy, chatty now. He was weaving the story told in the book he had referred to at the beginning of his speech. "This wasn't one of these 'how are you doing, how are old times, how is my brother doing,' conversations. This is literally a day and a half after Greg Harvey came over to find Karen Winslett before the police officers are involved. What does the defendant do? You guessed it. He creates a false alibi through his brother.

"He says, Todd, I have got this problem. I want you, if you are ever asked, to lie for me about where I was Thursday morning. Literally, I want you to create a story, a lie—in case anybody ever asks—that I went over to your house, spent all morning with you just kind of hanging around like a little brother ought to. Didn't leave there until 1:30 or 2:00 o'clock in the early afternoon. I need you to do this for me.

"His brother thought about it and when he talked to the cops he gave them that alibi. At least then.

"Why would a guy create a false alibi? What is the evidence in this case other than the fact that he lied to Greg Harvey about seeing Karen Winslett? What is the evidence in the case besides setting up and creating another lie at a critical time, a false alibi? Is that it?"

Statlin began to describe the reasons Paul Mack had to come up with lies. First, for the girlfriend he lived with who knew nothing of where or who'd he been with on the day of the murder.

He stared at Mack and dropped a bombshell.

"Another reason why he needed that alibi so terribly was because, as I told you, the body was found where the 260 Z was backed up into the parking lot of the motel at Madison and Hillsdale. Guess who was on foot and had to be picked up in the early afternoon the Thursday, February nineteenth, in the vicinity of that motel?" He pointed to Paul and nodded. "This defendant. Paul Mack."

Mack stared right back. The jury's heads moved back and forth watching the silent dialogue between the two men.

"How do we know that? Mack had an acquaintance, a guy named Chris Jackson. You are going to hear him testify. He will tell you, and he was certain it was that Thursday, February nineteenth, at about 1:30 in the afternoon he got a call from this defendant, Paul Mack. Mr. Mack told him that he was at the Arco station at the corner of Hillsdale and Madison, which, from the photographs, you will ultimately know is the Arco station right beside that Colonial Motel.

"He told Mr. Jackson he needed a ride, and asked if he would come and get him. Well, that wasn't that far from where Mr. Jackson lived, so he went over there and picked him up. By that time, the defendant had left the phone at the Arco station and was walking down Hillsdale in the general vicinity of his house, but Chris Jackson picked him up in the general vicinity of that intersection on foot at Madison and Hillsdale. That's why Paul Mack needs an alibi so badly.

"A false one at that.

"Is that it? Is that all the evidence? No." His voice had a razor edge. "The evidence will not only show you that at that critical date when you know the killer had to drive the victim's body over there and got out and walked and got picked up, he was there, and met Chris Jackson—aside from the initial lie, the false alibi, there is more. Clearly there is more.

"Let's talk about the weapon for a moment. What Paul Mack used to murder Karen Winslett. What is the evidence about that? Percodan.

"The evidence is going to show that Paul Mack uses Percodan.

"Why do I say that? He had a dentist friend named Dr. Ted Warren who treated him up for dental problems. Dr. Warren prescribed Percodan for Mack.

"Prescription records will show that defendant acquired sixteen tablets of Percodan some five months after he was last treated by Dr. Warren. In fact, one week before Karen Winslett died with it in her system, February thirteenth, 1987, this defendant gets Percodan by way of prescription from Dr. Warren. And, obviously, there is going to be evidence of prior prescription and his use, his drug of choice, of Percodan."

Speaking with cold distaste, Statlin drew his accusations together. "Well, lies, false alibis, he's in the vicinity of the motel, he has access to that type of weapon to kill somebody. What else? What is the other evidence?"

His voice dropped. "You remember I told you about those fibers, the kind of unusual fibers that were found on the clothing and literally on the outside of the socks that were inside the boots Mr. Winslett was literally wearing as she lay in the back of her car, dead? The police go to Mr. Mack's house and they had a search warrant. They go up into this man's bedroom, this defendant's bedroom, and they take carpet specimens."

As a bearded man walked out and held the courtroom door ajar, Margie heard Statlin saying:

"A criminalist compares the fibers that were found on Ms. Winslett when she was taken out of the back of that car and they compare that against the carpet that they get out of his master bedroom. And, you see, nobody in the whole world is ever going to be able to tell you that this particular piece of carpet came out of this particular location, but what they can tell you—a qualified criminalist—is that you can analyze these fibers and make a comparison based upon the presence or absence of certain characteristics within the fiber; its twist, its color, its melting point, and on and on and on."

Margie heard Statlin fire his next words out.

"It is identical. The carpet specimens, the fibers found on the clothing of Ms. Winslett match—not just similar to— match, in every important characteristic, with the carpet out of Paul Mack's bedroom, from his bedroom floor." An audible reaction rippled through the gallery. Robertson rapped his gavel and the door closed.

"That's not all the evidence. Because, you see, after Karen's body was found on March third, the police were talking to Chris Jackson, the guy that gave the defendant a ride.

At the same time, they are still trying to impress upon Todd Mack he really ought to be telling the truth.

"They even talked to the defendant's lawyer about now being the time for him to be arrested for the murder of Karen Winslett. The defendant flees. He absents himself from the jurisdiction. He remained at large for about a year. When they found him it was no longer Paul Steven Mack, the man responsible for the murder of Karen Winslett. He was, as Margie Danielsen, the woman he married, the woman he deceived, will tell you, Sean Paul Lanier of Salt Lake City, Utah. Hers is quite a story.

"He fled. That's what the evidence is about in this case.

"If you take a good, long hard look at it, a critical look, with your common sense and reason, there is only one reasonable interpretation that you will arrive at: This defendant murdered Karen Winslett. He induced her to come over to his house because she was a young, beautiful woman and he wanted to have sex with. He filled her full of Percodan. He killed her. He covered it up. He made a mistake of attempting to weave a web of deceit around it to cover it up, and that was his downfall. And when you look at those facts, there is only one reasonable conclusion: These charges, this defendant, he's guilty of them. And the evidence will prove it beyond a reasonable doubt.

"Thank you."

The judge called for a lunch recess. With that, spectators and reporters filed out into the hallway. Some pulled out cigarettes as they headed for the exit, others made quick trips to the restrooms and the rest stood around stretching their legs and chatting about Statlin's opening statement. Margie listened avidly, circulating among them, trying to get their perceptions not only of the prosecutor's words but of Mack himself. Most of the women thought him charming and earnest looking. "Do you think he could have done it?" was an often repeated question. Margie frowned, wishing they would ask her but no one did.

Then Margie spotted Nickie.

Margie and Nickie walked down the corridor, away from

the small crowd forming near the courtroom door. They found a bench in a quieter, less crowded area and sat down.

"The prosecutor's opening was tough," Nickie told her. "He said some terrible things about my father."

Margie looked at Nickie sympathetically. She knew the turmoil going through the young girl's mind. Her father was a man she didn't know but desperately wanted to love and believe in, just as Margie had wanted to love and believe in him. In the short reunion his daughter and he shared, he had seemed so wonderful to Nickie, just as he had seemed wonderful for a time to Margie. He had conned his daughter just as he had conned them all.

"Nickie, I know how difficult this must be for you," Margie said gently.

"My dad could not have done these things. I just know he couldn't," the girl said brokenly. Margie leaned over and put her arm around Nickie.

"Sometimes, the truth is very difficult to take. No one knows that better than I do," Margie said sadly. She looked into the girl's blue eyes, so like her father's. "But Nickie, if we live with lies, we must continually fight off the reality we can't help but see. It is an exhausting, but as I well know, in the end, decaying process where we are not only lied to but become liars as well. Liars to ourselves," Margie said gravely. "And that is the worst lie we can tell or accept."

"Oh, Margie, I hate this," Nickie cried.

"No more than I do," Margie said sadly. "But I know it's necessary so that we can all get to the other side and get back our lives." Margie paused. "And Nickie, one important thing to remember is we have the rest of our lives. That poor girl the trial is about lost hers."

Without answering, Nickie stood up and headed toward the front door of the courthouse to go out for lunch. Margie followed her silently.

# CHAPTER TWENTY-FOUR

## The Defense

THE lunch break was over. The two women hurried back to the courthouse. As Nickie opened the courtroom door, Margie could see the tall, blond haired defense attorney striding confidently up to the jury box. She wondered if the attitude he showed was for the benefit of the jury or if Jim Clifton really believed in his client and thought he could prove him innocent. Did he think Paul Mack had been condemned by a mistake of fate? How could he not know, as she did, that Paul was such a gifted liar he could even convince himself of the veracity of his claims? Margie sighed and gave the defense attorney the benefit of the doubt. Paul had the power to seduce them all.

The judge said, "Mr. Clifton, you may make your opening statement."

"Thank you, Your Honor."

"This is the opportunity for me to make an opening statement to you," Jim Clifton, an accomplished lawyer, was scanning jurors' faces trying to take their measure.

"I want to point out the purpose of an opening statement is not to argue the case to you. I will merely present some of the issues and describe some of the evidence I think is critical to you in consideration of this case. I will not tell you everything that will be presented; I will just give you enough information so that you can place all the testimony that you are going to receive in the proper context.

"You should be aware that you are not going to be hearing from defense witnesses for some time because the burden of proof is on Mr. Statlin and he will be calling his witnesses first. But you should keep in mind much of the defense will come out through the cross-examination of Mr. Statlin's witnesses."

The courtroom door seemed stuck a bit ajar and Margie heard Clifton's voice which had a kind of suppressed excitement. It was as if he knew a secret the others didn't.

"Let me start by telling you a little bit about the background of Paul Mack. Paul Mack had his own business. It was called Wholesale Sportswear and Silkscreen. That business involved selling items of clothing for promotional purposes, hats with emblems on them and T-shirts with logos and shirts with logos, suspenders, that sort of thing. He generally would work accounts at restaurants, bars, hotels, where he would approach people there and sell them these items for their business purposes. He would take orders from them and then arrange to have the goods manufactured and they would be delivered to whoever purchased them from him.

"He did live with his girlfriend, Stacy Carter, as Mr. Statlin stated."

A bailiff came and fastened the door shut. Margie was left alone once again with her thoughts.

"He first met Karen Winslett in September or October. She was working on promotions out of the Warehouse Restaurant, which no longer exists. He was trying to sell T-shirts, jackets, suspenders, that sort of thing, and he was put in contact with her as the Warehouse was interested in purchasing products from him.

"The manager of the Warehouse Restaurant agreed to purchase some jackets and shirts with logos on them from Paul. The order was a C.O.D. order, which, as you know, is an order that has to be paid for when you get the goods. Karen Winslett was the person whom he was dealing with at the Warehouse, the person who was kind of the liaison.

"Unfortunately, around that time the Warehouse Restaurant was experiencing a lot of financial difficulties and was not in a position to pay for the goods they had ordered from Paul Mack and were unable to deliver a check for the goods and Paul Mack ultimately had to go to court and sue them.

"During the course of his business dealings with the Warehouse Restaurant and Karen Winslett, she gave Paul her telephone number. Now this is a telephone number that was not listed to her. It was listed to Greg Harvey, at the residence that Greg Harvey and Karen Winslett had shared for a number of years.

"Paul also gave Karen an invitation to a Halloween party that he was sponsoring along with someone else at a friend's house. He told Karen she could come and bring her boyfriend. Karen nor Greg, neither of them actually went to the Halloween party.

"Greg Harvey will tell you Karen got party invitations all the time from different people and generally she threw them away. But in this particular instance this particular invitation was kept and in her car when her car was found.

"Early the next year, Paul had the opportunity to go into the beef jerky business. You all know what beef jerky is. The opportunity he had was to get involved in a distributorship where this product would be provided to supermarkets—convenience stores or supermarkets in other areas. This was an attractive opportunity for him. The problem was he needed someone to take over his sales business, his silk screening business—take over the sales aspect of that. So in February, he prepared a list of people who he thought might be interested in doing that and might be good at it. Karen Winslett's name was on that list."

The story Jim Clifton was weaving was very different from the one Gene Statlin had told, and he told it well. The picture of Paul Mack he painted was that of a serious, pro-feminist businessman who had tried to give a young woman he'd met a helping hand into the business world. As his tale wound on, he would place Mack's arrest record in the context of youthful indiscretion that explained his fear of and lies to the police.

"On Friday, before she disappeared, Paul called Karen's number, the one that Karen had given to him and a man answered. He asked is Karen there. The man said, no, she would be back on Sunday. She was out of town. The following Monday or Tuesday Mack called back to see if Karen might be interested in a sales job; taking over his sales business so that he could go into the beef jerky business. He talked to her that morning. It was left between the two of them that Paul would get back to her later in the week when he had more information about what the opportunity might be.

"The next time that he had contact with Karen Winslett was on the morning of February nineteen when she disappeared. He called her early that morning to find out if she was still interested in a sales job—in taking over the business that he had operated. She said that she was.

"Now, at this point I will jump from February nineteen to February twenty-first. The events that happened on the morning of the nineteenth, the twentieth and twenty-first are the heart of that case, and I'm not going to tell you at this point what I think the evidence will show about that period of time. I will let you hear that as it comes out.

"On February twenty-first, Paul Mack was contacted by the police regarding Karen Winslett's disappearance, and I will tell you right up front he lied to the police about his whereabouts on the morning of February nineteenth. I will also tell you right up front that he asked his brother Todd to lie about his whereabouts on the morning of February nineteenth. Paul will explain all of that to you."

As for Paul Mack's access to the drug found in Karen Winslett's body, Clifton admitted Mack sometimes used it but for a medical reason and never in excess.

"I will tell you also that Paul Mack had access to some Percodan, that he had had extensive dental problems, which Dr. Ted Warren will testify about, in the past, and that Percodan had been prescribed to him.

"I believe the evidence will be somewhat conflicting as to how much Percodan Dr. Warren had actually given Paul Mack, but I think it will be clear that he did not have the amount of Percodan given to him that the police thought was given to the victim.

"And I will also tell you that in late March, while Paul Mack was under suspicion for this crime, that he took the only course that he felt was open to him, and that is that he left the area. He established a new identity, as Sean Paul Lanier, as you have been told. He tried to build a new life for himself, and, as you know, all that ended when he was apprehended."

All through his lawyer's discourse, Mack was so innocently pensive that the jury, who seemed mesmerized by him more than Clifton's words, were quiet, still, absorbed.

"He will tell you from February nineteen until he left in late March he believed that the police already had made up their minds that he was guilty of this crime. And I believe the evidence will show that he was probably right about that in terms of what the police thought.

"You should be aware that there is very important evidence in this case that the police either never bothered to collect or seize and then released without any attempts to preserve. And we will be asking questions about that, and I ask you to be attuned to that.

"There were extremely promising leads which the police had which they did not follow up on. There was important evidence that pointed away from Paul Mack that was never followed up on. Paul will tell you that he has had many problems with the law, that he was convicted of theft-related offenses five times, three times in California and two times in other states.

"He will tell you that he had no faith in the courts, no faith in the police, and no faith in the criminal justice system that justice would be done. He had no reason to believe that the police would ever fully investigate the case to try and prove his innocence.

"Further, the media attention on this case had been extreme. There had been a lot of major television stories about the victim being missing and about the victim being found on March third. The police hadn't solved the case. As far as they knew, they were going to solve it by charging Paul Mack. In light of that, he left the area."

Clifton, perspiring a bit now, launched a different attack.

"Now I want to say something about what I think the evidence is going to show about Karen Winslett. From outward appearances, she was a wholesome, beautiful, young lady, a model and beauty queen with what appeared to be a promising career in modeling. She had had a long-term relationship with Greg Harvey. They had been living together for three years. Greg Harvey wanted to get married to Karen Winslett."

Margie, who saw the jury's faces each time someone left the room, felt her stomach clench. She knew they were trying to figure out, just as she had for so long, what the truth about Paul Mack was, how a man who seemed so earnest could do that of which he was accused.

"But I think the evidence will actually show that Karen Winslett was a troubled young woman, that she was not happy with her life with Greg Harvey, that she was far more interested in developing her modeling career, and she was trying to do that at a very dangerous pace.

"The evidence will show that she used marijuana upon a fairly regular basis."

Statlin, annoyed, stood up. It was par for the course to try to demean the character of a dead victim in order to exonerate a defendant, but Statlin hated the maneuver.

"Your Honor, I will object to relevance."

"Sustained."

Clifton pushed on. "Your Honor, may I be heard?

"You are requesting to be heard on that now?"

"Yes."

"Do you want me to excuse the jury for that purpose?"

"Well, let me go on to another point, and I may come back to it."

"All right. We can come back to that. I will let you be heard."

"At the same time Karen was trying to maintain a stable relationship with Greg Harvey, she was involved with other men."

Statlin stood up again and said angrily, "I will object to relevance."

"Sustained."

"Your Honor, I believe we have already been heard on this," Clifton said.

"I think this has a relationship to the subject we were discussing, but I don't think it is the subject we were discussing."

"Karen Winslett had a relationship with a man from San Diego."

Statlin again stood up. "Same objection, Your Honor."

"Your Honor, could I have a moment?" Clifton asked.

The judge spoke in a no-nonsense tone which indicated he wasn't going to permit this to go on much longer. "I will take that objection under submission and I will rule on it at the end of the opening statement. I don't know where Mr. Clifton is going with all this and how it is going to tie into some coherent—if it is going to tie into some coherent defense theory without electing to show how that will be relevant. With that, the objection is under submission."

Clifton responded, "Thank you, Your Honor."

Clifton went on raising questions about Karen Winslett's love life and character. It was particularly horrendous for some of her family who had gathered in the courtroom and who felt they did not recognize the vivacious girl they loved and knew so well in Clifton's demeaning remarks.

Clifton went on, "It is our position that the statements that Karen Winslett made in the Budweiser calendar note left on the bed in her house for her boyfriend were lies that she told to cover up from Greg Harvey what she was actually doing."

Judge Robertson's impatience was telling. "Would you explain that, please?"

Clifton answered, "Because she made so many different statements about this Budweiser calendar, because there is absolutely no evidence that Paul Mack was a photographer or was shooting a Budweiser calendar. And we will present evidence of at least one other photographer who was approaching people, including Karen Winslett, to shoot a Budweiser calendar. And her statement that she was going over to Paul Mack's house to shoot a Budweiser calendar is not—just not trustworthy."

"What is your theory of what she was covering up?" the judge asked.

"She was covering up where she was going that morning."

"What is your theory about where that was?"

Clifton said, "Well, I think at this point I'm hesitant to relate this much of the defense already."

"Well, you know, it is now or never. I'm going to rule on this motion about whether this evidence comes in or not. I can't do it in the dark. I need to know why it is relevant, why it is material. I will never know unless you tell me."

"Your Honor, may I have a minute?

"Yes."

The defense counsel conferred with the judge off the record.

"Okay, Your Honor, at this point, before I present more information about the defense in this case, I would ask that we go in camera and do that in private."

"You mean out of the presence of the district attorney?"

"Yes."

"What is your position in that regard, Mr. Statlin?"

"I oppose it," Statlin said firmly.

"Do you wish to be heard?"

"I have stated my reasons previously on why I don't think I should be removed."

The judge sighed. "Do you want to be heard as to why you should be allowed to make a showing in camera out of the presence of the district attorney, Mr. Clifton?"

Clifton wasn't about to give up. "Because it involves revealing our entire defense. I don't think we are required to do that at this stage of the proceedings. I don't think People versus Hall requires me to make this kind of showing in advance before I have asked the witnesses questions. As Mr. Statlin said, People versus Hall relaxes the standards on presenting other suspect evidence. All you have to do is create a reasonable possibility, grounds for a jury to conclude that there is a reasonable doubt about the defendant's guilt.

"That is not a very high showing. And at this point I've already revealed a substantial portion of our defense, and I don't think I should be required to reveal any further. I'm prepared to do that to the Court in camera, but I don't think I should have to do that in front of Mr. Statlin."

Judge Robertson made short work of the legal maneuvering

for position. "I deny the request. The district attorney has the right to due process and fair hearing. This is an important question. These are important questions. The district attorney ought to have the right to be present to respond. I deny the request.

"In terms of whether you are obligated to disclose now, you are not. You don't have to make an opening statement. You can defer an opening statement until the conclusion of the prosecution's case in chief, as you well know. If you choose not to cross-examine on these points, you won't be challenged on them now. But you have no right to make an opening statement or present evidence without regard to the rules of evidence."

Robertson rapped his gavel.

"You have got to comply with the rules of evidence, and that may require, if you choose, to make an opening statement now or choose to cross-examine on these points, that you make disclosure out of the presence of the jury. That is what Evidence Code Section 401 and following are all about. It is up to you. It is your choice. You don't have to disclose these things, but you have to disclose them if you want to make references to them in your opening statement or cross-examine prosecution witnesses about them."

Clifton raised his eyes and said very calmly, "Well, is it the Court's position that before I ask one single question that might lead to evidence of a possible other suspect, even though it is relevant on other grounds, that I have to make a complete showing?"

Robertson said sharply, "No, I'm going to rule on those matters on a case by case, matter by matter basis. If the district attorney raises an objection or makes a motion for request for hearing, I will rule on it. As to some matters, yes. As to others, no."

Clifton said in a thoughtful measuring expression, "Your Honor, I would ask that we break now so we can discuss this further."

\* \* \*

As the door swung open, Margie peered inside. Margie had decided it was like a baseball game in which she was turning her head each moment to watch the pitcher and the batter connect. Margie sat on the bench watching the spectators, reporters and lawyers file out. Suddenly, a friendly face walked up. Detective Frank smiled and called out, "Margie, are you okay? Quite an ordeal you've been through, I'm surprised you wanted to come out here before you're needed to testify."

"There are things I want to be certain of and people I need to talk to," Margie said. "Like Sean's, I mean Paul's, parents. And I have his daughter with me. She's inside. She never really knew him, and now she has to come to grips with all this. And, of course, I want to be sure the truth comes out."

"You're quite a brave lady," Frank said with admiration.

Margie sighed. "Don't misunderstand me," she said. "I don't think it's bravery that propelled me this far, but the need to set things right so my daughters and I can go on."

Detective Frank looked around as everyone made their way back into the courtroom. "I'll try to come out every now and then to let you know how things are going." He smiled.

"I really do appreciate that," she said. "You've been so kind to me and I thank you for it."

"No, it is you we all should be thanking. Without you, we wouldn't be here today."

A pang of regret struck Margie. "And how I wish none of it were true and that we didn't have to be here at all," she said softly.

"I know you do," Frank said.

When Detective Frank walked back in, Margie could see the seats in the gallery were all taken. Standees crowded the walls. The media had spread the word: this was a trial worth watching. Margie wished she could hear every word.

After lunch, in open court and with the jury absent, Clifton once again tried to cast doubt on Karen Winslett's good character and her relationship with Greg Harvey.

"At this time, for tactical reasons, we are not prepared to state any further information about what the defense evidence is going to be in this case. However, I want to make some comments about what I have already expressed by way of offer of proof.

"Let me modify that somewhat to say we do intend to present evidence that the victim in this case made a number of different statements to different people about the Budweiser calendar shoot. She told some people that her trip to Mexico was for the purpose of doing the Budweiser calendar shoot. She told some people that she had already taken the pictures for the Budweiser calendar shoot and they had been sent to Budweiser.

"She told other people that the Budweiser calendar shoot was some time in the future."

Clifton alluded to Winslett's planning to leave Greg Harvey and to Greg lying about their relationship.

But the judge didn't buy it. "You are losing me. Let's start again. You want to show evidence that she used marijuana, she used cocaine, she used methamphetamine, she used magic mushrooms, she went to Mexico for a week a short time before she disappeared."

The judge snapped. "I am going to ask you again how is any of that, even if true, going to bear on the victim as the author of the notes or shed any light on the credibility?"

Clifton argued on and on.

Finally, the judge glared at the defense attorney. "I conclude that none of the evidence covering the offer of proof has relevance for any of the grounds asserted. I sustain the objections."

Margie watched as the jury was brought back in and saw Jim Clifton continuing his opening statement. In the courtroom, Margie caught a glimpse of Paul Mack at the defense table, elegantly groomed as ever, wearing a black suit. The jurors stared at him as they walked in and he smiled that charming, infectious smile which she had once found so beguiling. Then once again, as the door was closing, she heard Clifton's voice.

"As with all witnesses, you will be asked to assess the credibility of the witnesses called by the People. I submit to you that you will hear evidence concerning the credibility of Greg Harvey that will call into question the credibility of the statements he makes to you in court, and I ask you to pay close attention to that." Clifton had walked toward the jury box and peered into their impassive faces. Now he tried to bring the autopsy results into question.

"There are other issues that are significant to this case, some of which I want to talk about. I believe the evidence will not show beyond a reasonable doubt that the victim actually died of a Percodan overdose."

Clifton, knowing the coroner's findings would be heavily weighted, told the jury that he would bring them experts to try to dispute him and to prove that Karen herself had ingested the drugs.

"Now you will be given evidence of other situations where a person has died from an acknowledged Percodan overdose, and there are very few of these because it is a fairly uncommon drug that results in death. You will be shown evidence of three suicides that took place when someone intended to kill themselves, obviously, by taking an overdose of Percodan.

"You will be shown what the drug concentrations are in those three cases that were thoroughly researched, and it will be apparent that the drug levels in the victim in this case were far lower—far lower than the levels in the three people who intended to kill themselves by taking Percodan.

"Thus, I believe the evidence will be consistent with a self-administered dosage of Percodan by the victim in this case. I don't think you will be able to rule that out as a reasonable possibility."

He told the jury that there was other telling evidence that someone else, not Paul Mack, had brought Karen Winslett's body to the motel where it was found.

"There will be evidence that on Friday morning, February twentieth, the day after Greg Harvey reported the victim disappeared, a man was seen getting out of the victim's car in the Colonial parking lot. There was a maintenance man that worked at the Colonial Motel. At about nine o'clock Friday morning, the day after the victim disappeared, he went into the office to get something and there was no car there. According to him, when he came out a short time later the Datsun was parked where it was ultimately found by the police. There was a person sitting in the Datsun. The person got out of the car, locked the car and left."

But, of course, what Clifton did not say was that the person was never found.

"Now the Budweiser calendar shoot. The district attorney will introduce notes that the victim wrote to Greg Harvey saying Karen Winslett was going to the defendant's house for a Budweiser calendar shoot. The evidence will show that Paul Mack was not the man who she was dealing with for a Budweiser calendar. The evidence will show quite the contrary."

Clifton's voice rose, penetrating the thick walls and streaming out to the hall. "The evidence will indicate that the victim's note to Greg Harvey about going to Paul Mack's house for a Budweiser calendar shoot was a lie.

"There will be testimony that the victim made many statements to many different people about the Budweiser calendar and what her position was with the Budweiser calendar.

"We will present evidence indicating that someone other than Paul Mack was the Budweiser calendar man who had been dealing with Karen Winslett about taking pictures of her for Budweiser.

"Finally, the evidence, I believe, will show that many of the witnesses to be called by the prosecution will have a hidden agenda, and that is that these witnesses—and this is relevant to their credibility—were involved in activities at the time all this was happening that calls into question the credibility of their statements to the police and presumably their statements here in court.

"In conclusion, I believe the evidence will show that Paul Mack was not with Karen Winslett when she died, will not show that he killed her, will not show that he raped her, and will not even show that Karen Winslett was murdered, beyond a reasonable doubt.

"Thank you."

The jurors stared at him poker-faced. Judge Robertson didn't wait a heartbeat. "Mr. Statlin, please call your first witness."

"I would like to call Mr. Greg Harvey, H-a-r-v-e-y."

# CHAPTER TWENTY-FIVE

## The Witnesses Speak

In the hallway, Margie saw muscular, blond Greg Harvey, Karen Winslett's boyfriend and the first witness for the prosecution, waiting nervously. She identified him from the pictures in the newspaper.

Margie stared at Greg, knowing nothing she could say could ameliorate the pain which showed on his face, but she wanted to tell him that it was an anguish all who had their lives touched by Paul Mack shared.

She got up and walked over to him. "I'm going to testify later. I was married to Paul Mack without knowing who he was," she told him. "So I know what you must be going through. I wanted you to know that and that I appreciate your effort to get the truth out."

"And I yours," he said, as the doors opened and the bailiff ushered Greg Harvey inside.

While Greg was being escorted down the aisle, he looked searchingly around the courtroom until his eyes met Paul Mack's. He took his seat in the witness stand, still staring at the defendant. The judge's words broke Harvey's silent, bitter gaze.

"Mr. Harvey, would you raise your right hand to be sworn, please?" asked the judge from the bench.

Harvey nodded.

The clerk approached Greg carrying a Bible and said, "Do you solemnly swear the testimony you are about to give will be the truth, the whole truth and nothing but the truth, so help you God?"

Greg sat up in his seat and responded, "Yes, ma'am, I do."

After asking Greg to spell out his name for the courtroom reporter, the judge then told the prosecutor to go ahead with his questioning. Gene Statlin thanked the judge and stood up from behind his table. He gave his black blazer a tug at the bottom, and looked at Greg.

Statlin walked around the table towards the witness stand. His voice was gentle. "I would like to direct your attention back in time, Mr. Harvey, to specifically around February of 1987. Do you have that approximate period of time in mind?"

"Yes, I do."

"Did you live with anybody at that time?"

"Yes, I did—my girlfriend for almost three years at the time, Karen Winslett."

Then Greg began to tell the jury through the skillful questioning of Gene Statlin about the young woman he had loved. As he spoke about Karen's budding modeling career, all in the courtroom could hear the pride in his voice.

"Did she model very often?"

"She did, yes."

"Did she ever get paid for that, Mr. Harvey?"

"Yes, she did. She usually got a couple hundred to five hundred dollars."

Statlin had an envelope marked as evidence and walked towards Greg with it. "Mr. Harvey, do you recognize the woman who is depicted in these photographs in this envelope?"

"Yes, I do," Greg said, hesitating as he gently ran his fingers over the photographs. Then he said sadly, "That's Karen."

"Did Ms. Winslett own a car?" Statlin continued.

"Yes, she did. A blue Datsun 260 Z."

Greg was then asked to identify Karen's car in a picture. Greg stared at the picture for a few moments and said, "That's Karen's hatchback." He gave a half-smile. "I remember the dents in the front bumper. I'm sure of it."

"Mr. Harvey, I want to talk to you specifically about a particular week in February of 1987, and specifically what I would like you to do is to direct your attention to the morning of February sixteenth, a Monday, of 1987. Do you have that date in mind?"

"Yes, I do, sir."

It was obviously painful for Greg Harvey to talk about the period leading to Karen's death. He closed his eyes as Statlin asked about that morning. When he opened them he answered softly, "She was still asleep when I got up, but she was talking on the phone next to our bed when I got out of the shower."

"At that point in time, did you know who she was talking to?"

"No, I did not, but while she was talking on the phone, sitting on the bed, she was pointing to a note on the little stand we kept the phone on. It was really just a napkin, actually. Karen used anything to scribble on when she was talking on the phone, and she was pretty excited about it."

"Did you pay any particular attention to what she was saying?"

Greg seemed lost in thought, as if he was picturing that last morning in his mind. Finally, he went on. "No. I was just trying to get dressed as fast as I could for work that morning."

"After she finished the telephone conversation, did you and Ms. Winslett discuss the note that she had brought to your attention during the course of her telephone call?"

"Yes, she did. She let me read the note."

Statlin pulled from a folder on his desk a clear plastic bag containing a handwritten note on a napkin. Scrawled on the napkin in blue ink were the words "Paul," "Budweiser girl's calendar," and "five thousand dollars." Greg identified it as the note that Karen called to his attention that morning.

"Mr. Harvey, did you have a conversation with Ms. Winslett about what, if any, plans she had, as indicated in her telephone conversation or in this note?"

"She told me that she got a telephone call and was a finalist for a calendar. She said they were going to shoot it later on in the week or another week. It all depended upon what time the photographer could do it."

"Did she tell you the name of the person who was going to do this calendar shoot?"

"Yes, she did," declared Greg, looking over at the defendant in silent accusation. "She told me his name was Paul and that it was for a Budweiser calendar. She was going to be paid five thousand dollars for the shoot."

"Is that what the note says?"

"Yes, sir."

"How would you describe Ms. Winslett's reaction to this five thousand dollar deal?"

"She was pretty excited. It was a lot more money than she had ever been paid before to do any photo modeling."

"Now, I would like to move forward to Thursday, February nineteenth of this same year, roughly three days after the telephone call on the sixteenth. What did you do on the morning of the nineteenth, Mr. Harvey?"

Greg bit his lip and his voice broke as he went on. "I got up at seven A.M., took a shower, had breakfast and went to work."

"Where was Ms. Winslett that morning at the time you got up?"

"She was still lying in bed."

"Did you discuss with her at all what her plans were for that day?"

"Yes, I did," Greg replied. "She told me she was going to have lunch with her friend, Liza Barnes, about noon and go work out afterwards before work."

"What time was it, approximately, that you left your house that morning?"

"It was quarter to eight when I left. Karen was still in bed."

"About what time did you get to work?"

"Nine A.M., an hour after I left home."

"And then what did you do?"

Slowly Statlin went over the morning of the day Karen died, reconstructing Greg's movements for the jury.

"I forgot something at home so I went back to the house to pick it up."

"About what time was it that you got back to your and Karen's house?"

"About ten A.M. or a quarter past ten."

"When you arrived back at the house was anybody home?"

"No one was there."

"And was there any indication once you got inside the house as to where Ms. Winslett was?"

Greg put one hand to his face looking numb.

Statlin inquired, "Do you want me to repeat the question?"

Greg shook his head.

"She left me a note stating where she would be. It was laying on the bed upstairs on her work clothes."

Statlin once again picked up a clear plastic bag from his desk. Inside the bag was a small, white piece of paper with another note written in blue ink. Statlin also reached for a poster board propped behind his chair, which was a large blow-up copy of the same note in this plastic bag. Greg identified these as the note Karen left on top of her work clothes that day.

"Now, this note, Mr. Harvey, referred to the Budweiser situation, did it not?"

"Yes, it did."

"It listed an address?"

"Yes."

"Now, at that particular point in time, were you concerned about whether or not she had gone over to participate in that Budweiser calendar shoot, as evidenced by the note?"

"No, I wasn't concerned at the time." Greg frowned, his voice bitter.

"Was it usual for her to go by herself to one of these shoots where she would be photographed when she modeled?"

"No, Karen usually took someone with her, like a friend or me."

"Now, after you saw the note that was on top of her work clothes on the bed upstairs Thursday morning, what did you do?"

"I kind of dismissed it and went to work."

"Did you notice if Ms. Winslett's blue Datsun was gone?"

"Yes, I did, and yes it was gone."

"Did you work throughout the day?"

"Yes, I did, until about three-thirty P.M."

"What did you do after work that afternoon, Mr. Harvey?"

Greg looked weary as he replied. "I drove straight back to Sacramento."

"Where did you go once you got back into Sacramento?"

"I stopped at Chadwick's Restaurant to see Karen. But when I got there, I didn't find her. I asked a couple of the waitresses and I talked to one of her managers, and nobody had seen or heard from her. It was unusual because Karen usually showed up for work and she always called if she was going to be late."

As Greg described his growing concern about Karen after he found out that not only had she not gone to work, but she had not come home, there was a taut undertone to his quiet voice that caused the jury to lean forward in their seats. It was almost as though they were rooting for the day to have turned out differently for this obviously in love and grief-stricken man.

Next, Statlin asked Greg to explain what happened when he arrived at the house—Paul Mack's house—that, according to her note, was Karen's destination.

"I knocked on the door, and a young lady answered. I asked if Karen was there and got no response from her. Paul Mack immediately came to the door after that."

"Is the man who came to the door in this courtroom today?" Statlin asked, stepping back so that Greg could look once again at Mack.

"Yes, he is," Greg said, and there was something in those words more volatile than grief. He pointed out Paul Mack and his identification of the defendant was added to the court record.

Statlin continued, "Did you have a conversation with Mr. Mack once he came to the door?"

"Yes, I did. I asked if Karen was there and he said no. I explained that she was supposed to be there for a Budweiser calendar shoot and told him that I had a map she had drawn showing the way to his house."

"So what did he say in response to that?"

The anger in Greg's voice was palpable. "He said he did

not know her, so I left and went back to my house. But when I got back inside my house, I was in there for about maybe five or ten minutes and I got a phone call from Paul Mack. I recognized his voice, and he also identified himself. He said, 'Oh, yes, I do remember a Karen. It just slipped my mind.' He then said Karen was supposed to show up for a job interview that day, but they discussed it and decided not to do it when he found out she was going to move to San Diego."

"Later on that evening, did Karen ever come back?"

"No, she did not, so I called the police to report her missing. When the officers came that night, I turned over the note Karen left me that morning and also told them about some articles of clothing, a bathing suit, a leotard, and a couple of handbags that were gone."

Now Statlin turned to Greg's next meeting with the defendant, setting up Mack's trail of lies.

"Mr. Harvey, after you went over and saw Paul Mack's house and met with Mr. Mack that Thursday evening sometime after five P.M., did you ever see him again?"

Greg nodded. "Yes, I went back the next day, Friday, after work and talked to him again because he was the last person I knew of who talked to Karen. He was going to do an exchange of a U-Haul trailer, so I went with him and asked him if he knew anything about Karen's whereabouts. He said she was supposed to come over that morning, but never did."

"Was this different from what he had told you either at the door when you first met him or in the telephone conversation the evening before?"

"Yes, because he stated that she wasn't supposed to come over at all. Then he said she was supposed to come over but never did."

"Thank you, Mr. Harvey. I have no further questions, Your Honor," Statlin announced.

After a brief recess, everyone returned to their seats and Greg Harvey was returned to the witness stand for his cross-examination by Mack's lawyer, Jim Clifton. Clifton was as meticulously dressed as his client in an expensive, freshly-pressed brown suit. Clifton spent his first minutes asking routine questions of Greg Harvey. Then Clifton, adjusting his tie, began to ask more probing questions, trying to get Harvey to recant some of the statements he had made incriminating Clifton's client. But he ignored the old lawyer's rule to never ask questions for which you don't already know the answers and Harvey not only stuck to his story, but expanded on it.

"Mr. Harvey, what efforts did Ms. Winslett make to get modeling jobs?"

"People would contact her or give her their cards with their phone numbers to call. That's how she got most of her jobs, I think. But she only accepted a few of those job offers."

"When Ms. Winslett got this call about a five thousand dollar modeling job, what discussions did you have about it with her?"

"She was kind of excited. She typically gets a couple hundred to five hundred dollars for a modeling shoot, so this was a pretty big deal for her. She said she was one of the finalists in a Budweiser calendar. She would find out more during the week. That's all she really mentioned—that and," he looked over toward the defendant and gave an angry scowl, "a guy named Paul."

"Did you ever ask her anything about this guy?"

"No, not at all really."

"Was that the first time she ever mentioned anything about a Budweiser calendar to you?"

"Yes."

"During that period of time, from Monday until she disappeared, did she ever say anything to you to the effect that she wanted either you or someone else to accompany her on this camera shoot?"

"No, because she didn't know when it was supposed to be, what day it was."

Clifton studied the ceiling for a moment and tapped his finger on his chin. "Let's move forward. On the morning of Thursday, February nineteenth of the same year, Ms. Winslett told you she was going to have lunch at noon with Liza Barnes and go to the gym before she went to work. As far as you know, was Ms. Winslett going to have lunch with anybody other than Liza Barnes?"

"No."

"I think your testimony on direct was that Ms. Winslett ordinarily would take someone with her the first time she went on a shoot. Is that right?"

"Yes," Greg replied.

"In the note she left Thursday laying on top of her work clothes, she says she is scared to go by herself. Is that unusual?"

Greg Harvey's face showed his anguish. "Yes. I noticed that when I originally read it."

"Had she ever told you before that she was scared to go by herself?"

Greg's voice turned very quiet. "Like I said, she usually has someone with her at all times, but if she goes by herself, she usually knows the person."

And so, with Greg Harvey, the witnesses began. Each, Margie knew, added a piece, sometimes vital, sometimes minor, to the circumstantial evidence methodically building the case for the prosecution that Paul Steven Mack was guilty of the murder of Karen Winslett.

Dr. Ted Warren was the next witness called on behalf of the People. He had been Paul Mack's dentist. Ted's dark brown hair was peppered with gray streaks, but he looked fit in his tan sports jacket and pressed khakis. As he took his seat in the witness stand, the judge addressed him, "Doctor Warren, would you raise your right hand to be sworn, please?"

The clerk handed Ted a Bible and asked, "Do you solemnly swear the testimony you are about to give will be the truth, the whole truth and nothing but the truth, so help you God?"

Ted responded gravely, "I do."

After asking Ted to spell out his name for the courtroom reporter, the judge then addressed the prosecutor, telling him to go ahead with his questioning. Statlin thanked the judge and sipped from a glass of water on the table. He stood, picked up a folder from his desk and walked towards the judge, handing him the folder for identification as evidence. After receiving it back from the judge, Statlin handed Warren the folder for reference.

"Doctor Warren, what do you do for a living?"

"I'm a dentist, have been since 1975."

"Do you know a Paul Mack?"

"Yes, Paul was a patient of mine."

"Is the Paul Mack who was a patient of yours in the courtroom today?"

"Yes, he is. He is seated at the table to my left, wearing a black suit and a white shirt."

"When did you first see Mr. Mack as a patient?"

"September 1985, on an emergency basis."

"Now, with respect to these particular dental records in the folder you have, can you examine them to see the last time you actually treated Mr. Mack?"

Ted looked through the dental records and responded, "The last time I saw him was on July thirty-first, 1986, when we cemented a crown."

"Aside from treating Mr. Mack over a period of time up to approximately July thirty-first of 1986, did your relationship with him become other than just professional?"

"He was a patient and we had several meetings concerning some business dealings as well. From that point, it became a more social kind of relationship."

"During the course of your treatment of Mr. Mack as a patient, did you prescribe for him any pharmaceutical, narcotic-type drugs?"

"Yes, I prescribed Percodan. It's a pain reliever of choice that we used in the office at that particular time. It is used for moderate to severe pain and is a controlled substance. It is required in triplicate, meaning that when I write a prescription for it, I keep a copy of it and the other copies go to the pharmacy and the Drug Enforcement Agency."

"Roughly how many prescriptions had you written to Mr. Mack between April and July of 1986?"

"Four or five. One was for Tylenol with codeine but the rest were for Percodan."

"Did you keep prescribing Percodan for him after the last time you actually saw him formally in your office in July?"

"Yes, I did, about four or five times."

Warren went on describing a succession of Percodan prescriptions culminating in one for sixteen tablets on February 13, 1987.

"I would like to have you think ahead from the last date we discussed, February thirteenth of 1987, about eight days later to February twenty-first, 1987. Did you have occasion to go to Mr. Mack's house?"

"Yes, I did. I was asked by Paul to stop by when I called him on the phone. As soon as I got there, he told me that the police were coming."

"What was Mr. Mack's demeanor like before the police officers arrived?"

"He was somewhat agitated because a local girl was missing and he was supposed to have met with her the day she was reported missing."

Statlin then called Ted Warren's attention to the night of March sixteenth when he went to Mack's house and they left together.

"How was Mr. Mack acting? What was his demeanor like when you went with him in his car?"

"He was nervous and upset. He said that his ex-girlfriend and his ex-wife had been called down to the police department, and the police were trying to put some pressure on him."

Statlin now tied the Percodan prescriptions to Paul Mack and to Karen Winslett. "When you were having this ride with Mr. Mack, did the subject of your being a dentist having to prescribe Percodan ever come up in the conversation?"

Warren cocked his head and looked at the prosecutor. "Yes, it did. Paul asked me what I had prescribed to him in the past, and then he wanted to know if there would be a doctor-patient relationship in case the police talked to me. He didn't specifically come out and say, 'Would you do me a favor?' He asked me if the police spoke to me, if it was possible I not be specific with them." And so Paul Mack once again had maneuvered for another lie.

Then Statlin paused for a few moments after, and almost as an afterthought asked, "Did the subject come up of where the victim's body was found?"

Warren nodded. "Yes. I asked him where this woman had been found dead and Paul told me that she had been found at the Colonial Motel. Since we weren't that far from the motel, we drove by it and he showed me. As we passed the Colonial, he told me to turn in behind the Arco Station and said that they found her back there."

There was a stirring in the courtroom. Paul Mack had maintained that he didn't even know the location of the motel where Karen Winslett's body had been found. Warren's testimony showed that Paul did indeed know the place. It remained for another witness still to come to link him more ominously with it.

Statlin looked towards the judge. "No further questions, Your Honor."

The judge looked over towards Jim Clifton and asked him to begin.

"Dr. Warren, I want to ask you some questions about the date that you went over to Mr. Mack's house and the police showed up, February twenty-first. Did you follow any of the publicity about Karen Winslett being missing at that time?"

"Not prior to my arriving at Mr. Mack's house that afternoon."

"What was Mr. Mack's demeanor when he asked you to come over on February twenty-first when the officers came?"

"When I talked to him on the telephone, his demeanor was very calm, but when I got over there, he was highly agitated. I walked in the door and Paul was pacing, his face was white and he was talking very fast. He constantly looked out the window and started to tell me what was going on. He said that the police were sending a detective out to interview him about the missing girl, Karen Winslett. He also said that the day she was supposedly missing, her boyfriend came by asking whether Karen had been there for a meeting or not. Paul told me that she never made it to the meeting and had told him the same thing."

"And were you present when Mr. Mack talked to the police?"

"Yes, I was. The interview was about twenty minutes to a half hour."

"How many times did you see Mr. Mack socially between February twenty-first and the end of March?"

"We either talked or saw each other every other day at least."

"Had you treated him since July of 1986?" Clifton asked.

"Not in the office. He was a patient of record."

"So you had not treated him at all since July, yet you continued to prescribe narcotics to him?"

"I saw him all the time. I could monitor him," Gary rationalized.

"And what sorts of things did you do to monitor him?"

"First of all, I would watch his eyes and his demeanor. You can tell when somebody is on Percodan over a long period of time. Their eyes are dilated, fixed and agitated, but Paul did not appear to have been abusing Percodan."

"As far as you were concerned, Dr. Warren, all the Percodan that you gave Mr. Mack was required by his dental condition, correct?"

Warren wanted to make sure his reputation stayed intact. "That is correct, sir."

Clifton gave a wry smile and looked at his notepad on the table. "Now, you testified before that you ordinarily would not give more than twelve tablets of Percodan at a time. Is that correct?"

"Yes, normally ten tablets at a time. One tablet every three to four hours as needed for pain."

"What was Mr. Mack's dental condition that caused all this pain?"

"When I first saw Paul, we started root canal therapy on one tooth. We then started it on another tooth. His dental condition was that he had a lot of missing teeth and a lot of problems. Incomplete, partial dentures were made for him. His condition was such that I would expect him to have continually been in a lot of pain."

"Do you recall talking to the police on March eleventh, the day after the victim's body was found?"

"Yes. They advised me that they thought the victim had died of a Percodan overdose."

"Did you ever meet Karen Winslett?"

"Not that I was aware of."

"Was Paul Mack a photographer?"

"No, not that I knew of."

"Did Mr. Mack ever talk to you about a Budweiser calendar?"

"No."

"And you were in communication almost every other day during this period of time, the first couple of months of that year?"

"Yes."

"Thank you, Dr. Warren." Clifton faced the judge. "That's all the questions I have, Your Honor."

"No questions." Statlin signaled to the judge.

The judge turned his chair towards Ted Warren and looked down at him. "Thank you, Dr. Warren. You are excused, but you must hold yourself available for recall if that becomes necessary. You must return to court on reasonable notification if either side requests that you return."

Ted nonchalantly gave his thanks, stood up, stretched his legs and was escorted out of the courtroom by the bailiff. Although he did not look at Paul Mack, he had to know that his revelations linking Mack to the drug that had killed Karen Winslett did his former patient and friend no good.

Hours passed. As the men and women who were to testify stood in the hall waiting, then strode in and out of the courtroom, Margie tried to figure out what the jury's impression of each of them would be. By the end of the first day, Margie was very anxious. She didn't know if she could wait until the end of the trial to learn what was happening in the courtroom.

As the days wore on, Margie's mood was too serious for small talk. At lunch and back at the hotel with Nickie, Margie was often silent, wanting to put her own thoughts in order.

Every night and morning, she watched the television reports

and read the newspaper accounts. They, too, added to the emerging picture of the devious man she had married. She grew to dread the next day when more witnesses would shed light on the man she had fallen in love with, Sean Paul Lanier. A man whom she felt more and more sure, she knew not at all.

# CHAPTER TWENTY-SIX

## More Truths

It was Liza Barnes, Karen Winslett's good friend, who added a revealing personal dimension—that of warmth and spirit—to the impression of the young murdered woman.

This portrait began to take shape after the preliminaries, when Statlin's questions turned to Liza's last conversation with Karen Winslett.

"During the course of your telephone conversation with Ms. Winslett, did she discuss with you any plans concerning a modeling job?" Gene Statlin asked.

"Yes."

"Could you—"

Liza's lip quivered. "She was very excited and proud she was going to meet with Paul Mack on Thursday morning to do a Budweiser calendar commercial and we were going to meet for lunch after that."

Judge Robertson interrupted, "Hold on just a moment, please. Mr. Reporter, would you read the last question and answer, please." The reporter read back the question and answer.

"All right," the judge stated and motioned for Statlin to continue.

Statlin moved in. "When you say 'do'—she was going to do, what was she going to do?"

"Do, as far as the calendar promotion? She was going to model for that commercial."

"Was it your understanding she was going to be photographed?"

"Yes."

"Did she tell you specifically who set this up?"

"She said that Paul Mack had arranged it."

"Did she ever talk to you about how much money she would make for doing this?"

"No. No." Liza shook her head. "Just that she couldn't believe her good luck and I told her she deserved it. She had worked so hard for a chance."

"Did she discuss with you her plans for later on that day? That is, after she would meet you for lunch?"

"I think she had to be at work, and that was my day off, so, no, that was pretty much it."

"Whereabouts did you make arrangements to meet her?"

"Over by the Chowder Pot and Ruby's Cafe, right there in the parking lot."

"Did you often have lunch with Ms. Winslett over the course of your relationship with her as friends?"

"Oh, frequently, yes, and we would talk and kid each other a lot," Liza said, brightening, as if remembering happier times.

"That Thursday, at the time when you were supposed to meet her, did you go to that location that you have described?"

"Yes, I did."

"Were you alone?"

"Yes."

"Did Karen show up?"

Liza bit her lip and a tear rolled down her cheek. "No, she did not."

"Did she call?"

She shook her head, the tears coming faster now. "No, she did not."

"Was that unusual, either for her not to show up or not call?"

Liza took a deep breath trying to calm herself. The bailiff handed her a tissue.

"Yes, it was very unusual."

"Why do you say that?"

"Well, she was sometimes late, but she always showed up when we made appointments or agreements to meet each other or whatever. She—or if she couldn't make it she would call and say she couldn't and be genuinely sorry she had put the other person out. Karen was very thoughtful, you know."

Statlin asked his final question. "Did you ever know Ms. Winslett to use or take the prescription drug Percodan the whole time you ever knew her?"

"No, I didn't," Liza said firmly. "Never."

Statlin smiled at Liza as if to say, You're doing fine, and then turned toward the judge. "I have no further questions."

Although Defense Attorney Jim Clifton tried to shake her testimony, Karen Winslett's quiet, sincere best friend made a lasting impression on those who heard her words.

With the next witness, another piece of the puzzle fell in place. This one not only put Mack in a location where he professed several times he never was—the area where Karen Winslett's car with her body in it was found—but it placed him there the day of the murder. This testimony was furnished by Chris Jackson, an old friend of Paul Mack's in California before the con man had fled to Utah. It was Chris who, at the time Paul disappeared from Sacramento, felt compelled to give the police critical information.

After the preliminaries, Statlin asked a few questions about Chris's relationship with Paul Mack and how they met. Then he zeroed in on the time of the murder.

"On February 19, 1987, in the afternoon hours at about 1:45 did you receive a telephone call from anybody?"

"Yes I did."

"Who did you receive it from?"

"It was—Paul called me that day."

"When you say 'Paul,' the person you know as Paul Mack, is he in this courtroom today?"

"Yes, he is."

"Can you tell me where he is located and what he is wearing so the jury knows who you are talking about please?"

Chris looked at Paul. "He's at the table, wearing a dark gray suit and a white silk shirt."

"May the record reflect he has identified the defendant?"

Judge Robertson answered, "Yes."

"Now when you talked to Mr. Mack on the telephone on the nineteenth at about 1:45 did he ask you to do anything?"

"Yes, he did."

"What did he ask you to do?" Statlin's voice had a razor edge.

With a quick glance at Mack, Jackson replied, "He asked me to come to the service station, the Arco service station at Walerga and Hillsdale, and give him a ride home."

Statlin paused a moment, letting the jury absorb this critical piece of evidence. Then he went on. "Did he indicate to you where he was calling from, specifically, when he made this call?"

"Yes, he said he was calling from the Arco station."

"And did he tell you the intersection, the specific intersection that he was at, at that Arco station?"

"Yes, he did."

"Which one was that?"

"Hillsdale and Walerga."

"Right." Statlin once again turned toward the jury. He did not have to remind them that the cross street was very near where Karen Winslett's body was found. He just paused for a moment and looked tellingly at Paul Mack.

"Now what did he say?"

"He told me that he had had an argument with a person that he was riding with, some female, and she let him out at that intersection and he needed a ride home."

"Was that essentially the extent of the conversation that you had with Mr. Mack?"

"Well, I told him that I was busy and I had some customers over there, and he told me that he had an appointment at approximately 2:30. I don't know where. And he needed a ride. So I told him I would do my best to give him a ride."

Statlin prodded him. "What did you do after you talked to Mr. Mack and told him that you would use your best efforts to give him a ride home?"

"I told him to go ahead and start walking down Hillsdale and I went back in the garage and I told the people I was with

I had a friend that was stranded and I was going to leave and give him a ride home."

"Did you do that?"

"Yes, I did."

Statlin fleshed out the scene. "About what time did you leave your house?"

"Oh, approximately two o'clock."

"Roughly ten or fifteen minutes after you originally got the call from Mr. Mack?"

"Probably ten minutes."

"Where did you drive to?"

"Toward the Arco station at Walerga and Hillsdale. Probably three quarters of a mile approximately."

"And did you stop and pick him up?"

"Yes, I did."

"Once you picked Mr. Mack up, did you take him anywhere?"

"Yes, I took him to his house."

Having finished his questions, Statlin waited wearily as Jim Clifton tried to shake Chris Jackson's testimony in his cross-examination, returning to the moment at which Jackson had picked Mack up.

At first Clifton tried to show that Mack was calm, not distraught and so didn't have the state of mind of a man who had just committed a murder.

"And what was his demeanor at that time?"

"I didn't think it was anything—I didn't really notice anything different."

"He didn't seem excited or anything?"

"No, I don't recall."

"Did he seem out of breath?"

"No, I don't believe so."

"Did he seem fairly just routine, the way you had seen him before?"

"Yes."

"Now he indicated to you on the telephone that he had had an argument with the person he was riding with and that person kicked him out of the car; is that correct?"

"Yes."

"Did he give you any more details than that?"

"No."

Clifton's questions and Chris Jackson's answers about the pick-up continued for a short while longer. When Clifton was unable to shake the man's testimony, he turned to another subject, trying to show that Jackson was involved in Mack's purported drug use.

"Didn't you sell him cocaine on a regular basis?" Clifton asked suddenly.

"No," Jackson responded.

Statlin stood up. "I'm going to object and move to strike."

Judge Robertson shook his head. "I sustain the objection. I would like to go into that after the jury is excused this afternoon. I don't want this witness asked any further questions on that subject."

"May we approach the bench?" Clifton asked.

"Yes," Judge Robertson answered, motioning them to come forward.

The two attorneys went back and forth in hushed tones with the judge acting as referee. Finally, the judge made a decision on the matter and sent the two attorneys back to their tables.

Robertson then announced, "Ladies and gentlemen of the jury, I will ask you to step in the hallway for just a moment, please.

"Please remember and heed the admonition," the judge continued. "Return to court when the bailiff asks you to. This will not take very long, just a very few minutes."

The jury and alternates quickly filed out of the courtroom.

In the hallway, Margie looked at the men and women of the jury. Their impassive faces masked their emotions. They looked weary and beleaguered, as she knew she must look. Trying to figure out the real identity of Paul Mack was a tiring and long procedure in which one had to separate what only seemed real from what actually was real. She felt sorry for them all and for a moment, she felt sorry for herself. But she refused to give in to that. She was here, as the members of the jury were, to get at the whole truth.

Inside, as soon as the courtroom closed, Judge Robertson said, "We are meeting in open court out of the presence of the jury. Both attorneys are present. Mr. Mack is present. The witness is present."

The judge turned toward Chris Jackson. "Mr. Jackson, you know under the fourth and fifteenth amendments to the United States Constitution and under the California Constitution, you have the privilege against compelled self-incrimination and you can not be compelled to incriminate yourself. That means you have the right not to answer the last question about selling cocaine and any related question. And you have the right to consult with an attorney if you think you need to do so before you decide whether you want to answer any such questions.

"Do you understand what I have told you?"

Chris looked up at the judge. "Yes, sir," he said soberly.

"All right." Judge Robertson nodded his approval. "Bring the jury back, bailiff, please."

The bailiff stepped outside and then, as quickly as they had left, the members of the jury and the alternates entered the courtroom and returned to their seats. Clifton continued his cross-examination of Chris Jackson.

"Did you sell or provide cocaine to Mr. Mack in 1987?"

"No," Jackson said confidently, looking right at Mack.

Mack glared back at him.

Clifton took a deep breath and let it out. "Did you ever come forward and tell the police about this telephone call, or did they contact you?"

"I came forward."

"Who did you come forward to?"

"The man that introduced me to Paul, the police—the Sheriff's Department was going to interview him and so I told him to go ahead and have them contact me while he was being interviewed so I could go ahead and tell them what had happened."

Clifton glanced down at his notes. "That wasn't until April twenty-first; correct?"

Jackson looked thoughtful and then slowly replied, "I don't remember, really. It was shortly after he left town."

Clifton finished up his questions. Now Statlin would take the opportunity to ask Chris Jackson some more questions on redirect examination. He told the judge he only had a few questions to ask.

Statlin began, "Mr. Jackson, until Mr. Mack fled, you had no idea he was a suspect in this case; is that correct?"

"That's correct," Jackson replied without hesitation.

"So you didn't know that you had information that was important until he took off and it was in the news; right?"

Clifton was up. "Objection. Leading."

"Sustained," Robertson called out.

"When was it that you realized that this incident on the afternoon of February nineteenth was truly important to the cops?"

"It must have been just about the time—the date on that interview."

"Was that after the news hit that he had fled?"

"I'm sure it was."

"No further questions."

Another long day of testimony came to an end. For Margie, it was an exercise in patience and endurance. Seeing all the people with their grim faces being called to testify, some with familiar names and faces, others unknown to her, made Margie anticipate her chance to tell the truth on the witness stand all the more. As much as she wanted to hear what the other witnesses had said, she felt sure her testimony was vitally important. Difficult as it would be to sit in the same room with the husband she never really knew, she looked forward to her chance to let the jury hear the truth as she lived it. In fact, the knowledge that her chance would come was one of the few things that helped her get through each day sitting outside the courtroom. Margie was anxious, but she told herself over and over, *My turn is coming very soon.*

## CHAPTER TWENTY-SEVEN

# Gerry Sue

As time went on, many of the witnesses blurred together in Margie's mind. Some of the witnesses that appeared Margie knew or read about. Some, like Greg Harvey and Gerry Sue, Margie had known would be testifying. Others, like Dee Taylor, whom Paul Mack had told about the photo session with Karen Winslett that he later denied, were surprises. Nevertheless, Dee Taylor, Todd Mack, Chris Jackson, and the others, for Margie, added segments of the awful truth about Paul's actions the day Karen Winslett was murdered.

The witness who provoked the most comments was Paul Mack's Salt Lake City roommate. Dressed in an attractive gray suit and red satin blouse, Gerry Sue Conway stood outside the courtroom one afternoon, her face puckered in thought. She was so engrossed she did not see Margie, who had been to the ladies room and was returning to her post outside the courtroom. She passed so close Margie could have reached out and touched her. Unlike Margie, Gerry Sue ignored the people passing in and out and kept her large and expressive eyes riveted on the door to the courtroom. Gerry Sue was tall enough that each time the door opened she could see Paul at the defense table. She had eyes only for him.

Margie sighed. It was hard to break Paul's spell. No one knew that better than she.

After she was called into the courtroom and the routine preliminaries were completed, Statlin asked Gerry Sue, who had settled herself in the witness chair, crossing her legs demurely, "Ma'am, I would like to have you think back in time to about April, May, 1987. Can you tell us where you were living during that period of time?"

"I was living in Salt Lake City at the Timber Creek Apartments," she said in her deep, throaty voice that attracted and held attention.

"In approximately late April of 1987, early May of 1987, did you come to meet a man known to you as Sean Paul Lanier?" Statlin asked.

Her eyes still on Paul, Gerry Sue replied, "Yes, I did."

"Could you describe the circumstances under which you first had contact with this man known as Sean Paul Lanier?"

"It was in answer to an ad in the newspaper for a roommate."

"Did you respond to that ad?"

"Yes, I did."

"Your Honor, I will object to the relevance of this testimony," Clifton declared.

"Would you approach the bench please, counsel."

The two attorneys conferred with the judge at his bench for a few minutes. When they were finished, the judge called out, "The objection is overruled."

Statlin stroked his chin, obviously unnerved by the interruption. "I forgot where we were, but I think I asked you if you responded to the ad?"

"Yes, I did."

"And who did you contact when you responded to the ad concerning whatever it was, the apartment?"

"In the room here?"

"Yes."

"The gentlemen in the gray suit."

Statlin raised his eyes and said calmly, "May the record reflect she is indicating the defendant?"

Robertson nodded. "Yes."

"Did he introduce himself to you?"

"Yes, he did."

"What name did he introduce himself by?"

"Sean Paul Lanier."

"Did he ever refer to himself as Paul Mack?"

"No."

"Now, did you enter into an arrangement whereby you shared the apartment pursuant to that ad?"

"Yes, I did."

"Approximately when did you move in with and share the apartment with Sean Paul Lanier, Mr. Mack?"

"March or April of that year, 1987."

"Now approximately how long did you live with Sean Paul Lanier in that apartment?"

"It is difficult to remember. I would say six months."

"During the time that you stayed or shared the apartment with Mr. Mack, our defendant, known to you as Sean Paul Lanier, did he ever ask you to obtain any medication for him?"

"Just one," Gerry Sue said glancing over at the defendant while biting her lip.

"What medication?"

Gerry Sue hesitated before answering grudgingly, "Percodan."

"Approximately how many times did he ask you to do this?"

She sighed. "I couldn't remember the number of times."

"Was it more than once?"

"More than once." She nodded.

"Did you ever know him to take Percodan?"

"I never observed him taking it," she said very softly, looking at Mack sympathetically.

"I'm sorry?" Statlin said.

Judge Robertson inclined his head. "I didn't hear you either."

"I never observed him taking it," Gerry Sue repeated a bit louder.

"Did you have any friends who had access potentially to drugs like Percodan?"

"Just one who could possibly get it."

"Did you ever have discussion with Mr. Mack as to your friend's access to Percodan?"

"Yes, I did."

"What were those discussions?"

Clifton stood up. "Objection. Hearsay."

Robertson said curtly, "Overruled."

Then the judge turned to the witness and said, "Answer the question, please."

Gerry Sue replied softly, "He just wanted to know if I could obtain some for him and if I had any friends who could do so."

"Did he refer to this drug specifically by name?"

"Yes, sir."

"What did he call it?"

"Either Percodan or perks. I don't remember."

"No further questions."

Judge Robertson looked at the defense lawyer. "Cross-examine, Mr. Clifton."

Clifton walked toward the witness chair and gave Gerry Sue a cool, wary gaze.

"Ma'am, did you ever actually see him take Percodan?"

"No, sir."

"Did he tell you what he wanted Percodan for?"

"No, sir."

"Did he suffer from migraine headaches?"

"I don't recall any discussions about headaches."

"Do you recall any discussion about dental pain that he suffered from?"

"No, sir."

"How long did you say you lived with him?"

"Approximately six months."

"Ms. Conway, I apologize for getting personal, but what was the name that you were using at the time that you were living with Mr. Mack?"

"I object to relevance."

"Overruled. Answer the question, please."

"The same name that I have now."

Clifton drew a deep breath, paused to look at the defendant and fired his verbal bullet. "Wasn't your name Gary David Conway at that time?"

"No. It was Gary Davis Conway."

"You were a man at that time; were you not?"

"Yes, I was."

There were audible gasps from the spectators and even the jury.

"I object on relevance. What does this have to do with anything?"

"What is the relevance, Mr. Clifton?"

In what must have been tongue in cheek, Clifton said, "I think the impression has been created that this witness and Paul Mack were boyfriend and girlfriend, and I think I need to dispel that impression."

Robertson was not amused but relented. "The objection is overruled. The answer stands."

"You weren't living together as boyfriend, girlfriend; were you?"

"No."

"You had separate bedrooms?"

There were more whispers from the spectators, this time growing louder. Robertson rapped on his gavel sharply.

"Yes, sir."

"Thank you. That's all I have."

"No questions," Statlin said on redirect.

The judge looked down at the witness. "Thank you. You are excused."

"Thank you."

"Do you want this witness subject to recall?"

"No," Clifton said firmly. Quiet laughter hung in the courtroom. Though there was much to admire in Clifton's deft handling of a difficult case, this was truly not one of his finer moments.

Nickie came out to tell Margie that Gerry Sue's testimony produced the only moments of levity in the otherwise tense proceeding. Nevertheless, Margie knew what for some were a few moments of fun must have left the person at whose expense they were filled with pain. Nickie sat down and went on to tell Margie about Gerry Sue's testimony. At that moment, one of the officers opened the doors to the courtroom and Gerry Sue swept up the aisle. Margie looked in and got a good look at the jury. All sixteen rapt faces were riveted on the departing witness. In fact, even Judge Robertson, who always conducted himself with dignity, looked taken back. He rested his forearms on the bench and clasped his hands together in what looked like a prayer for decorum. Despite this, loud murmurs erupted all over the courtroom and the judge snapped to attention, bringing his gavel sharply down. The bang echoed through the corridors.

# CHAPTER TWENTY-EIGHT

# *Unraveling Lies*

ON the day when Margie saw Paul Mack's brother, Todd, his resemblance to Paul gave her heart a pang and identified him immediately. In that moment, a gust of intermingled emotions filled her: regret, excitement, curiosity, and something deeper than interest for she knew he had first lied for his brother and then recanted. His words that morning, she knew, would be devastating for his brother. He looked over at her with a cool, wary gaze. *I know he must recognize me from the wedding pictures Sean sent him. He must be thinking, This is one of the many women who shared Paul's life.*

She got up and walked over to him. "Hi. I'm Margie," she said quietly.

"I know," he replied.

"This must be as hard for you as it is for me."

He nodded.

"But I feel this is the way it has to be," she said. "We all need the truth no matter how difficult it is to tell."

"It's hard though."

"Very hard," she agreed and looked into his eyes, so like Sean's in color, but otherwise so different. When Todd's eyes met hers, she saw a grieving soul.

In moments, the doors opened and she heard his name called. As he turned to go, Margie gazed after him, wondering what it would be like for him in the courtroom.

Judge Robertson called out to Todd, who was slowly making his way from the back of the room, "Step forward, please."

Todd did as he was told. When he reached the witness stand, the judge told Todd, "Raise your right hand."

The clerk holding the Bible then said, "Do you solemnly swear the testimony you are about to give will be the truth, the whole truth, and nothing but the truth, so help you God?"

Todd Mack looked toward the hallway and then answered quietly, "I do."

"Have a seat, please. State your full name and spell your last name."

Todd cleared his throat. "Todd Michael Mack, M-a-c-k."

"Mr. Statlin, go ahead," Judge Robertson advised.

"Thank you," Statlin responded.

"Mr. Mack, do you know Paul Steven Mack, the defendant in this case?"

"Yes, I do."

"Is he in this courtroom today?"

"Yes.

"Could I have you describe what he is wearing?"

Todd looked at his brother. "A gray tweed coat, black pants, and what looks like a white shirt."

"May the record reflect he has indicated the defendant and described his clothing?"

Judge Robertson nodded. "Yes."

"What is your relationship to the defendant in this case?"

"Paul is my brother." Todd again looked sadly at his brother.

"I want to have you think back to around February of 1987. Do you have that approximate period of time in mind, sir?"

Todd's attention went back to the prosecutor. "Yes, sir," he said politely.

"Can you tell the jury where you were living?"

Todd began explaining his living arrangements and discussed the fact that he still held the same job. Todd then revealed that he did not see Paul on the day of the murder—as Paul had claimed—but that the next day he received a telephone call at work.

"Who did you receive the telephone call from?" Statlin probed.

"My brother," Todd answered.

"And what was the conversation that you had?"

"That he wanted me to meet with him at the Roseville Auction the following morning after I got off work."

"Did he indicate to you anything further than what you have related; that is, as to whether it was important, unimportant? What did he say?"

"He mentioned it was very important."

"Did you agree to do that, sir?"

"Yes."

"The following morning would have been February twenty-first," Statlin noted and then continued. "Did you go to the auction in conjunction with a conversation that you had with your brother the night before?"

"Yes, I did."

"About what time did you arrive there?"

Todd paused a moment and then answered, "It was sometime around nine, ten A.M."

"Were you alone or were you with anybody?"

"No, I was alone."

"Did you meet with your brother at the auction on Saturday the twenty-first?"

"Yes."

"When you met with your brother on that Saturday morning the twenty-first, did he ask you to do anything?"

"Yes."

"What did he ask you to do?"

"He asked me to alibi for him for the Thursday."

"Tell me exactly what he said to you with respect to how this alibi was to be, what it consisted of?"

Todd looked uncomfortable as he shifted in his seat. "Basically that he was with me that Thursday morning from approximately nine until about one o'clock in the afternoon."

"That was not true?"

Todd bit his lip. "No. He hadn't been with me that day."

"Did you agree to do that alibi for him?"

Todd looked down. "Yes," he said quietly and sighed.

"Now did he tell you why he wanted this alibi?"

"Yes."

"What did he say?"

"He mentioned the fact that the boyfriend of Karen, I believe, went over to see him."

Pausing, Statlin gestured to the jury. "What else did he say was the reason for the need of an alibi?"

Todd look at his brother and took an audible rumbling breath. "Basically he was concerned because of his past with the law, and that he had—she hadn't actually shown up. There was mention of a telephone conversation, that he was thinking about the possibility of hiring her for some work—sales work with the firm he was working for, and that she had not—or she had made plans, mentioned something to him about moving to San Diego, so he had told her that there was really no reason for her to come over. And—"

Statlin wasn't going to take a chance that there would be an objection. "Let's take it one step at a time as to what he told you," Statlin interrupted. "First of all, did he indicate whether or not somebody was looking for a particular person?"

"Yes."

Statlin's eyebrows knit together as he continued to rapid-fire questions which one by one dismantled Paul Mack's claims. "Who was the somebody who was looking for a particular person?"

"Paul mentioned her boyfriend."

"Did he know the person by name that the boyfriend was looking for?"

"Yes."

"Did he indicate to you if he knew her before, and, if so, where he had met her?"

"Yes, he indicated that he had met her, I believe it was at the Warehouse Restaurant."

"Did he discuss with you whether or not he actually spoke to her on Thursday morning a time that—which he needed an alibi?"

"Yes, he mentioned that he had talked to her on the phone."

"Did he tell you the substance of the phone conversation that he had with her?"

"Yes, he did."

"You can go ahead and tell us."

"It was basically that he had been considering her for a sales position and that she had mentioned during their conversation that she was thinking about moving to San Diego and that he had, in turn, told her that the appointment—it was unnecessary to keep the appointment because he needed somebody that was going to be around for a while."

"Did he mention anything about modeling?"

"No." Todd shook his head.

"Did he mention anything about a Budweiser calendar or Bud advertisement to you?"

"No, he didn't."

"Did he tell you to whom you were supposed to relate this false alibi?"

Todd sat back, answering slowly but clearly. "I believe it might have been, you know, the police."

Clifton shot up from his chair. "I am going to object. Move to strike. No foundation that he knows that. He said that he just believes it might have been."

Judge Robertson nodded. "The motion is granted. The last portion of the answer is stricken from the record and must be disregarded by the jury trial."

Statlin let a moment or two of silence fill the courtroom. He knew as Clifton and the judge did, it was too late. The jury would remember. He continued. "Did he tell you what he actually did that day?"

"Yes, he mentioned that he had been at home, that he had gone out to run a couple of errands and was back at the house and then later that afternoon he was going to a hair appointment, I believe."

After asking a few more ancillary questions, Statlin moved in once again.

"This false alibi that he asked you to back up for him, did you later—when you were interviewed by the police, give them that false alibi?"

"Yes."

"In other words, you lied for your brother?"

"Yes."

"Did there come a point in time in approximately April—

late March or April of 1987, a little over a month later that
you later told the police the truth?"

The eyes of every juror were fixed on the ashen face of
Todd Mack, who, like the brother of the Unabomber Ted Kac-
zynski, had tried to support and then came to terms with his
brother's guilt.

"Yes."

"Todd, what prompted you to tell the police the truth finally?"

"Basically," Todd Mack sighed heavily and then went on,
"two reasons. One is that he was going to turn himself in, and
he didn't. He fled town. And the other being that an arrest
warrant was issued for him."

"You realized this was now serious and you decided you
better tell the truth?"

Clifton said, "Objection. Leading."

But Todd answered, "Yes."

"Sustained," Judge Robertson declared, but the telling effect on the jury was still evident.


On the day when Dee Taylor, an old friend of Paul Mack's,
was called as a witness on behalf of the people, even the bailiff
spoke to the petite blond softly.

"Would you step right up here, ma'am, please?"

"Do you solemnly swear the testimony you are about to
give will be the truth, the whole truth and nothing but the
truth, so help you God?"

"Yes I do."

"Have a seat, please."

"State your full name and spell your last name."

"Dee Taylor, T-a-y-l-o-r."

"Thank you."

Statlin followed suit. "Ms. Taylor," he said gently, "do you
know the defendant in this case, Paul Mack?"

"Yes," she said quietly.

"Is he in this courtroom today, the man you know as Paul
Mack?"

"Yes."

"Could I have you describe what he is wearing today?"

She looked at Paul and sighed. "Black suit, gray shirt, boots."

"Is he seated at counsel table here to your right, my left?"

"Right."

"And did there come a time in approximately May 1987 where you received a phone call from Paul Mack?"

"Yes."

"During that call, did he sound to you to be depressed or down?"

"Yes" she said, so softly, the jurors all bent forward in unison.

"And did you ask him why he was depressed or down?"

"Um-hmm. Yes, I did."

"And what did he say?"

The questions seemed to startle her. "Well, at first he, you know," she gave a shy smile, "just said he wasn't feeling, you know, too good. He was depressed. And I kept asking him what was wrong and different things. And he said, you know, that he didn't want to tell me. Because he didn't want to involve me in anything. And finally, I talked to him and got him to tell me what was wrong."

"Did he begin to tell you what was wrong?"

"Yes, he did." She nodded.

Statlin pried the answers from her in measured pace. "Did he go on to tell you about the girl that he was involved with in this California trouble?"

"Well, he had told me that there was an incident there and that they were claiming that he did something that he didn't do."

"Did he tell you what the girl did?"

And now Dee hesitatingly added her piece to the puzzle. For Paul Mack had denied knowing anything about Karen Winslett's modeling. "Well, it was to do with a modeling appointment of some—some photo session or something where he was going to promote shirts and suspenders and different things."

"Do you remember talking to the police about this telephone conversation? They came back and visited you, two cops?"

"Uh-huh."

"Answer yes or no, please," Judge Robertson requested.

"Yes," she said a little nervously.

Statlin prodded. "On or about November 6, 1988?"

"Yes."

"Do you remember telling them about this telephone conversation?"

"Yes."

"And did you tell them the truth at that point in time?"

"From what I could remember."

Dee Taylor told the filled courtroom how she talked to Paul Mack about Karen Winslett's modeling—another identification Mack denied ever making.

It was obvious that like many who had known and cared about Paul Mack, Dee Taylor was a reluctant witness. But this did little to ameliorate the impression of Paul Mack which was being constructed piece by piece. Still, the jury just kept glancing over at the relaxed, smiling Mack as if trying to decide if he really could have done it.

# CHAPTER TWENTY-NINE

## *Walking Alone*

ON the morning Margie was supposed to testify, Detective Frank stood beside her in the hallway as she waited to be called.

"I thought you might need support," he told her. "Just remember, you're strong, you'll do fine."

The bailiff opened the courtroom door and motioned for Margie to enter. Margie looked at Detective Frank and said, "This is it," and drew in a deep breath. Detective Frank smiled as he took Margie's arm and led her toward the courtroom door. At the door, he let go.

Keeping her head up high and stiffening her back, Margie walked into the courtroom alone. The bailiff then motioned for her to go to the front of the courtroom. Everyone in the room turned and gazed in her direction. The experience was like walking into a party crowded with revelers, and suddenly the music stops and everyone turns to stare at you. Margie's knees shook and her heart pounded.

She made her way to the front, taking deep breaths to try and remain calm. Then, she was there. She stood in front of the witness chair ready to begin her next and hopefully last involvement in the life of Paul Mack, alias Sean Paul Lanier.

"Raise your right hand and repeat after me."

Margie repeated the oath in a quiet voice. Then the bailiff said, "Take the stand."

Margie's eyes scanned the jury. She caught a glimpse of Paul out of the corner of her eye. Everyone watched Margie intently.

The prosecutor began his questions. "Please tell us where you met Paul Mack."

Margie answered with a meek voice. "I met him in Salt Lake City, Utah."

Gene Statlin smiled and said, "Another quiet one."

Margie assumed the other quiet one was Stacy Carter who had testified just before her. The judge asked Margie to speak up and she tried as Statlin led her through the preliminary questions. Finally he brought her to the reason she had come: her relationship with the defendant. She looked over at Paul Mack and her heart beat so loudly she was sure they all heard it.

"What did he tell you his name was?" Statlin asked.

"Sean Paul Lanier."

"A little louder," Judge Robertson interrupted.

"Sean . . . Paul . . . Lanier!" Margie almost yelled as she paused between each name. "It was his first lie, followed by many others," she added. For Margie, it was a moment of truth. A moment she had been waiting for.

And then, with Statlin's careful prodding, she began to discuss how Paul Mack had "met me under the assumed name of Sean Paul Lanier, never told me what his true name was or where he was from. Instead, what he did was tell me a series of stories about his background, how his parents were killed in a plane crash, his daughter was killed in a car wreck, his brother and sister were killed in the same plane crash. He worked for the CIA. He was a government documents carrier. On and on and on.

"He literally created things like a false hospital death certificate to show me to prove, for example, that his daughter died."

Judge Robertson shook his head. "You lost me. Are you saying he did that—as a metaphor, or are you saying he did that, made up a false death certificate to show that his daughter died?"

"Yes."

Robertson was incredulous. "Made up a false death certificate to show that the daughter died."

Statlin intervened. "On the daughter's death certificate—Ms. Danielsen has now met that daughter and knows her to be alive."

Walking up to the judge along with Clifton, Statlin said quietly and out of earshot of the jury, "I think it a fair inference from the evidence the so-called sales people list which was provided to the police by the defendant on February twenty-first was nothing more than a cover-up to try and explain, if you will, with legitimate circumstances, how the defendant could have had contact with Ms. Winslett, Karen Winslett.

"It is our position that from the evidence that the Court has heard in this case that is a false document, it is nothing more than a cover-up, just like the false alibi and that this subsequent evidence shows that this is what Mr. Mack would do, the lengths that he would go to create false documents to support what we know to be lies."

The prosecutor asked the judge to allow Margie to amplify her testimony about all the rest of Sean Lanier's lies.

Gene Statlin resumed his examination of Margie. He next instructed her to point Paul Mack out. The fear left Margie's voice and a quiet strength jumped to her eyes as she looked at this man, this stranger, she hadn't seen for almost two years.

Margie pointed her finger right at Paul and said, "That's him."

"Does he look the same?" Statlin asked.

Margie responded, "Somewhat, except grayer." Paul smiled.

Margie was so nervous her mind was spinning. *When I knew Paul, his hair was wavy and light brown with just a touch of gray. In fact, he had joked about his gray being my fault.* She looked closer. His muscles had been huge, like the muscle-bound hunk on her postcard. She'd known him once but now, like a chameleon, he was a thin man with straight, dark gray hair parted on the side. And yet there was something about him that would never change and Margie knew what it was—those eyes. Those eyes which could be so beautiful and so cruel all at the same time.

Statlin's next question broke Margie out of her thoughts. "Did he ever tell you the truth about who he was?"

The courtroom was hushed, expectant.

"No, never," Margie answered, the strength of her words echoing in the hushed courtroom once again. She stared at Paul Mack and this time he was the one who looked away.

Gene Statlin was through with his questions. James Clifton announced, "I have no questions at this time."

Judge Robertson informed Margie, "You might be requested to testify again at a later date. You may step down."

Outside the courtroom, Detective Frank walked up to Margie and put his arm around her as he asked, "How did it go?"

"I think I did okay," Margie said.

"Oh, I'm sure you did fine." The detective smiled and said, "Just remember if it wasn't for you, we wouldn't have found him. You're a brave lady."

Frank was called into the courtroom next and Margie again sat alone on the bench in the hallway.

A little while later the courtroom door burst open as everyone rushed out into the hallway. Nickie walked up to Margie. She did not ask how Margie felt about her testimony. "Lunch break," she told her.

As they stood there, a man and two women walked up to Nickie and Margie. Nickie introduced Paul's parents and his sister to Margie. It was easy to see who Paul got his good looks and personality from. Paul's father, Robert Mack, was a very charming man with a great sense of humor. His head was topped with thick, gray hair. His features were the same as Paul's with those same charismatic blue eyes. Peter's mother, Frances Mack, seemed tired and nervous. It's *no wonder*, Margie thought, considering the stressful circumstances Paul's mother was under. Her hair was short, stylishly cut and light brown. Her eyes were a beautiful, clear green and she wore little makeup. Carly, Paul's sister, was outgoing and easy to talk with. She was plump but pretty with short dark hair and eyes that shone with the same beautiful color of blue as Paul's. Todd, Paul's brother, had not come back to court since his testimony.

The group walked outside together, pausing before walking down the stairs to the street. They took in the California sun and felt the wind gently blow across their path. Paul's father seemed to want to lift their spirits. He joked about California drivers and the smog. Paul's mother was still serious and forlorn. Paul's sister laughed at her father's remarks. Carly left to retrieve their car from the parking garage. The rest of the group sauntered down the cement sidewalk, pausing often to chat and waiting for Carly to pull up.

Suddenly, as they stood there, Paul's attorney, Jim Clifton, walked up. He shook Robert Mack's hand and commented on the beautiful day. Clifton said hello to Margie and handed her a note from Paul before leaving. Shocked, Margie opened the piece of paper cautiously.

The note read, "You're so much prettier than Stacy."

Margie rumpled the note up, walked over, and threw the paper in the garbage can.

*Another con*, she thought.

As she walked back to where everyone was standing, Margie saw Paul's mother, who had heard the exchange, watching her wistfully with tears in her eyes.

When Bob Mack asked them to dinner, Margie quickly agreed. It would be a chance, she hoped, to get answers to some of the questions she'd had for so long.

After Bob and Frances got in the car and Carly pulled away, Margie and Nickie went to a little Mexican restaurant nearby. Once inside, their conversation consisted of everything except Paul Mack. They talked about the lovely California weather, a trip they were planning, and Nickie going to college. It had been a long morning and Margie felt that Nickie had enough to dwell upon after hearing Margie's testimony. She didn't want to add to what she knew must be one of the most difficult days of Nickie's life.

That night, Margie sat next to Bob Mack at dinner and listened to his every word with interest. Bob was as charming as before. Frances sat quietly, deep in thought, yet it was only she who spoke at all of Paul's childhood in response to Margie's questions.

"Was he a happy child?"

"I thought so," his mother murmured.

"Had he been close to his siblings?" Margie asked

"Yes, for a while," Frances answered quietly.

Margie continued probing. "When had he first gotten into trouble?"

"He finished high school in prison, in prison," Frances told her brokenly. "He was only fourteen," she continued. "We just didn't know." She wiped away a tear.

Margie knew that every family had secrets, some of which they couldn't handle, some locked away never to be told.

It was obvious Paul's parents, and particularly his mother, were suffering and found it painful to remember. Finally, Margie gave up. If the secrets to Paul's criminal behavior lay in his childhood, his parents didn't know, or perhaps, didn't want to know.

Instead, Margie listened and watched these people, strangers really, except for Nickie, and quietly wondered about their lives. Paul's parents began to relax as they talked about their travels in their motor home. Nickie talked with them about going back to school.

As soon as Margie and Nickie returned to their hotel room, the telephone rang, breaking the silence.

Nickie picked it up as Margie stepped into the bathroom. "Margie, the phone is for you," she called. Surprised, Margie walked over to where Nickie was standing.

"It's my father," she whispered, her hand covering the speaker.

Margie sat down on the edge of the bed to try to calm herself. Then she motioned to Nickie to hand her the phone. "Hello," she stuttered.

"Hi, honey. How was dinner?" Paul asked calmly.

Startled, Margie managed to mutter, "Fine." Then she added, "You find me wherever I go! I want it to stop!"

As if not hearing what she had just exclaimed, Paul said, "Why don't you have Nickie bring you over to see me tonight? I'd like to see you before you leave tomorrow."

"I don't think so," Margie answered disgustedly.

There was a pause. "I have to go," Margie said quickly and hung up the phone.

After Nickie had gone to sleep, Margie phoned Darrel. "He wants," Margie said, "to see if the rest of the world can be as easily conned as those of us who were so charmed by him."

She knew, as always, Paul Steven Mack would have answers for everything.

The prosecution's presentation of witnesses and evidence was over. Now it was time for the defense. Clifton tried to attack every aspect of the prosecutor's case he could, even bringing in an expert who attempted to dispute the coroner's findings. However, the question on everyone's minds—the media, the spectators, and the jury—was, would Jim Clifton put Paul Mack on the stand? It was debated on the front steps of the courthouse, in the hallway where Margie sat each day, and by the media on the television and in the newspapers.

The answer finally came. Paul Mack wanted to testify and what Paul Mack wanted, Paul Mack got.

# CHAPTER THIRTY

## *The Chameleon*

DRESSED in a British-cut navy blazer and gray pants, looking relaxed and attractive as always, Paul Mack walked to the stand while spectators gawked. Settling himself in the witness chair, his manner was casual, as if he was the gentlemanly neighbor so many had thought him, coming over for a chat. Even on trial for murder, Paul Steven Mack, as Margie well knew, had style and charisma.

All the jurors, leaning forward in their chairs, looked at him expectantly, eager to hear what he had to say. Turning his head toward them for a moment, Paul smiled, and at that moment was eminently likeable. Spectators had jammed the courtroom to see him. People stood along the back and sides of the room. The door was slightly ajar. Margie could see Paul and he obviously enjoyed all the attention.

Even as his lawyer began to bring out the shady elements of his past, that aura of guilelessness, that somehow fate had badly treated him, still hung on.

"Paul, between 1971 and 1983 were you convicted of five felonies involving theft?"

"Yes, I was," Mack said shyly, as if he had played boyish pranks.

"Were you convicted of specifically forgery in 1971 and 1975?"

"Yes," he answered demurely.

"And were you convicted of theft on two occasions in 1980?"

"Yes," he said, looking innocent. And then he shrugged as if to say, *Boys will be boys. We all get in trouble when we're young*, and the spectators seemed to respond in kind.

"And were you convicted of possession of stolen property in 1983?"

"Yes."

Several jurors shook their heads in amazement. They all looked at him expectantly, leaning forward in their chairs, anxious to hear more about him.

"Since 1983, have you been convicted of any felonies?"

"No."

With that answer, Paul Mack settled back in his chair and became his affable self, relieved perhaps that the shortened laundry list of his past sins was out of the way.

Clifton took a quick glance at his notes and visibly relaxed himself. "Now, in late 1986 what was your occupation?"

"I had my own business," Mack replied, smiling just a little bit at the women in the audience who smiled back at him.

"What kind of business was it?" Clifton was energized by the spectators' response to his client.

"Originally I started with a company I called Suspender World." Mack leaned back in his chair.

"And what did that business do?"

"Basically, sales of suspenders to businesses with their names, their logos, and things like that on them," Mack said as if chatting with a friend, instead of sitting in a courtroom on trial for murder.

"The company was Suspender World?" Clifton confirmed.

"Yes."

"Did you own that company?"

"Yes." Mack smiled.

"And did you have any other business in 1986?"

"I also began a business called World Advertising."

"And what did that business do?"

Paul had easily made the transition from felon to respectable businessman. "You have to appreciate his chutzpah," Statlin murmured to his assistant as he watched the master showman on the witness stand.

"We basically picked up advertising items that I hadn't sold before," Mack said proudly. "I found when I went to the clients, they wanted a lot more than just suspenders, so I began covering everything I could from pencils to matchbooks to T-shirts, jackets, hats."

"And generally how did you get clients for that business?"

"Cold calling."

"What does that mean?"

"Just contacting businesses. I would start with people I knew in different businesses and then try to get referrals from them and got involved with the softball teams in Sacramento and the Pig Bowl and police olympics, all kinds of things."

"Your client base was made up of what kind of businesses, generally?"

"Any kind of business," he answered nonchalantly.

"Did you do business with hotels and motels?"

"Yes, hotels and restaurants, I would suppose would be primarily because of my background in that business."

"And you have a background in the restaurant business?"

"Yes."

"In what capacity?"

"As a chef," Mack said, his pride evident.

Clifton shifted gears. "Now in the second half of 1986, did you have occasion to contact the Warehouse Restaurant?"

"Yes, I did."

"And what was your purpose in contacting the Warehouse Restaurant?"

"I was referred to the restaurant by a gentleman I was working with."

"And what was that person's name?"

"Ben Collins."

"What kind of business did he have?"

"He owned a company by the name of S.M.I. which is Sportswear Media Incorporated."

"And what did he do?" Clifton gently prodded.

"What—well, I had met him because whenever I had T-shirt accounts, I would be kind of the middle man. I would sell or I would get the business from you and then take it to him to be printed. He had somebody that did the printing on the shirt or on the jacket or whatever and we ended up being together, working together. I even had a desk in his office."

"Now when you contacted the Warehouse Restaurant, did you meet Karen Winslett?"

"At first I—I went out there to meet Jim Walker." Mack seemed a bit flustered at the mention of Karen Winslett's name, but he quickly regained his composure.

"Who was Jim Walker?"

"He was the manager of the restaurant."

"Now when you went to the Warehouse and talked to Jim Walker about placing an order with you, do you remember what month that was?"

Paul hesitated for a moment. Then, in his most sincere tone replied, "I just feel that it would be after July, like maybe August."

"And did you meet Karen Winslett out there?"

"He brought her out and introduced her to me, yes." Mack gestured as if to say the meeting was inconsequential, hardly enough to take note of.

Clifton nodded and went on. "And what was your understanding of what her capacity was?"

"He asked her to go over the design that they already had from previous business with S.M.I. and decide whether she wanted to stick with that design or redo it for the order that he was placing at the time."

"And what were they ordering at the time?"

"I believe at first it was jackets."

"And so you talked to Karen in person on one occasion at the Warehouse, correct?"

"Just as he introduced me to her and told us to make arrangements to get together."

"And did you at some later time get together with her about this order?"

"Yes, she came to S.M.I. at the office."

"And did you have any telephone contact with her?"

"Probably to arrange her coming down to look, you know. They had—S.M.I. had folders with everybody's previous business in it."

"And did you have any conversation, telephone conversations with Karen between the time you first met her and when she came down to S.M.I. of any significance?"

"Just to have her come in, I guess," Paul said genuinely.

"And when she came in to S.M.I. was she by herself or with anybody?"

"Well, she was by herself. She came in the office there. There were like four or five people that work there."

"And how long did she stay there?"

"I don't know. Fifteen, twenty minutes." Paul, ever the actor, was relegating Karen Winslett to minor player here, likable, but barely noticed by him.

"Did you have any conversations with her about anything other than the order for jackets?"

"Not at that time, that I can remember, no."

"Up to that point had you had any discussions with her at all about another job?"

"No," Paul said firmly.

"At some point did you have problems with respect to the money that the Warehouse owed you?"

"Yes."

"What sort of problems?"

"We couldn't collect," Paul answered smoothly, relaxed and confident. He explained, "Basically, they owed S.M.I. fifteen hundred dollars, and I was trying to collect because I couldn't get paid if I didn't collect."

"Did you have conversations with Karen about your trying to collect money from the Warehouse?"

"Yes, I did," he said genially, implying that would be the natural thing to do.

"And was that in person or on the phone?"

"On the phone."

"About how many conversations would you estimate you had with her about that?"

Mack replied cogently, "I have no idea."

"And what was the nature of the conversations that you had with her?"

"She was friendly. She appeared to be trying to help."

"Did she at some point give you her telephone number?"

"Yes."

"Why was that?"

"During one of the final conversations we had, she basically said, it doesn't look like we are even going to get paid, and I need a job. And you know, she asked me if I thought a woman could sell and so on and so forth in the type of business I was doing. It was just a very brief conversation." Paul stressed the word brief. "She gave me her number and said, Hey, if you have anything, let me know."

"What did you tell her, if anything, definite?"

Ever the nice guy, he had, of course, tried to help her, was the impression he seemed to be trying to convey. "I told her, from what I had been told, a woman could definitely sell for S.M.I. because I was informed on many occasions by Ben Collins that a woman had built this business in the past."

"At some point did you have to sue the Warehouse?"

"Yes, we did," Mack said regretfully.

Clifton moved to another subject.

"Now, do you know Ted Warren?"

"Yes," Paul answered, rolling his eyes. The spectators were with him now, shaking their heads in unison as if to cast aspersions on the dentist. There was no doubt Paul Mack had star quality.

"Did you obtain Percodan from Ted Warren?"

"Yes, sir."

"Prior to the time that you met Ted Warren, had you ever used Percodan to your knowledge?"

"Not to my knowledge," Mack stated, though others had testified he used the substance years before.

"Now, why did you contact Ted Warren the first time?"

"Bad dental problems."

"What sort of dental problems were you having?"

"Root canals more than anything. Just bad teeth."

When Clifton asked if Mack was having difficulty sorting out what his recollections were from the reports put before him of what he's said, Mack nodded and said, "At times." It was the understatement of the trial.

Mack explained that Warren originally gave him Percodan

for his dental work and that he definitely needed it for that. According to Mack, he also had migraine headaches a lot. But then Mack slipped in a bombshell, saying, "I also took it because I was using cocaine at the time."

Though Mack's cocaine use had been mentioned by prosecutor's witnesses, the spectators either had forgotten or found it shocking and in contrast to their impression of Mack himself. Now the intake of breath was audible. Like so many others they were obviously asking themselves who Paul Mack really was.

"When did you start socializing with Ted Warren?"

"Well, there was a period of time that I didn't come in for dental work because I couldn't afford it. And then I started going back in. We began—we would have lunch, talk about business, just hit it off."

Statlin stood up. "I will object and move to strike as non-responsive."

Judge Robertson swiftly declared, "The motion is granted. The answer is stricken from the record."

Clifton tried another tack. "Was there a distinctive time when you started socializing or—and stopped being treated by Ted Warren, or did it all merge together?"

"When I began being treated again it was March of 1986— I believe. From January to March I didn't see him. Then I began seeing him again and we immediately started socializing then."

"You indicated one of the reasons you took Percodan was because you were using cocaine. What did you mean by that?"

"I had begun using cocaine within a number of months prior to this and I would do cocaine on the weekend. I would stay up too long. I would be tired come Monday. And I would take a Percodan and it would get rid of any headache I had, and it seemed to give me energy."

"And what effect did cocaine have on you?"

"It didn't have the effects that I thought it would have. I mean, I could eat, I could sleep at times. Depends upon how much I did. It caused sexual arousal. It made you talk a lot."

"During this period, where did you get your cocaine?"

"Chris Jackson."

Skillfully, Mack had brought into question the validity of Chris Jackson's testimony by labeling him a drug dealer, though Jackson had adamantly denied it.

"Are you aware of any other income other than selling cocaine that he had prior to that time?"

"No."

Now Clifton, with Mack's help, brought another witness's testimony into question.

"And at what point did you start using cocaine with Ted Warren?"

"Right after we became friends and began our, you know, social relationship."

"Did he use cocaine frequently?"

"Yes."

"What was your understanding with Ted Warren about giving him cocaine for the Percodan prescriptions?"

"Well, he knew that the Percodan prescriptions weren't being written for a medical reason, per se, so he would write me the prescription, and I would give him a quarter ounce, which was twenty-five dollars, and we basically just had a mutual agreement that that would be our trade off."

Just as he had done with Chris Jackson, Mack was now trying to demolish Ted Warren's credibility and testimony, not to mention his professional reputation, by implicating him in drug trafficking.

Then Clifton turned to Mack's relationship with Karen Winslett.

"Incidentally, have you ever been a professional photographer?"

"No," Paul said calmly, returning the glances shot at him from the jury box. He seemed so truthful that it made even the prosecutor shake his head in wonderment.

"Have you ever represented yourself as being a professional photographer?"

"No."

"During this period of time, did you have any camera equipment?"

"I think my girlfriend Stacy owned a thirty-five millimeter or something like that."

"Other than that, did you have any lenses?"

"No," Paul said, a sincere smile on his face.

"Any flash attachment?"

"No."

"Any of those kind of umbrellas photographers use, any equipment like that?"

"No."

"Calling your attention to around February thirteenth, 1987, did you have telephone contact with Karen Winslett?"

"No."

"Did you attempt to contact her?"

"Yes."

"What was your reason for trying to contact her?"

"To see if she was still interested in looking for a job, if she was considering looking for a job."

"Had you mentioned to Stacy that you were going to contact her?"

"Yes." It was something Stacy had denied.

Clifton's questions were offered at a staccato pace, as were Mack's answers, as if to say, How could these be lies, I don't even have to consider my reply.

"Did you mention Karen Winslett by name?"

"Yes."

"What number did you call and where did you get the number?"

"It was the number Karen gave me."

"And who answered the phone?"

"A gentleman."

"Did he identify himself at that time?"

"No."

"What did you say to him?"

"I asked him if Karen was there."

"What did he say to you?"

"He said, 'No, she won't be back until the first of the week' or Sunday. One or the other. He said either Sunday or the first of the week."

"Do you remember what day of the week that was?"

"I believe it was Friday."

"Did you attempt to contact her again the following week?"

"Yes."

"What day?"

"Monday or Tuesday, one or the other."

"And were you able to contact her at that time?"

"Yes."

"What did you say to her? What did she say to you?"

There were no stumbling replies, the interplay between client and attorney so smooth it could have been a game of ping-pong or a courtroom scene in a TV drama. And yet, despite this edge, there was something about it that seemed to make the jury uncomfortable now. They were fidgeting in their seats. Margie of course knew what it was. She had felt it—so long—an instinctual feeling of discomfort at what one was hearing over and over without being able to put one's finger on just what wasn't right.

"The conversation was very brief. I simply asked her if she was still looking for a job and she said yes. And I said, I am considering hiring somebody to take over my accounts for sales, and I will get back to her at a better time when I would want her to fill out an application. Basically, that's all it was."

Then in a second call, according to Mack, "She told me she was still interested. The main thing, she just asked me, you know, the idea of—for some reason the idea of a woman being able to do that type of work."

"And what did you tell her?"

"I reiterated what my friend had told me about this gal that had sold for him, and that's all I ever heard about at S.M.I. because every time I contacted a customer of his from the past they asked where this gal, Fran, was."

"Now, did she say anything to you during that telephone call about moving to San Diego?"

"As the call progressed, yes, she did."

"What did she say?"

"I had told her I would like her to come over and pick up an application. And we talked about her schedule and then some—I don't know why, but I gave her directions to the house, but it seemed like there was something that clicked and all of a sudden she said, 'Oh, by the way, I might be moving to San Diego.' "

"What did you say when she said that?"

"I said, 'When?' And she said within the month."

"What did you say?"

"I said, well, if you really are sure of that, then I just want you to understand, I would rather not go through all of this, because it would really be a waste of both our time."

"What did she say to that?"

"She understood."

"How did you leave it on that telephone call with her in terms of her filling out an application?"

"I had told her if she changed her mind and if she found she still needed a job, to let me know."

"Did she indicate to you that she was definitely moving to San Diego or was it kind of tentative?"

"I don't know. She just mentioned—when I said are you sure, and she said—I don't know. I can only say, I think."

"What did you do after the telephone call?"

"Got ready to go to work and go get my hair done."

Now the jury would see the day of the murder from Paul Mack's perspective. Margie prayed they'd know he was lying.

"Did you see Karen Winslett that morning?"

"Yes, I did." His eyes, his voice asked for understanding.

"Where did you see her?"

"At my house."

"How did she get to your house?"

"She drove."

"About what time did she get to your house?"

"I was just walking out the door to my hair appointment so it had to be 9:00, 9:15."

Paul explained that Karen, not knowing what she would be doing in the future, had decided to stop by his house for a job application and he had asked her in. The jurors stopped squirming. They were watching him now. The courtroom was quiet with anticipation.

"Now, when Karen came into the house, where did you guys go?"

"Into the kitchen."

"And had you used any cocaine that morning?"

"Yes."

"Now at some point did the conversation turn to cocaine?"

"After a while, yes."

"Who brought up the subject of cocaine the first time?"

"Karen did."

"And how—was there something that prompted her to mention cocaine?"

"Well, I had a little thing sitting on the counter right by where we were sitting that was a grinder that you use for grinding cocaine and she saw it."

"And was there cocaine in this grinder at the time?"

"Yes."

"What did she say about it?"

"Well, she noticed it. And, I mean, anybody that has ever used cocaine is going to know what it is," Mack said matter-of-factly, insinuating that Karen was a drug user, a claim all her friends and family denied. "And she just asked me if I did cocaine."

"What did you say?"

"I said, 'Yes.' "

"What did she say?"

"She asked me if I had any."

"What did you say?"

"I said, 'Yes.' "

"What did she say?"

"At that point I don't know if I offered or she asked or what. All I know is we ended up doing cocaine."

In the same casual tone he had been using all along, Mack accused Karen of using cocaine on the day of her death.

"Now did she have any difficulty snorting the cocaine herself? Did she seem to know how to do it?"

"Yes."

"Did you have to teach her in any way?"

"No," Mack said ingenuously.

"Did she appear to enjoy it?"

"Yes."

"Did the cocaine affect you in any way?"

"Just as usual, I suppose, talking. We both got giddy, you know, talking and laughing and joking about whatever."

"Did the conversation turn toward sex?"

"Yes."

"And what effect did the cocaine seem to have on her?"

"I guess it had the same effect on both of us."

"Were you aroused sexually?"

"Yes."

"Did she appear to be as well?"

"Yes."

"Did you make love?"

"Yes."

A spectator walked out of the courtroom and Margie heard Paul's words float out through the open door; words so believable that even Margie was momentarily tempted to suspend judgement.

However, the newspaper reports of the coroner and toxicologist's testimonies which she held in her hands refuted this temptation. No cocaine had been found in Karen Winslett's blood sample nor had the metabolite that would show up if cocaine had been present. What was present, according to the toxicologist, was evidence of Percodan throughout Karen's body. Much more than a casual dose in the frivolous morning of sex and cocaine Paul Mack described.

Moreover, there was the mysterious bruise on Karen Winslett's throat which the coroner said had to be inflicted before death and might have resulted he said, "from someone putting their hand on someone's throat"—a throat which perhaps had been held open as Karen Winslett was forced to take pills.

"At some point did both of you get dressed?"

"Pardon?"

"At some point did both of you get dressed?"

"Yes."

"Can you put any kind of time frame on when you got dressed?"

"After we had sex, she asked about the restroom, availability of a restroom, and there was one right downstairs right around the corner. She went into the restroom. I was getting dressed in the kitchen–family room area where we were and she came back out and we had a little bit more of a conversation and then I went upstairs."

"Now, during this morning period, where was your Percodan?"

"Sitting on the counter in the kitchen."

"In what kind of container?"

"A little, brown prescription bottle."

"Would that have been the prescription that Dr. Warren gave you on the thirteenth of February?"

"I assume so."

"Had you been getting Percodan from anyone else other than Ted Warren?"

"No."

"Now, where was the vial of Percodan in relation to where the cocaine in the grinder had been?"

"On the same counter."

"At some point, did Karen ask you about the bottle?"

Mack nodded, speaking directly to the jury. "After she came back out from the restroom she asked me—I don't know if she asked me about the bottle first or about cocaine, about having more cocaine. One or the other, but, yes, she asked me about it."

"What did she ask you about the bottle?"

"She asked me what it was."

"What did you tell her?"

"I told her it was Percodan."

"What did she say when you told her that?"

"She asked me why I had it."

"What did you tell her?"

"I told her what I used it for and then I was going to go upstairs to clean up and also look for some cocaine, because we had also got into the conversation about cocaine. She asked me if I had any. I said I would look. I didn't think I had any more. And I told her what the Percodan had done for me and she said, can I try one? I said yes, you know."

"Did you see her actually take any?"

"No, she was holding, you know, the bottle. We were talking about it as I walked out of the room."

There was no way around it; Paul Mack, alias Sean Paul Lanier, had not only a way with words but of looking so earnest, so forthcoming that it was hard to believe that there was seldom a word of truth in the things he claimed. For he had such a genteel way about him that it was hard to conceive him a man of violence. Surely such a man would show signs of beastliness and not be matter-of-fact, offering explanations which sounded so plausible, memories which sounded so real. And it was this, Margie realized, which made the man she had once loved for the image he created, even more dangerous.

"When you came back downstairs was there more discussions about drugs?"

"Yes."

"Who said what?"

"I said I didn't have any upstairs, and I began looking around. And we began talking about cocaine and everything else again. It just went back into general conversation as I was looking. It was more than apparent I was looking to see if I had any because I thought I might have some downstairs."

"Did she express any desire to have more cocaine?"

"She had already expressed that desire before I went upstairs, asking me if I had any more."

"And when you were not able to find any more cocaine, what discussion did you have at that point?"

"I brought up the fact that, you know, if she wanted some more, I was willing to buy some more because I was out anyway, and we could drive over there and I would get some."

"And by driving over there, what were you referring to—who were you referring to?"

"The two of us driving over there."

"Over where?"

"Oh, I'm sorry, to Chris Jackson's."

"Now, at some point, did you drive over to Chris Jackson's?"

"Yes, we did."

"Do you remember about what time you left your house?"

"It was after twelve. I know—it was probably close to one o'clock."

"Was she fully dressed at that time?"

"Yes."

"Was she fully conscious?"

"Yes."

"Did she appear to be sedated at all?"

"No. We were both probably kind of high and still giddy, I guess is the word for it. We were just joking with each other and teasing with—teasing about—just—"

"Go ahead," Clifton cajoled.

"Well, it was like two kids teasing each other and stuff, I guess." Paul Mack's voice was all childhood innocence. He sounded almost shy. "I mean we were just laughing and joking about things."

"Who drove the car?"

"She did."

"Is there any reason why you didn't take your car?"

"As we walked out the door, hers was right there in front. I don't know that she suggested or I suggested it. We just walked toward her car and got in."

According to Mack, when he and Karen reached Chris Jackson's house, other cars were there. Mack then waited until they had passed Jackson's house to tell Karen that they had passed it and that they couldn't go in because other people must be there. Winslett suddenly turned on him, furious.

Clifton, inclining his head as if finally getting at the truth, asked, "What did she say?"

"It was like all of a sudden she is mad, acting like she is expecting me to interrupt this person or whatever, but she said, that's fine, I can get my own cocaine," Paul looked at the jury, his face expressing a naive inability to understand Karen's anger. Then he told them that she said, "Why don't you just walk back?"

"What happened then?" Clifton asked.

"Well, I was kind of dumbfounded," Paul said with another innocent look towards the jury. "We were at the corner—by then we were at the corner of, I guess it is Hillsdale and Walerga. There is an Arco station there. I got out of the car and she drove away."

Then Mack told the jury how he had called Chris Jackson, his friend and dealer, to get a ride home. And again, Mack was able to make Chris Jackson look like the villain, painting him as a drug-dealing, reckless driver.

"He told me he had somebody there. I said, Chris, I have got an appointment I need to get to. Can you please give me a ride? And he said, all right, I'll be right there."

"And did he pick you up?"

"Yeah."

"What was his demeanor when he picked you up? Happy, sad, mad?"

"He obviously wasn't real happy. He was agitated, I could tell, but he wasn't going out of his way to be nasty or something like that. He was speeding. I think he was in a hurry."

"Speeding, meaning driving fast?"

"He was driving real fast, and I mentioned it to him. I said, Chris, take it easy. Slow down. He said, well, I have got somebody at the house. I want to get back."

"Did you go to your house?"

"Yes."

Next, Clifton turned to the subject of Mack's encounters with Karen Winslett's boyfriend, Greg Harvey.

"When he knocked on the door, what happened in the house?"

Mack set a scene of domesticity. "Stacy and I were both in the kitchen, and we both ran for the door. It is just something we did."

"And who got their first?"

"She did," Mack said, sounding regretful.

"What happened after she got to the door?"

"When Stacy opened the door and saw it was a man, she

just automatically let me talk to him. She didn't know who it was, so she wanted me to take it from there."

"And what did Greg Harvey say to you?"

"He said, is Karen Winslett here?"

"What did you say?"

"I said no."

It was a typical Paul Mack answer, almost but not quite true.

"Did you lie to him?"

"She wasn't there at the time."

"What else did you say?"

"He said something about I have a note. I think he said Budweiser. She's supposed to be here. And I said she is not. I said I don't know what you are referring to."

"Why didn't you tell him that Karen had been there that morning?"

"I was standing in the door. I thought Stacy was standing right behind me. What am I going to say?" Mack nodded his head at the spectators and the jury as if to say, 'Come on, I had no choice. What would you have done?' Once again, it all seemed so logical and Mack so candid that one might wonder how it could all be lies.

"When you called him on the phone—about how long after he had left did you call him on the phone?"

"Five minutes."

"Why did you call him on the phone?"

"After he left it just—it occurred this was probably her boyfriend. I started thinking maybe she had gone home and told her boyfriend that something had happened and he was coming over to play against me or to me or whatever, to see what I was going to say. And I just thought I better say something to him, so I called back and talked to him."

"And when you called him back, what did you tell him?"

"First I said is this the guy that was—I'm Paul Mack. You were just at my house in a blue truck? And he said yes. And I told him I had talked to Karen about a job, sales, and that she had told me she was going to move to San Diego so we didn't keep the appointment."

"Now did you have contact with Greg Harvey at any time on Friday?"

"Around six o'clock that evening."

"And what happened?"

"I was outside and he drove up. Well, he got out of his truck, and his mannerism was—it seemed aggressive and it just kind of stuck out to me."

"How did it seem aggressive?"

"His walk, his mannerism. He seemed like he was mad or upset about something."

"What did he say to you?"

"He said, 'I just want to talk to you some more about Karen.' He basically asked me the same questions. He asked me what our conversation had been. He asked me about Budweiser."

"What did he ask you about Budweiser, if you can remember?"

"He asked me if I knew of Budweiser or if I knew anything about them."

"What did you say?"

"I said the only thing I knew was that Budweiser was obviously a beer company, and, because of having dealt with the different beer companies from being in the restaurant business, I told him if I was him I would check with Coors, Markstein, or whoever might handle the Budweiser account."

"At that point in time, had you done any work for Budweiser?"

"No." Mack looked at the jury steadily.

"Did you ever do any work for Budweiser?" Clifton gestured toward Mack.

Slowly Mack shook his head. "No."

"Had you ever worked on any kind of calendar promotion for Budweiser?"

"I never worked on any kind of calendar promotion."

"Now, did he mention anything in that conversation about the police?"

"Yes, but I don't know in what context. I just remember it. I don't know if it was the missing person report or it was something else. I just don't remember what exact context."

"What did you tell him about Karen during the conversation?"

"I told him the same thing I had told him before on the phone."

Clifton paused for a moment to write something on a legal pad and then continued. "Now, did you at some time Friday night or Saturday morning talk to your brother, Todd?"

"Saturday morning."

"What did you tell him when you called him?"

"I told him I needed to talk to him and there was something bothering me. and I needed to talk to him," Mack said anxiously. "It was important."

"Did you make arrangements to talk to him?"

"Yes, I did."

"Where were you going to talk to him?"

"I asked him to come out to the flea market."

"At some point, did Todd come out?"

"Yes."

"What time?"

"I don't know. Nine o'clock. Ten o'clock."

"Did you ask him to lie for you?"

"Yes."

"What did you say to him?"

"I basically just told him that I was home, and I didn't think anybody would believe it and that I was worried about the boyfriend, the police and what was happening. I wasn't aware. I was scared. I thought I would be put in the middle of something."

"Did you tell Todd what you actually had been doing Thursday morning?"

"No, I did not."

"What was your reason for asking him to lie?"

Mack looked at the jury pleadingly. "Because I was scared."

"What were you scared of?"

"Just everything going on. I was uncertain of what was happening, but between the boyfriend and the mention of the police, I felt somebody was trying to tie me into something."

Once again, Mack seemed almost credible. Wouldn't any-one be frightened under the circumstances? Wouldn't anyone ask an innocent favor of their brother? Wouldn't anyone . . . and Mack was so deft, so soft-spoken, you could almost imagine what had never occurred and almost forget the horrible reality that had. Almost . . . For Paul Mack's calm, earnest veneer never faltered, at least not while his own attorney questioned him. In fact, at this point, hours into his testimony, he exuded an air of such self-assurance that he appeared, to those who knew the distinction, to believe his own lies were the truth.

"Now at some point, the police came and talked to you?"

"Yes."

"Do you remember when that was, for the first time?"

"When I came home from the flea market on Saturday, I received a call. I believe it was Detective Frank. He asked me to come downtown. I said I had a previous engagement planned for that evening. He said, How long will you be home?"

"I told him. And he said, Well, we will come out there.

"I said fine."

"What effect did that have on you?"

"Well, first of all, the first thing he did was tell me he was a homicide investigator. And I didn't know why a homicide investigator would be missing—you know, asking me questions about a girl that was supposedly just missing."

Paul stumbled over his words, seeming to relive his sense of fright all over again. But was it fear from his memory or a current fear of being found out, being found guilty of murder? Margie would never know. That was the most chilling thing, Margie thought. The way Paul Mack told lies, the tearful entreaties, the shocked disbelief, the intense feelings. It could have been the cries of an innocent man being tortured. Instead, she knew his were the damning words and screams of a demon with angelic looks and manners.

"What effect did that have on you?"

"It scared the hell out of me," he said defensively.

"And did he come and talk to you?"

"Yes, he did."

"Was anyone present when he talked to you?"

Mack nodded. "Yes."

"Who was present?"

"Stacy Carter."

"Why was she present?"

"When Frank called me, I picked up the phone after he talked to me and I called my attorney to ask his advice and he told me to be sure and have somebody present and be sure the conversation was recorded."

"Did you lie to Detective Frank?"

"Yes," Paul said quietly, as if he could not believe his own transgression.

"Why?"

"I had—I had said—I had made the statement I had made and I was too scared to change it. I was too scared to think that I could be believed. Stacy was sitting there. I was still trying to protect the relationship. Mainly, I was scared."

Mack kept looking over at the jury with large, innocent eyes, the eyes of a child being punished for something he did not do.

"Now, when the police came and talked to you the first time did you make any plans to leave?"

"No," Mack said, sounding proud of himself.

"When did you start making plans to leave?" Clifton questioned.

"I never made the plan to leave," Mack said self-righteously.

"When did you decide to leave?"

"When they asked me to surrender."

"What did you do?"

"I called Stacy at work. I told her what was happening. I asked her to come home. I just threw a bunch of clothes in the car. She came home and I left."

"What was your state of mind that day?"

Paul turned to look at the jury with a pathetic, scared expression. "I felt penned in. I felt everything had been tossed on me because of the past. I just felt it was wrong. I felt defenseless."

"After you left Sacramento, were you prepared to return to Sacramento and surrender yourself?"

"Yes," Mack said contritely.

"Why didn't you?"

"Because the—according to my lawyer, the District Attorney, or whomever he was conferring with, and the Court would not allow him to be appointed as my attorney."

"At some point, did you decide that you were just going to stay away?"

"I had to."

"Do you remember about when that was?"

"About a month after I left."

"And did you establish new identity at that point?"

"Yes, I did."

Clifton moved in for his final moments, trying to elicit sympathy by looking penetratingly at the jury. Then he turned back to Mack.

"Did you kill Karen Winslett?" he boldly asked.

"No, I did not," Mack said, thrusting his chin forward to punctuate the importance of his statement.

Clifton moved closer to the witness stand. "Were you with her when she died?"

"No, I was not," Mack said adamantly.

"Did you see her either alive or dead at any time after she dropped you off near Chris Jackson's house?"

Mack looked directly at the jury. "No, I did not," he said with conviction.

"That's all I have," Clifton announced and returned to his seat. And with that, the jury and all in the courtroom had a moment of respite after spending several hours watching the chameleon try to remain smooth and composed while showing the appropriate emotion—from shame, to fear, to sadness—at the right time. Paul Mack had given a brilliant performance, one designed to elicit the utmost sympathy and understanding.

Judge Robertson looked grave. "Cross-examination, Mr. Statlin."

Gene Statlin rose from his chair. "Thank you, Your Honor," he said, moving forward with a determined look on his face. He had a lot of respect for Clifton's ability as a defense attorney, but he wasn't about to let Clifton get away with this travesty. He intended to unmask Paul Mack.

# CHAPTER THIRTY-ONE

# *Lie Upon Lie*

As Gene Statlin slowly approached Paul Mack, the prosecutor's face had a thoughtful measuring expression. He looked hard at the jury, pausing for a few moments before beginning his first question. Then he struck. In seconds, Statlin cleared the stagnant air and changed the atmosphere of the room. Excitement was tangible as the two men started to clash.

"Did you suffer a felony conviction for forgery in Sacramento, California?"

"I believe so, yes."

"Four years later, did you suffer another felony conviction for forgery in Sacramento, California?"

"I was under the impression—I don't know if it was forgery." Mack became cagey.

"These were multiple charges, were they not?"

Mack shifted uncomfortably in his seat. "I don't remember."

Statlin's mouth formed a smile of derisive anger. "You don't remember the felonies that you were found guilty of?" Statlin said incredulously, looking at the jury.

"I don't recollect exactly what they were for."

"In 1975, did you suffer a felony conviction in Sacramento, California?"

"For forgery? I guess," Mack said vaguely.

Statlin gave a shocked expression and asked, "You don't remember suffering a felony conviction in 1975 in Sacramento County Superior Court?"

Mack's answer came out in jumble. "The conviction that I have suffered, when Mr. Clifton named them off I said the same thing. I can't say exact dates and times," Paul said defensively. "I'm saying, yes, I have been convicted."

Statlin nodded. He wasn't about to let Clifton's scanty enumeration of Mack's past crimes stand. "In 1980, did you suffer a felony conviction for theft in a state outside of California?"

"Yes."

Statlin shot out the next question. "In 1980, didn't you suffer another felony conviction for forgery in a state even outside of that state outside of California?"

"I'm not sure what it was for. I just know it was at the same time."

Inclining his head, Statlin said, "Pardon me?"

Mack looked around the courtroom like a cornered animal. He struggled to remain composed. "I'm not sure what it was for. I just know it was for the same thing."

"You were being prosecuted by two different jurisdictions; isn't that true?"

"Yes."

"And you suffered a felony conviction on those counts?"

As soon as Mack admitted something, Statlin went on, bringing up one conviction after another until the effect was dizzying.

As Statlin questioned him, Mack began to slump, almost shrink inside his well-pressed clothes as if he were warding off the blows of what was coming next. But there was nowhere to hide.

Statlin turned to the night Mack met Greg Harvey and fired his next questions one after another.

"Now, when Greg Harvey came to the door, you said you didn't know a Karen; isn't that what you said?"

"I believe so."

"In other words, right at that moment in time you decided to lie to Mr. Harvey, didn't you?"

"Yes."

"In fact, you knew Karen, didn't you?

"In what way?"

"You knew who he was looking for, didn't you, when—when you lied to him?

"When he said Karen, the first thing that I thought of was Karen that had been there that day."

The damning rhythm of the questions and replies went on.

"So you lied to him right off the top, right then, the first time?"

"Yes, I did."

"You were caught a little bit by surprise, weren't you, Mr. Mack?"

"Yes."

Statlin asked his next question with a cool, appraising look of distaste. "You didn't expect Mr. Harvey to show up looking for Karen, did you?"

"No, I did not."

"In fact, you had no idea she had left a note describing where she would be?"

"No."

"In fact he told you he had a note, didn't he?"

Mack looked pale, lost. Clifton made no objection, as if he didn't want to worsen the inevitable. "I don't remember whether he mentioned a note or not. He said something about Budweiser, but he said something about I have directions to your house. I don't know if he said note, per se."

"You recall him talking about having directions to your house?"

"I had given directions to Karen."

"Do you recall him telling you about the Budweiser ad?"

"He said something about Budweiser. He didn't specifically say what it was."

"Right at that point in time was the first time that you recognized that Karen Winslett in fact had left a note as to her whereabouts that morning; isn't that true?"

Statlin was firing his questions so quickly that Mack, perspiring now, wiped his forehead and took several nervous audible breaths. "No, it is not."

"Didn't he tell you previously she had left a note?"

"No, he didn't mention a note, per se."

"Did you ask him where he got the directions?"

"No, I didn't."

"Now, when you walked back inside the house, you immediately told Stacy Carter that you knew who this boyfriend was looking for, didn't you?"

"Not immediately, no."

"When you walked back inside the house to where Ms. Carter was in the kitchen, didn't you tell her, hey, this guy is looking for Karen, the gal that used to work at the Warehouse?"

"No, it was about five minutes later when I got my phone book and decided to call."

"You lied to Stacy Carter at that point in time, too, didn't you?"

"In what respect?"

"You didn't tell her Karen Winslett, the gal this boyfriend was looking for, had been over to the house that morning?"

Only Mack's lips moved. "No, I did not."

"You didn't say that?"

"I didn't—"

"Pardon?" Statlin's voice hardened.

"—say—"

"Pardon me?"

"You asked me if I told her, and I said no, I didn't tell her."

Mack was obviously rattled, his air of confidence visibly shaken. Statlin pressed on.

"So at the point in time Mr. Harvey came over and you had told him this lie, you had no idea whether or not Karen Winslett had walked into Mr. Harvey's house two and a half hours later; isn't that true?"

"I'm sorry, I didn't hear the question."

"The moment you lied to Mr. Harvey about not knowing who Karen was, you had no idea at that point whether or not she was alive or dead, right?"

"No, I didn't."

"So for all you knew she could have walked back in the door over at the Harvey house an hour and a half later, isn't that so?"

"Right. I thought he was there because maybe she had told him what had happened."

"He told you she was missing, didn't he?"

"No, he asked if Karen was there and said he had directions to the house."

"So this was the first lie. You made that up right at the spur of the moment; is that so?"

"Yes, I did."

"Let's talk about the next lie." Statlin paused for a moment to let his words sink in. "The next lie to Mr. Harvey was about ten minutes later?"

"After he left when I called?"

"Sure."

"Yes."

"So this was the next lie to him, not counting what you spoke to Ms. Carter about, right?"

The self-assured Paul Mack had been replaced by a man with a nervous wariness forced to answer quickly, not knowing where the next trap lay.

"Uh-huh. Yes."

"Now, when you talked to Mr. Harvey this next time, this is the second time you went to the trouble to lie to him; is that so?"

"Yes."

"When you talked to him the second time it was—oh, I do recall Karen. I recall her. I had talked to her on the phone about an appointment and she didn't show up. Isn't that in essence what you said?"

"Yes, it is."

"You didn't tell Mr. Harvey the truth that time either, did you?"

"No, I didn't."

"You didn't tell him that you had seen her?"

"No."

"You chose to lie to Mr. Harvey again?"

"Yes, I did."

"Wasn't this appointment about a sales job a lie too?"

"No."

"That part was true?"

"Yes."

Statlin smiled and looked over at the jury. They were with him now. There was heat and passion in his voice as he continued.

"Was that the only part that was true that you talked to Mr. Harvey about?"

"I don't know."

"Didn't you get on the phone and ask, hey, Mr. Harvey, have you found her yet? Has she shown up?"

"No."

"You didn't do that, did you?"

"No."

"Why did you bother calling over to Mr. Harvey's after he left your house if you didn't think she was missing?"

"Because I was scared and I was strictly trying to go into detail about the fact that I had an appointment with her and what the appointment was about."

"You weren't so scared that you couldn't think up a lie, were you?"

Clifton called out, "Objection. Argumentative."

Judge Robertson nodded. "Sustained."

Still, the jury had heard, but just to be sure, Statlin reformulated the question.

"Were you so scared that you couldn't think up a lie?"

Once again, Clifton objected, and once again, it was sustained.

"What you were thinking of doing is try and invent a story to cover up your having seen her in the morning; isn't that what you were doing?"

"Yes."

"The Karen that you are referring to is the one who had helped you before when she worked at the Warehouse, right?"

"She had been helpful."

"You thought enough of her to want to give her a job, Mr. Mack?"

"I thought enough of her in the sense of other people that

I was needing somebody possibly in the near future." Mack's answer came out in a nervous jumble.

"You liked her enough to have sex with her that morning?"

"Pardon?" Mack looked taken aback by this sudden foray into his sexual encounter with Karen Winslett.

"You liked her enough to have sex with her that morning? That's what you testified." He looked at Mack, who was silent. Mack gave the prosecutor a trapped look.

"Mr. Mack, are my questions real hard for you to understand?"

Judge Robertson interrupted. "I don't think he understood, so why don't you repeat the question, please."

Statlin nodded and did just that, but Mack still was having trouble answering. Statlin looked over at the jury. For the first time, they were nodding at him.

Statlin went on. "You essentially told the cops on the twenty-first when you talked to them the same lie you told Mr. Harvey on the nineteenth, the evening of the nineteenth?"

"Yes."

As Statlin moved Mack through the days preceding his arrest, Statlin punctuated his time line for the jury by a phrase which almost served as a chorus. For the jury, he believed, could not fail to see how many opportunities Mack had to tell the truth and on how many of those opportunities he chose to lie. "Now at that point in time," he began the chorus to let his words sink in, "you didn't know, according to your version, if Ms. Winslett was alive or dead, did you?"

"No, I did not."

Statlin looked in Mack's direction as he continued his questions.

"You had no idea whether she was alive and going to return on Sunday or what, did you?"

"I had no idea." Mack's voice was oddly hollow.

Karen Winslett's father, who had been sitting in the courtroom, could not seem to take any more and was quietly weeping. He stood up and walked outside to try to compose himself.

"Instead, you chose to perpetrate a lie, didn't you?"

"Yes."

"You told Mr. Harvey during that conversation that she had never shown up, didn't you?"

"I said we cancelled the appointment."

"Did you ask him if he had found her yet?"

"No."

"You weren't concerned about that at that point in time, were you?"

"It just never came up."

"But you knew you wanted to make a call to him to allay his suspicions?"

"I didn't know she was missing. I still felt he was confirming something that she may have told him. I didn't know what he was thinking or what he was doing."

"The story you gave Mr. Harvey on the telephone about her never showing up, was a complete lie too, wasn't it?"

"Yes, it was."

"This was just something that you invented right then to cover yourself; is that true?"

"Yes."

"Now, when you saw Mr. Harvey again Friday evening, at that point in time he made it clear to you that he still had not seen Karen Winslett; isn't that true?"

"He was looking for her, yes."

"At this point in time, you had no idea, did you, whether or not she was alive or dead?"

"No, I didn't."

Pausing, Statlin asked softly, "Yet you chose to perpetrate your lie, didn't you?"

"Yes," Mack conceded.

Statlin moved closer to the witness stand.

"When did you decide you needed a false alibi?

"When I called my brother."

"At the point in time, when you decided you were going to call your brother to set up a false alibi, you didn't know that Karen Winslett was alive or dead, did you?"

"I had no idea."

Statlin said with a look so grave as to appear angry, almost fierce. "You had no idea whether she would walk in the door on Sunday, did you?"

"No, I did not."

"But you were going to go to the trouble of making up this false alibi and have your brother lie to the cops. Is that what you are saying?"

"I told him I wanted to talk to him and at that point that's just what I wanted to do. I didn't know for sure what I wanted to do."

"You told him it was important, didn't you?"

"Yes, it was."

Once more, Statlin surveyed the jurors, his hawk-like eyes demanding their attention. He turned back to Mack. "So you went to your brother and said, I need to create this false alibi? Is that what you did?"

Mack looked down, not meeting his gaze. "I told him what happened and told him what I wanted him to say; yes."

"And you invented the false alibi, didn't you?"

In the momentary silence, Mack nodded and said a barely audible, "Yes."

"You invented this false alibi just like you invented the initial lie to Mr. Harvey when he was at your door, the second lie over the telephone; you invented it, didn't you?"

"Yes."

"Mr. Mack, let's go on to the next lie that you told on February twenty-first; the day the cops came out. Do you remember that point in time?"

"Yes."

"Detective Frank came to see you; isn't that true?"

"Yes."

"It was a tape-recorded interview; was it not?"

"Yes."

"Now, at this point in time, you realized this was serious, did you not?"

"Well, he said he was from homicide."

"He told you he was investigating a girl who was supposed to be missing and they didn't know where she was; isn't that why he was talking to you?"

"He said he was from homicide and said he was reporting or investigating a missing girl or something. I'm not sure the exact—"

"Are you saying you misunderstood why he was talking to you that day?"

"No, I'm just saying it was basically something like that. But the thing that stuck in my mind is he said he was from homicide."

"Now, at that point in time, when you talked to Detective Frank on the afternoon of the twenty-first, you lied to him. In fact, on a whole bunch of occasions during that interview you lied, did you not?"

Mack hung his head. "I lied to him about the same thing."

Statlin shook his head, giving Mack the measured look of someone trying to maintain his patience. "You weren't going to give him information to try and help him find Ms. Winslett's whereabouts, were you?"

"I didn't know her whereabouts."

"You didn't mention anything about Chris Jackson, did you?"

"No."

"You didn't mention anything about even seeing her that morning, did you?"

"No."

"So, in other words, you essentially lied by not telling them the truth as to those points in particular; isn't that true?"

- "Yes."

"Let's talk about the affirmative lies that you told the detective. First thing you told them was that the last time you saw Ms. Winslett had been several months before; isn't that what you told him?"

"Yes."

"That was a lie, wasn't it?"

"Yes."

"What you were trying to do was throw the focus off of you and get it somewhere else. Isn't that what you were doing with this detective?"

Though Clifton objected, the judge overruled him. Regardless, the damage was already done; the relentless layering of fact after fact by Statlin had penetrated Mack's veil of deception. Even the spectators were silent.

Mack, confused, said, "I don't know that that is—that is hard to answer yes or no. I wasn't trying to throw it on somebody else. I was trying to say the same thing I had already said all along."

Statlin was not about to let Mack off so easily.

"You just wanted to be consistent in your lies. Is that why you continued lying to him?"

Mack's voice was flat, as if too many rapid questions had winded him. "I lied about the same thing I had lied about before, yes."

"Now, it was also during this conversation with Detective Frank that you lied about not seeing her; you lied about her car not being there, you also lied to the detective and gave him your false alibi, did you not?"

"Yes."

"Did you kind of invent and embellish this little false alibi story as you went along in explaining to it Detective Frank?"

"I just gave him the story."

"Well, didn't you tell Detective Frank that? He was asking you whether or not you were involved in this and didn't you tell him that, no—well, I was with somebody the whole, you know, the whole time. And he says, well, who? And you say, my brother. You told him that, didn't you?"

The question stopped Mack, who looked at his lawyer. Clifton stirred but said nothing. At last Mack replied, "I—I was stating what I had talked to my brother about."

"Pardon me?" Statlin said condescendingly.

"I was reiterating what I had talked to my brother about."

Facing the jury, Statlin, maintaining his tone of calm relentlessness, asked, "This is the story you invented, was it not? You were embellishing your story to make it sound believable to Detective Frank; isn't that true?"

"Yes."

"You wanted Detective Frank to believe your lies, didn't you?"

"Yes."

"You were trying to be convincing just like you're trying to be convincing here; isn't that true?"

Clifton rose to object, but the jury had heard it all. Though his objection was sustained, Statlin knew the sixteen men and women would not forget.

"In approximately April of 1987, you fled the jurisdiction, did you not?"

"Yes, I did."

"And at the time that you fled, you knew the cops were going to arrest you for the murder of Karen Winslett; isn't that true?"

"They asked me to surrender."

"And in fact, they had told your lawyer to be down at the Sheriff's Office, otherwise they were going to come get you; isn't that the story that you got?"

"Yes."

"And you chose not to do what they wanted you to do, so you took off, right?"

"Yes, I did."

"Now, at the time that you took off, you were engaged to marry Stacy Carter, were you not?"

"Yes."

"At this point in time you figured out that your brother wasn't going to stand up behind the alibi anymore; isn't that true?"

"No."

"Did you talk to your brother before you fled about whether or not he was going to back your alibi once the police were going to arrest you?"

Statlin watched Mack's throat work as he struggled for self-control. "No, when I was told—I didn't know I was going anywhere until I was asked to surrender."

"Did you talk—did you know at the time that you were fleeing, or getting ready to flee rather, that the police had found Chris Jackson?"

"No."

"At the time that you fled, didn't you know that the police

had a witness to put you in the vicinity of the motel?"

"No, I don't believe so. No."

"You fled ultimately to Salt Lake City, didn't you?"

"Yes."

"And essentially what you did in Salt Lake City was to daily live a lie, did you not?"

"I guess, yes."

Statlin's eyes glinted. "Well, you certainly fooled Margie Danielsen, the wife that you married; isn't that true?"

"In what respect?"

"Lied to her about who you were and what you had been doing?"

"Yes."

"And you lived that lie daily with her and convinced her of it, didn't you?"

"Yes." Mack's body sagged against the chair as if the nakedness of his admissions deflated him.

"Did you try and be convincing with Margie Danielsen, the lady who you married under the name of Sean Paul Lanier?"

Clifton looked at the Judge. "Objection. Argumentative."

Judge Robertson responded, "I sustain the objection."

But once again the jury heard and would not forget. Statlin was satisfied.

"Now, you still continued to lie at the point in time of your arrest, didn't you?"

"How is that?"

"About whether or not you saw Karen Winslett on the morning of the nineteenth?"

"Yes."

"And at this point in time, this wasn't a deal where Stacy Carter was still your fiancée and you were worried about keeping her out of it; you no longer had her interest to protect in the matter. You had left that, had you not?"

"Yes."

"And it was too late to protect Margie Danielsen, to stop her from thinking badly of you, that consideration was gone. You could now tell the truth, couldn't you?"

Clifton objected, but Robertson called out, "Overruled. Answer the question, please."

Mack gave a disjointed shake of the head. "I didn't feel I should be discussing anything with them."

The courtroom door opened as several people entered. Margie listened intently for the few moments it was held ajar.

"You proceeded to tell the cops lies after they gave you your appropriate warnings and you waived them; you told them lies, right?"

"Continued to say the same story, yes." Mack took a heavy breath.

Statlin was on Mack before he could let the breath out. "Well, they specifically asked you—they told you, look, this is your last chance. Give us what you know. Didn't they tell you that?"

"Yes."

Looking at the prosecutor and watching how he worked, Margie thought Statlin reminded her of the television detective Columbo. When she had first met him, he seemed so humble and dignified, like a country preacher naive of big city evils. She had thought almost anyone sophisticated could fool him. However, as she heard him dissect Paul Mack's testimony and expose him for what he really was, she realized that beneath that exterior was a crusader so tenacious that he could cut right through deceit.

As the door slowly closed, Margie strained to hear the next question and felt a growing relief that Gene Statlin was on her side.

"Didn't they tell you that you were in serious trouble?"

"Yes."

"Now, at this point in time, you didn't know that the cops had the fiber evidence, did you?"

"No."

"This is something that is a new revelation since you told the cops all the lies and they arrested you on March twenty-eighth; isn't that true?"

"Yes."

"At that point in time, you also didn't know that they had evidence of your having sex on the victim?"

"No."

"You didn't know that when you talked to the cops on March twenty-eighth; isn't that true?"

"No, I didn't."

"Did you deny seeing Karen Winslett that day when—"

"Yes, I denied seeing her."

"That was a lie, wasn't it?"

"Yes."

"At this particular point in time, you also denied ever having seen her car, too; isn't that true?"

"Yes."

"That was a lie, too, wasn't it?"

"Again, yes." Mack gave a fleeting, incongruous smile, but it looked more like a grimace.

"You denied ever having been in her car?"

"Yes."

"That was a lie, too, wasn't it?"

"Yes."

"So you kept perpetuating these lies, did you not?"

"Yes."

"This point in time was your last chance; they told you that, right?"

"Yes."

"And you continued to lie?"

"Yes," Mack said dejectedly, but the look in his eyes as he peered at the prosecutor was close to hatred.

"Did you ever, in all the contacts that you had with the cops, ever tell them that you were with Karen Winslett on the morning of the nineteenth?"

"No, with an explanation." Mack's voice was filled with resentment.

Statlin shook his head. "Your Honor, I am not into these explanations. My preference is if he wants to amplify it, he can. I'm not asking for these things."

Robertson turned toward Statlin. "Well, my belief is that if the explanation is responsive to the question, he's entitled to make it. If it is not responsive, you are entitled to have it stricken from the record.

"Go ahead," Robertson said firmly, motioning to Mack.

"When they interviewed me in Utah after the arrest, at the very end of the conversation I remember telling them that there was something else I needed to talk about, but I didn't know how. I was scared, and I felt that I should wait until I had an attorney to decide what I should do."

Statlin stared at him. "Are you saying that these Sacramento police officers exploited you in any fashion because of your criminal record?"

"I believe they did, yes."

"How?" Statlin's voice was taut.

Mack made one last try at eliciting sympathy. "They told me that they were going to dissect my life. They told me they were going to talk to my business clients, my neighbors, and anybody else because they felt I was involved."

"And they were right, weren't they?" Statlin's voice thundered through the courtroom.

"No, they weren't," Mack said, his eyes flat and narrowed, a bitter smile on his face. He looked anxious and agitated but he kept repeating the same rationalizations over and over as if he could not, would not, let them go.

Clifton stood up. "Objection. Argumentative."

Statlin delivered his last words. "No further questions."

He looked over the jury to see if they were with him. He hoped they would be.

After Statlin finished cross-examining Paul Mack, he told Margie in the hallway, "For now, I've done all I can. I'll make my closing argument tomorrow. We've made our record— with your help." As he turned to leave, he looked back at her and said, "Thank you."

"Thank you," she called after him. She rushed out of the courthouse to catch up with Nickie, who had gone ahead to wait outside in the sunshine.

The closing arguments, when they came, were anti-climactic. Not that worthy adversaries, Jim Clifton and Gene

Statlin, did not give their best. But what everyone who would admit it knew—the spectators, the attorneys, the jury—was that what was finally Paul Steven Mack's undoing were his own lies.

# CHAPTER THIRTY-TWO

## *Final Encounter*

"WE, the jury, find the defendant, Paul Steven Mack, guilty of the crime of murder in the first degree as charged," read the jury foreman in a sonorous voice. He went on: "We, the jury, find the defendant, Paul Steven Mack, guilty of the crime of violation of section 261 of the Penal Code of the state of California, rape as charged in count two . . ."

For the first time, Paul Mack did not smile, show emotion, or even look in the direction of the jury as he stood to hear the verdict read, but several women in the courtroom could be heard crying.

Mack had been convicted of murder and rape but not the "special circumstances" that could have meant the gas chamber.

Once the jury had been dismissed, the prosecutor walked out of the courtroom over to Margie who embraced and thanked Gene Statlin. He whispered to her, "Call me later if you have any questions," then slipped away rather than talk to the crowd of reporters gathered and to avoid the photographers who tried to surround him and snap pictures.

Defense attorney Jim Clifton, when he came out, said he was surprised by the guilty verdict and thought that the jury had concluded Mack gave Winslett the overdose of prescription drugs that killed her. "They appear to think that he administered Percodan to the victim to have sex with her and then she got sick and died and he didn't do anything to help her."

Despite her feelings of relief and thankfulness at the verdict, Margie's thoughts turned to Sean. He had been her fantasy, her dream come true except for the fear—the fear she now knew had been occasioned by some primal instinct of survival for her and her daughters, an instinct, regretfully, she had blindly pushed away in the beginning. The truth had now been made known to her and this trial had been its final catalyst. The long mass of confusion was completely clear now and had given her back the life she had lost, but at a price: the disillusionment of her dreams. Oh, the hidden, terrible beauty of truth!

Back at the hotel, Nickie and Margie flopped on their beds. They were both exhausted. The phone rang and Nickie lazily answered it.

"Hi, Dad," Margie heard Nickie say.

There was a long silence as Nickie listened to her father on the other end. She began to look upset.

She looked at Margie and pleaded, "You don't want to go see Dad, do you Margie?"

"No," Margie said firmly.

Nickie continued arguing the point with her father. Eventually she hung up the phone.

A few minutes later, the phone rang again. Nickie ignored it this time, but when the incessant ringing would not stop, she picked it up in frustration.

"What?" she shouted.

Again, the debate raged back and forth between father and daughter. The tears, the pleading, the discouragement. Paul wasn't about to give up until he won.

The conversation ended when Nickie was fed up and slammed the phone down. However, a few minutes later, the phone rang a third time.

Nickie, exasperated, announced loudly, "Oh my God! I am not answering the phone!"

"He won't give up, Nickie," Margie told her, because she knew from experience Paul's determination.

"I'll take the phone off the hook then!" Nickie decided.

"He'll call the police and send them over. He's done that to me before," Margie replied. "You have to learn to deal with him. It's hard but necessary."

Picking up the phone and holding her hand over the receiver, Nickie suddenly made a startling request. "I'm going to go see my dad. I want you to come with me."

"Go to the jail?" Margie asked, incredulous.

"Yeah, I know he wants to see you. I know you don't want to. But he needs us now," Nickie pleaded.

"I don't think Paul Mack needs anyone, least of all me," Margie responded. Then she paused and looked thoughtful. "Let me think about it for a few minutes. I have to go downstairs to the hotel shop. I'll be right back."

As Margie left, she heard Nickie speaking to her father.

In the lobby, Margie phoned Gene Statlin. He told her, "Mack could receive a prison term of thirty-four years to life for both the rape and murder."

"His daughter wants me to go see him with her," she told him.

"What do you want?"

"I'm conflicted. On the one hand, I never want to see him again, but on the other, I feel bitter, frustrated, and angry because I want to tell him how I feel and put these feelings to rest so I can move forward."

"Go with your gut," he advised. "It's always worked for you before."

*Yes, that is true,* Margie thought. It was her instincts that had saved both her and her children.

"Gene, thanks," she said warmly.

"Good luck, Margie," he said, adding, "Again, thank you."

Back in the hotel room, Nickie was anxiously waiting for Margie's answer.

"Let's go," Margie said.

"Aren't you going to change?" Nickie asked.

"No." Margie shook her head. "Let's just get this over with."

County Jail, where Paul was being held without bond, was a foreboding gray building in the middle of the city near the courthouse. Black wire was strung over every window, giving the place the appearance of a fortress. The strange thing was,

Margie thought, as she walked up the front stairs, the fortress armament was not to keep people out, but to keep those imprisoned there in. Nickie stepped forward and opened the heavy mahogany door.

Inside, she and Nickie gave their names and signed forms at the front desk, indicating the inmate they wanted to see. An armed guard stood nearby. Then they went to the back of a line and waited behind family members and friends of other prisoners. Margie hated being there but she was determined now.

The line started to move. Margie followed Nickie and the crowd. Men in navy blue uniforms checked their identification and the two women walked through a steel door. An officer led them upstairs, down a hallway, and through another steel door. He pointed to a chair that faced a window with a phone on the wall. The officer turned around and left through the steel door. The door locked with a thud and Margie's heart jumped. Nickie was already seated in the chair. Cautiously, Margie walked toward Paul's daughter and stood behind her. She looked through the window down below to the jail cells. The shadowy forms of men were visible looking out through the bars. A few minutes passed and Paul walked up the steel stairs from below and approached the window. He was all smiles as he picked up the phone to talk to his daughter. He glanced at Margie from the corner of his eye.

Margie studied Paul's face. He didn't look like a killer. Yet she knew how deceiving his good, normal appearance was.

Paul asked to speak with Margie. Nickie handed her the phone and stood up, offering the chair to Margie. Margie sat down, face to face with her ex-husband through the window, looking at Sean or Paul or whoever he was.

Paul immediately started to weave his spell of charm.

"You look great," he said. "Then of course, you've always been beautiful."

Margie was impervious to his flattery now.

"I'm trying to stay in shape for when I get out of here," he told her. "I am innocent. You know that, don't you?"

"No, I don't know that at all," Margie replied curtly.

"You'll see when we appeal," he responded. "I want to come back to you. I'm going to come back to you." Paul's voice was cold now. He had ceased smiling.

Margie shivered. "No, I don't think so," she said firmly.

"Well, I'm going to see you and the girls one last time. You can bank on that," he told her, his tone clearly expressing the seriousness of his intentions.

Margie knew he meant what he said. The words, "one last time" echoed over and over in her mind, yet she pushed her fear aside, determined not to let him get to her.

Paul's controlling eyes searched Margie's for submission, but he was disappointed by the defiant, unwavering gaze she returned. For a moment, he looked annoyed and then he smiled.

"What's wrong, Sweetheart?" he asked, his voice softening.

"You must be kidding. You were convicted of murder today," she replied.

She felt the renewed chill of his eyes upon her, but she still did not falter or retreat. She looked back in his eyes. Silence filled the air for what seemed like an eternity in Hell.

"Well, it's good to see you," he finally said in a cordial way, as if he were running into an old acquaintance at the corner convenience store.

His nonchalance fueled Margie's determination. "I want you to know I'm not afraid of you any longer."

"No," he said quietly.

"No." She thought of the power he believed he had. If only he knew the strength she now had and that continued to grow within her. She would play this game and win. After all, he was behind bars, not her.

The bright lights glared all around them. Neither of them spoke for several minutes. Margie felt drops of perspiration on her forehead from the heat. The window between them was caked with fingerprints. How many prisoners and their wives and girlfriends touched their hands together on the glass showing their love? How many hearts were broken and lives destroyed?

Paul broke the silence. "So, are you going on with your life?" he asked sarcastically.

"Yes. I'm reclaiming it . . ." she looked straight in his eyes, "from you."

"Well, I'm moving on, too," he told her smugly.

Margie looked at him and said with determination, "I think that's for the best."

"You know it's not for the best," he said softly. He smiled. "I do understand, though."

"I don't think you do or ever have. How many times have you twisted the truth? You are an expert at disguising lies and making yourself appear innocent."

The hard knot of anger which Margie had for so long carried in her stomach burst from her lips. "Do you know what you did to us?" she almost shouted. "To all of us who believed in and loved you?"

"I loved you and the girls more than anyone ever could," he argued. "I tried to give myself to you in every possible way—"

Margie interrupted his monologue.

"By lying and cheating us of everything we had—our home, our trust, our faith?"

Margie's hand tightened around the phone. She wished his lies would strangle him the way they had her, yet she was struck by a feeling of loss: not of him, but of her own innocence.

"Sean, I mean Paul, you're the most insidious liar who ever lived. You don't know the meaning of the word love."

He stared at her in disbelief, shocked by her determination and strength. He continued to try to win her over with words of devotion. "Whatever I did before I met you had no bearing on how I felt toward you or what I gave in trying to be a faithful, hardworking committed husband and father."

"Like you were faithful to Stacy Carter? And what about your seven wives?" she shot at him. Before he could answer she went on. "Paul, you murdered two women."

He did not answer her charges, but went right on as if he hadn't heard her.

"And look what you did to me." His voice was laced with honey venom. "You made calls and inquiries. You went to the police when no one had any idea where I was. Was that being faithful to me? They would never have found me if it weren't for you."

His eyes held daggers of cruelty, but his voice was soft, almost gentle.

"I'm not blaming you nor do I love you any less for these things, but I won't forget," he said, glancing over at the guard and then back at Margie, "what you did."

Margie stared into those ice blue eyes now but would not allow herself to shudder or look away. "That is just the point," she said. "I do blame you. You have been found guilty today and you will be forever. Nothing will change that."

"Like I said, you'll see when we appeal," he told her with a smirk.

"I see the truth now," she replied as she stood up.

"You will see," he repeated as he too rose from his chair. "I will always love you."

There was no more to be gained here, she thought. "I've got to go," she said. "Goodbye."

"Bye, Sweetheart." He smiled.

Margie hung up the phone. Now she could leave the anger and the bitterness here. She could finally walk away from the nightmare Sean Paul Lanier, or Paul Steven Mack, had brought to her and her daughters' lives.

She looked one last time at the man she had once believed in and loved. The stranger at the glass partition. And then her eyes, tearless and steady, turned away from the past as she took her first step toward the future.

# Epilogue

"HE'S impossible," Nickie stated when they got back to their hotel room.

"Yes, he is," Margie agreed.

Sleepy and weary, they fell on their beds. Several minutes passed in silence.

"I get to go home tomorrow!" Margie said with a smile. She looked over at Nickie, who had already fallen asleep. Margie got up, retrieved a blanket from the closet and walked over to Nickie's bed. Covering the girl, Margie bent down and looked at her face, whispering, "Sleep well" and, thinking of her own girls, said a prayer for her.

For the first time in over a year, Margie slept well that night. Her thoughts were on the next day when she would see her daughters.

Margie felt enormous relief when she left the hotel the next morning. At the airport, she hugged Nickie. "I'm glad we've been together during this difficult period. I'll be there for you whenever you have sorted all this out and feel the need to talk, Nickie. Please call. I'll be thinking of you often."

Margie felt good as the plane soared into the blue sky. *I'm on my way home*, Margie thought. *The journey's over. I left the state I was born in for the second time and now I'm returning wiser and stronger. I've faced the enemy. I looked him right in the eye and told him and the world the truth and I survived. Now the girls and I can live without fear.*

When the plane landed in Salt Lake City, Utah, Margie was filled with joy. She wanted to kiss the ground and embrace the mountains. Nila, who was waiting for her at the airport, ran up to Margie and hugged her. "You look different. Are you alright?" she asked.

"Nila, I did it." Margie's face lit up and she smiled. "I stood my ground and found courage. I'll tell you all about it on the way home."

When they arrived at Margie's house, her daughters, who had been anxiously awaiting her arrival, ran out to hug their mother. As they walked, wrapped in each others' arms with the youngest straddling her, Margie saw the banner over the front door. "Welcome home, Mom." A huge, yellow ribbon decorated the mammoth oak tree nearby.

Tears fell down Margie's cheeks. "I'm so glad to be back with you," she said to Julie, June, and Jessi. "And I have so much to tell you, but most of all, the most important thing is I love you and always will."

And with those words, their healing began.

Ideas about the future filled Margie's head as she fell asleep that night. She awoke the next day to the smell of coffee brewing and bacon frying. Julie, June, and Jessi had made a special breakfast for their mother. They all seemed so happy as they sat at the kitchen table together in their pajamas. Margie felt normal and peaceful.

"It's time," she said, "to get on with our lives, and I'm excited."

"I'm excited too." Jessi smiled, revealing a new tooth missing.

"Then let's begin today," Margie said, kissing her youngest daughter.

That day, Margie found and joined a women's support group. She was determined to find emotional health and wisdom. In the weeks that followed, she digested information on co-dependency and the loss of self, which cause so much difficulty in all areas of life. She felt the definition of co-dependent people, those who are controlled or manipulated by another person who is afflicted with some condition, like addiction, fit her earlier personality. They believe they are not worthy of life, happiness, friends, or being treated well, just as she had believed in the past.

As a small child in an alcoholic family, Margie had learned to keep the peace by keeping quiet and doing what she was told. She learned to fear people and the outside world. She wanted to please, to be loved. This was her way of surviving and she carried this way of behaving into adulthood. She believes she looked for similar relationships with men and that was why she became involved with Sean Paul Lanier alias Paul Steven Mack—a liar, a thief, a drug user, and now, a convicted murderer.

Despite the fact that Margie now was making every effort to face reality, the past, at moments, haunted her. Sometimes Margie thought she saw Sean lurking in the shadows and wanted to hide. Sometimes she thought she saw his face in a crowd and felt a sudden lurch of fear. However, each time she retreated from reality into fantasy she stopped to tell herself it wasn't real. Then she propelled herself forward, and continued to free herself from the demon. Today, the bad memories are fading for her and for her daughters.

In a real sense, it has been an education on good and evil—one whose lesson she wishes to share, for Margie has learned con men are highly intelligent. They find out everything about you and use it to their advantages. To avoid being taken advantage of, Margie believes you must use your heart, but also listen to your instincts, for your mind and emotions can play tricks on you by rationalizing something bad into something good. Your instincts, she feels, will not lie. Don't let your heart convince your brain to make excuses. In the past, Margie had made up many excuses to settle the uneasy feelings she had about Sean Paul. She would tell herself, "Oh, he's just had a hard life. It's just my imagination. I shouldn't be suspicious. He's better than being alone. Oh, but I love him." She has vowed to make excuses a thing of the past and to instead cope with the good and bad of each day without illusions.

Each and everyone of us has a weapon inside of us counteracting the illusions of our heart and brain. This weapon is one of our greatest assets. It is called instinct, gut reaction.

Margie has come to feel you must listen to your instincts, even if your heart and mind are saying something different.

Instead of living the unfavorable lessons of the past over and over, Margie has learned to change her behavior. She has discovered her strength, her endurance, and begun to live a normal, healthy, and enriched life. In doing so, she has found the inner peace of being in control of her own life, her own destiny, and not to be afraid. Every single day she vows again to learn, grow, and live. She listens to her inner soul. She is proud of who she is. She doesn't accept just anyone in her life. She knows that she has the right to say no and not allow people to control or hurt her. These are the hard-learned lessons she now lives by.

Margie's children, old friends, and new friends stood by her in her quest for a better life. Neither she nor they live in the eye of the storm anymore. Her life today is so much better than she ever imagined. She is happy and content. She is financially and emotionally healthy. Her children are strong, healthy, and independent. She has tried to set an example and her children have followed. Julie has graduated from college with a bachelor's degree and is happily married to a wonderful, healthy man. June has graduated with honors with an associates degree and is a freelance writer. Jessi is working her way through college.

Today, Margie no longer chases the adventure of chaos. She no longer fantasizes. She consciously accepts reality. She has turned her horrible experience into power and strength. She has recovered and lives a life full of love, a life worth living. She helps other women to become their own powerful beings. She has broken the chains of the past, which once imprisoned her, and found freedom.